ACZ-9/19

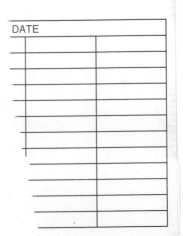

| DATE | |
|---|---|
| | |
| | |
| | |
| | |
| | |
| | |
| | |
| | |
| | |
| | |
| | |
| | |

# Bloom's Modern Critical Views

# Bloom's Modern Critical Views

*Bloom's Modern Critical Views*

# HERMANN HESSE

*Edited and with an introduction by*
Harold Bloom
Sterling Professor of the Humanities
Yale University

CHELSEA HOUSE
PUBLISHERS
A Haights Cross Communications Company

Philadelphia

©2003 by Chelsea House Publishers, a subsidiary of
Haights Cross Communications.

A Haights Cross Communications Company

Introduction © 2003 by Harold Bloom.

Printed and bound in the United States of America.

10  9  8  7  6  5  4  3  2  1


Library of Congress Cataloging-in-Publication Data

Hermann Hesse / edited and with an introduction by Harold Bloom.
    p. cm. -- (Bloom's modern critical views)
Includes bibliographical references and index.
  ISBN: 0-7910-7398-X
 1.  Hesse, Hermann, 1877–1962--Criticism and interpretation. I.
Bloom, Harold.  II.  Series.
  PT2617.E85 Z72154 2002
  838'.91209--dc21

                                2002152671


Chelsea House Publishers
1974 Sproul Road, Suite 400
Broomall, PA 19008-0914

http://www.chelseahouse.com

Contributing Editor: Jesse Zuba

Cover designed by Terry Mallon

Cover photo © Bettman/CORBIS

Layout by EJB Publishing Services

# Contents

# Editor's Note

My Introduction attempts an aesthetic appreciation of Hermann Hesse's masterwork, *The Glass Bead Game* (known to some readers as its the earlier translation into English, *Magister Ludi*).

The historical sequence of criticism begins with E. R. Curtius, one of the great modern critics, in my judgement. Curtius, in a careful overview, accurately distinguishes Hesse from Proust and Joyce, epic writers who make new aspects of reality visible to us. Something of this status is granted by Curtius to *Narziss and Goldmund*, which seems to me generous overpraise for a beautiful book that I find as much a "transposed life history" as *Demian*, *Steppenwolf*, *Rosshalde* and so many other lyrical narratives by Hesse. *The Glass Bead Game*, which I perhaps rank higher than Curtius does, seems to him essentially another lyrical "self-cure."

Thomas Mann, who sometimes named Hesse as an alter ego, introduced *Demian* in 1948, almost a quarter-century after the book's first publication, affirming his permanent esteem for Hesse's work, particularly the introduction to *The Glass Bead Game*, which Mann felt was a part of himself, and related to his own *Doctor Faustus*.

The biographer of Rilke, Ralph Freedman, centers upon Hesse as lyrical novelist, akin to André Gide and Virginia Woolf, though Freedman rightly emphasizes the intense romanticism of Hesse's lyricism.

Theodore Ziolkowski provides a very useful interpretation of *The Glass Bead Game*, exemplary in its comprehensiveness and sympathy. I find memorable Ziolkowski's ironic observation that the book's "shift of allegiance away from aestheticsm to human commitment is reflected by artistic shortcomings in the form."

*Narziss and Guldmund*, Hesse's other major achievement, is viewed by Mark Boubly as a very dark parable, of Hesse's sense of his own *human* failure, as opposed to aesthetic success.

*Steppenwolf*, once a counter-cultural favorite, is read by Henry Hatfield as Hesse's own crisis, transmuting his psychoanalytic treatment (Jungian variety) into novelistic archetypes, and arguing for a joyous acceptance of life that (in my judgement) it cannot demonstrate.

Joseph Mileck returns us to *Narziss and Goldmund*, which he finds favors Goldmund over Narziss, whose story cannot truly be told until *The Glass Bead Game*, interpreted next by Martin Swales as *Bildungsroman*, but one that undermines that literary tradition from within.

Hesse's poetry is analyzed in the context of the Wordsworthian crisis-lyric by Eugene L. Stelzig, while Hesse's publisher, Siegfried Unseld, writes a defense of his author's ethical influence. In a final essay, Stelzig praises the legendary art of Hesse's *Siddhartha*.

# Introduction

When I was young, both Thomas Mann's *Doctor Faustus* (1947) and Hermann Hesse's *The Glass Bead Game* (1943) were accepted as the two indubitable post-World War II German classics. Hesse, on the strength of *The Glass Bead Game*, his final novel, joined Mann as a Nobel laureate. The two novels seemed the last words of an older, Liberal Germany upon the dreadful debasement of the German spirit under the Nazis.

Mann's *The Magic Mountain* and Hesse's *Steppenwolf* each attracts more readers today than *Doctor Faustus* and *The Glass Bead Game*, at least in the United States, if not also in Germany. The ironies of both Mann and Hesse have obscured their comedic aspects: Thomas von der Trave in *The Glass Bead Game* is a parodistic portrait of Thomas Mann, while Hesse's Fritz Tegularius plainly parodies Friedrich Nietzsche, and his Father Jacobus is an ironical version of Jakob Burckhardt.

Hesse had a posthumous revival in the Counter-Cultural American Seventies, when *Demian*, *Suddhartha*, and *Steppenwolf* suited the *Zeitgeist*. The complex allegory of *The Glass Bead Game* attracted far fewer readers, though for a time *Doctor Faustus* had a substantial audience. Today both books, though admirably composed, are rather neglected, and rereading demonstrates that each remains considerably more than a Period Piece. The dumbing-down of high culture makes the survival of either book somewhat problematical, alas.

In some ways the Glass Bead Game, the game rather than the book, can now be regarded as a synthesis of Western literary and musical culture akin to the Western Canons of literature and of "classical" music. The imaginary province of Castalia (the fountain of the Muses) is a science-fiction projection into a non-existent cultural future. Joseph Knecht (whose name means "servant") is both the fulfillment and the reduction of the Castalian aesthetic ideal.

I find myself, in 2002, regarding Hesse's Castalia with a certain nostalgia, for its equivalents in literary criticism—such as the work of E. R. Curtius, Northrop Frye, Kenneth Burke—largely have been replaced by the curious entity now called Cultural Studies in most Anglo-American universities. As a strenuous opponent of Cultural Studies, I myself have just published a vast book that is a kind of Kabbalistic Glass Bead Game, *Genius: A Mosaic of One Hundred Exemplary Creative Minds*. Hesse is not among those minds (though Mann is) but I find myself ironically wondering if my book is not, after all, another vision of Castalia, another metaphor for a waning, soon perhaps to be lost high culture.

Aestheticism, in the face of the Nazi horror, seemed not a pragmatic possibility for Hesse and for Mann. Without necessarily regarding both *The Glass Bead Game* and *Doctor Faustus* as more than great but flawed fictions, Aestheticism in 2002 hardly seems a useless alternative to the Age of Information, Corporate corruption, and Bushian bellicose santimoniousness. Bach, Mozart, Shakespeare, and Dante seem absolute goods in themselves, even when cut off from our dwindling cultural possibilities.

Castalia, rejected by Knecht, looks very different to me in 2002 than it did in the 1940's. The American equivalent of the musical aspect of the Glass Bead Game is the jazz of Louis Armstrong and Duke Ellington, Charlie Parker and Bud Powell, Charles Mingus and Thelonious Monk. An American Castalia might counterpoint classic jazz with the superb American poetical tradition: Walt Whitman and Emily Dickinson, Robert Frost and T. S. Eliot, Hart Crane and Elizabeth Bishop, James Merrill and John Ashbery and A. R. Ammons. Our Glass Bead Game might fuse Charlie Parker and Wallace Stevens, thus synthesizing an art of nuance that transcends the concerns and the capacities of Cultural Criticism.

In 2002, the sacrifice of Joseph Knecht seems to me a spiritual mistake. The cultural commissars of Resentment regard Knecht's demise as another proof of their polemic that all art must be political. Hesse, a sensitive lyric novelist, was not an adequate prophet of the cultural malaise we all need to combine to defeat.

E. R. CURTIUS

# Hermann Hesse

November 1918.... Leaden despair weighs upon men. For the old generation, Germany is shattered, because to them Germany means the empire of the Hohenzollern. There are dignitaries of the fallen regime who do not wish to survive the entry of the occupying forces. But the younger generation do not mourn the passing of this unreal world. To them Germany was, in George's words, "the land still imbued with great promise." Through the collapse of the regime all the progressive forces had been set free. In the German universities great teachers were functioning at the height of their powers: Ernst Troeltsch in Berlin, Max Weber in Munich, Max Scheler in Cologne, Wilhelm Worringer in Bonn, Alfred Weber and Friedrich Gundolf in Heidelberg. A springtime of the mind, lavish in its wealth, had begun to blossom. Students, still wearing their field-gray uniforms, crowded into the lecture halls, the most open-minded student generation since the summer of 1914. In many of them the spirit and the traditions of the *Freideutsche Jugend* were still alive. Their sacred texts were the parables of Chuang-Tsu, Plato, Hölderlin, Nietzsche, and George. Their attitude was a wonderful cosmopolitan openness, an awakening to a new day.

It was this generation that Hermann Hesse addressed in the periodical that he edited in collaboration with Richard Woltereck, *Vivos voco*. It bore witness to a new spirit, a spirit striving to overcome the evil forces of national

From *Essays on European Literature*. © 1973 by Princeton University Press.

hatred. In 1920, I had the opportunity to report on "a voice from the youth of America" in its pages. Hesse's literary work had made no impression upon the young. That was to change as by magic with the appearance of *Demian* in 1922. This work spoke directly to the students in field-gray. Here were the sufferings of school; the perplexities of sex; the experience of myths and mysteries; the War, felt as a premonition, endured, paid for in death. The dying Demian to his wounded friend: "Little Sinclair, pay attention! I shall have to go away. Perhaps you will need me again some time.... If you call me then, I shall not come again so rudely, riding on a horse or on the train. You must listen to what is inside yourself, then you will see that I am within you." A message as simple as it is profound. Nothing else in Hesse's work attains the level of this utterance. You say something like that only once.

In the same year, 1922, I was surprised by a letter from T. S. Eliot. His friend Hermann Hesse had brought me to his attention. Whether I would like to contribute to *The Criterion?* The first number (October 1922) contained Eliot's *The Waste Land*—and an essay by Hermann Hesse on "New German Poetry." In the notes to *The Waste Land* we read that several lines were inspired by Hesse's *Blick ins Chaos [A Look into Chaos]*. A single crossing of the paths. But how many paths and encounters there were in the spiritually relaxed Europe of the time! Rilke translated poems by Valéry, who showed them to me in manuscript. At Scheler's I saw the first issue of Ortega's *Revista de Occidente*. Valery Larbaud introduced Joyce in France. Sylvia Beach's bookstore, "Shakespeare and Company," was an international meetingplace as was that of her friend Adrienne Monnier diagonally opposite. From 1922 on the "Décades" at Pontigny were taking place again. The Pen-Club was founded.... A Europe of the mind—above politics, in spite of all politics—was very much alive. This Europe lived not only in books and periodicals but also in personal relations. One visited the venerable Ivanov in Rome. In Heidelberg, one saw Thomas Mann and André Gide during the same week. "European Conversations" (*Europäische Gesprache*, the title of a Hamburg periodical) were conducted in those days....

Hermann Hesse no longer took part in them. It was not his way. He was the hermit of Montagnola: gardener, dreamer, painter and writer—"the literary man Hermann Hesse" (as he styles himself in *Kurgast [A Guest at the Spa]*); an idler, a timewaster, an easygoing, work-shy man, to say nothing of his other vices" (*Nürnberger Reise*) [*The Journey to Nuremberg*]. Meanwhile he turned fifty (July 2, 1927). For this date an official biography appeared from the pen of Hugo Ball (1886–1927), that profound and solitary spirit, who had found his way back from Dadaism to *Das Byzantinische Christentum* (1923) and the Roman Catholic Church. His *Kritik der deutschen Intelligenz* (1919) was an apocalyptic cry of alarm which has not even now reached its destination. Ball's biography may be called official because it is illustrated "with fourteen photographs from the family collection," and is based on a great deal of information furnished by the poet himself. The account of Hesse's home and family, of his Germano-Russian and his Swabian grandfather (two splendid characters), of the Hindu-Pietistic atmosphere of the Basel mission, is vivid cultural history. At thirteen, the gifted boy broke out of this protected world. It is the decisive break, which the poet himself, in a later retrospect (*Kurzgefasster Lebenslauf* [*Life Story Briefly Told*], *Neue Rundschau* [1925]) merely notes, without explaining it. "When I was thirteen, and that conflict had just begun, my behavior at home and at school left so much to be desired that I was exiled to the Latin school of another town. One year later I became a pupil in a theological seminary, learned to write the Hebrew alphabet, and was well on the way to grasping what a *dagesh forte implicitum* is, when inner storms suddenly broke over me, leading to my flight from the monastery school, my confinement in the 'dungeon,' and my expulsion from the seminary. For a while I made an effort to continue my studies at a Gymnasium, but the outcome, confinement and dismissal, was the same there too. After that I was a shopkeeper's apprentice for three days, ran away again, and to my parents' great consternation disappeared for several days and nights. I was my father's assistant for half a year, then, for a year and a half, a locksmith in a machine shop and clock-tower manufactory. In short, for more than four years everything they tried to do with me went awry—no school would keep me, and I couldn't stand any apprenticeship for long. All attempts to make a useful person out of me ended in failure, sometimes in ignominy and scandal, at other times in escape and expulsion. And yet people were ready to grant that I had ability and even a certain amount of sincere good will!"

Conflict with the school is a normal experience and since 1900 had become a popular subject for literature. *Flachsmann als Erzieher* [*Flachsmann as Educator*] by Otto Ernst (1901) and Wedekind's *Frühlings Erwachen* [*Spring's Awakening*] ran to full houses. Emil Strauss (*Freund Hein*, 1902), Hermann Hesse (*Unterm Rad* [*Beneath the Wheel*], 1905), Heinrich Mann (*Professor Unrat*, 1906), Robert Musil (*Die Verwirrungen des Zöglings Törless* [*Young Törless*], 1906) were the classics of the *Schülerroman*, the novel of student life. Even *Buddenbrooks* concluded with the catastrophe of little Hanno's schooldays. Thomas Mann himself got no further than the "Einjährig-Freiwilliger-Examen" (high-school-leaving examination),[1] with which one could bid school farewell at the end of the sixth year. But the rare combination of talent, determined application, and luck led him rapidly to success, esteem, prestige. "Gustave Aschenbach, or von Aschenbach, as his name has been officially known since his fiftieth birthday"—thus begins *Der Tod in Venedig* [*Death in Venice*] (1913). This Aschenbach, "the author of the lucid and powerful prose epic on the life of Frederick the Great of Prussia," at the age of forty already had "to cope daily with post that bore the stamps of every country in the world." The school authorities have included selections from his writings "in their prescribed textbooks." Early in life he had chosen Munich for his place of residence, "and lived there amid such civic honor as the intellect may in rare instances be privileged to enjoy." When Thomas Mann was fifty years old in 1925, there was a banquet in the Munich Town Hall and many other corroborations of civic honor. Thomas Mann knew the value of representation as well as Senator Budden-brook.

Hermann Hesse's fiftieth birthday passed without ceremony. He would not have had it any other way. As a "reply to the greetings" he published, in 1928, the angry volume *Krisis*, forty-five poems only fifteen of which were later included in the collected edition (*Gedichte* [Zurich, 1942]). These verses give utterance "to one of those stages of life where reason becomes weary of itself, abdicates its authority, and leaves the field free to nature, chaos, and the animal instincts." Animal instincts, in this context, mean the shimmy, whisky, cognac, bars, and hangovers. *Armer Teufel am Morgen nach dem Maskenball* [*Poor devil the morning after the costume ball*] ends:

> Ach wäre dieser Sonntag schon vorbei
> Und ich und du und dieses ganze Leben.
> Ich höre auf, ich muss mich übergeben.

[If only this Sunday were over at last, and you and me and this whole dreary life. I've got to stop, I'm going to be sick.]

But that is still too tame. Everything must come out, though it were in the diction of a schoolboy:

> Das Leben ist darum so beschissen,
> Weil wir doch alle sterben müssen.

[The reason why life is so shitty is that we all must die.]

Even in the charming *Nürnberger Reise* we hear of the "peculiar sadness and, pardon the expression, shittiness of life." In such moods Hesse crossed the threshold of his sixth decade, "more concerned with the fear of aging and dying than with the pleasure of celebrating" (*Krisis*, postscript). *Krisis* is the birthday child's sullen requital: a document of emotional stresses but a gesture of provocation as well. The revolt of the thirteen-year-old has turned into a defiance of social conventions. It makes the aging man into an "unsociable hermit ...., who is deeply pained when he has to obtain a certificate of residence from the local authorities or even to fill out a census slip" (*Kurgast*, 1928).

Hugo Ball informs us that in Switzerland, in 1916, Hesse suffered an acute nervous crisis. Psychoanalytic treatment, administered by a student of C.G. Jung, provided relief. Between May 1916 and November 1917 there were more than seventy sessions. The fruit of this period was *Demian*: release of new creative power and depth perception. Psychoanalysis, as we have seen, was unable to resolve the tensions in Hesse's nature, or even to prevent their recurrence. But neurotic conflicts are not operable injuries or unmitigated disasters. They are part of the very substance of life and therefore part of the material and the problems to be shaped by life. That this is true was demonstrated in Hesse's finest book, *Narziss und Goldmund* [*Narcissus and Goldmund*] (1930). We know that Hesse's early novel *Unterm Rad* depicts his escape from the monastery school at Maulbronn. After a quarter of a century the poet returned to this theme, but transposed now to a timeless Middle Ages, and purged of all the passions of youthful revolt. Goldmund, a student at the monastery, admires his teacher, the ascetic young monk Narcissus, with a shy and worshipful love. He wants to devote his entire life to the Order. But Narcissus explains to him that that is not his destiny. "You are an artist, I am a thinker. You sleep at the mother's breast, I watch in the desert. For me the sun shines, for you the moon and the stars. Your dreams are of girls, mine of boys." Narcissus awakens Goldmund to a knowledge of his own nature. Instead of study, monastic discipline, and virtue, powerful instincts take possession of Narcissus: sex, love of women, longing for independence, travel. He roams through woods, mountains, towns, cities; women's favors accompany him on his journey. He knows how to fend off treacherous companions with a knife. He sees whole territories laid waste by plague; orgies of brutality and lust at the edge of the grave. He becomes a woodcarver and is about to be inducted with honor into the guild. But restlessness drives him to seek new adventures. He is on the point of losing his shirt and his head when Narcissus, the powerful abbot, intercedes for his release and brings him back to the monastery. The whole thing is a wonderfully colored picture out of the German Middle Ages, in which romanticism and realism are blended. Fruity, fragrant, round, self-contained, neither didactic nor problematical; a variegated tapestry of the ever-lasting powers of life, steeped in magical essences that recall Arnim, Tieck, Novalis—but as a result of a secret affinity of blood, not of literary borrowings or an overlay of antiquarianism. No single work of Hesse's has a greater claim to a place in the heritage of German literature. It is a completely German book, unaffected by the lure of the Orient to which the poet was succumbing even then.

Hesse's maternal grandfather, Dr. Hermann Gundert, was one of the first pioneers of the German evangelical mission in India. Upon his return he worked for thirty more years on a dictionary of one of the Indian dialects, on behalf of the Basel mission. He had married in India; Hesse's mother was born there. All the thoughts of his parents and of their friends from the mission revolve around the fabulous land. So it is not surprising that in 1911 Hesse embarks on a journey to India. He has personal reasons for going, were it only the need to see India with other eyes than those of his parents. His book *Aus Indien* [*Out of India*] appears in 1913. Around the same time Waldemar Bonsels (*Indienfahrt* [*Voyage to India*], 1916) and Graf Keyserling (*Reisetagebuch eines Philosophen* [*Travel Diary of a Philosopher*], 1919) had visited India. Thus, with his book on India, as with his school novel and psychoanalysis, Hesse had unwittingly and unintentionally set foot on a terrain that was soon to become a playground of intellectual fashion (Rabindranath Tagore's *Gitanjali* had appeared as early as 1914). Hesse's encounter with India proved a disappointment. He thought that he would find there the innocent and simple children of paradise. "But," the travel book concludes, "we ourselves are different. We are strangers here and have no rights of citizenship. We lost our paradise long ago and the new one that we wish to have and build is not to be found on the equator or beside warm Eastern seas. It lies within us and in our own Northern future."

The next book about India, *Siddhartha* (1922), is merely a transposition of Hesse's revolt against his pietistic home to an Indian setting. Siddhartha, the devout son of a Brahmin, can find peace neither in the teachings of his ancestors nor in asceticism nor in sensual pleasure. Nor can he accept Buddha's doctrine: "No, a seeker after truth cannot accept any doctrine, not if he truly wishes to find. One who has found, however—he can approve of every doctrine." In the end the seeker finds peace by listening to the great stream, "surrendering himself to its streaming, at one with Oneness." A rather more novelistic than philosophical solution to the problems posed. A stage, of which there are many in Hesse's work, destined to be superseded by more impressive elaborations. *Die Morgenlandfahrt* [*Journey to the East*] (1932) is pretty much along the same lines. The East here is "not only a country and a geographical location but rather the homeland of the soul's youth, the everywhere and nowhere," "the union of all the ages." The travelers to the East are an Order;[2] all disclosures regarding the secrets of the Order are forbidden. The journey takes place for the most part in Europe (a proceeding justified by the indication "everywhere and nowhere"). The narrative is confused, with no attempt at construction. "How to make the story of our Journey to the East tellable? I don't know." A significant admission. In this instance Hesse availed himself of the literary puzzle in the manner of E. T. A. Hoffmann in order to legitimate the irreality of his account. The narrative ends in Basel, where it turns out that Leo, "the perfect servant," is at the same time the head of the Order. The "servant" might easily be a preliminary version of Joseph Knecht of *Das Glasperlenspiel* [*The Glass Bead Game*], whose name means squire or servant. Hesse likes name symbolism, and he also likes to play hide-and-seek with names. One of the officials in *Das Glasperlenspiel* is called Dubois—like Hesse's grandmother. Her first husband, Isenberg, lent his name to Knecht's friend Ferromonte. Thomas Mann appears in the book as Meister Thomas von der Trave, Jacob Burckhardt as Pater Jacobus. Knecht's friend Designori ("of the nobles") is of patrician stock; his name is the antithesis of "Knecht." Such playing with names may be regarded as a system of correspondences invented by the writer for his personal use. It enables him to establish cross-connections between widely separated periods in his life and work. Its function is similar to the interweaving of themes that is so typical of Hesse's literary technique. In *Rosshalde* (1914), little Pierre wants to know what carnations are called in the language of the bees and what the robin redbreasts say to each other. On his wanderings through the woods Goldmund would have liked to become a woodpecker, perhaps for a day, perhaps for a month. "He would have spoken woodpecker language and extracted good things from the bark of trees." Among the travelers to the East is one who hopes to learn the language of the birds with the aid of Solomon's key. And now the same thought without the dress of fiction: "To feel life throbbing in me... to have a soul so nimble that by the play of hundreds of fancies it can slip into hundreds of forms, into children and animals, and especially into birds, that is what I want and need in order to live" (*Wanderung* [*Tramping*], 1920). To understand the language of the birds—eternal motif of fairy tale, of legend (cf. Wagner's Siegfried), of dream; the longing to be in harmony with all living creatures, not merely with the birds. One of Goldmund's wishes is never to find his way out of the forest, never to see people again, never to love another woman—to become an animal, "a bear or a stag." In the tale *Der Wolf* [*The Wolf*], the hero is the wounded animal: driven off and sad, on the heights of the snow-covered mountains, the wolf feels the approach of death and sees the red moon rise. The singer Muoth (*Gertrud*, 1910) "had been emaciated by solitude like a wolf." The motif is transformed and developed fully in the novel *Der Steppenwolf* (1927).

Fish too are fraught with symbolism for Hesse. Fishing in the Nagold, depicted by the painter Veraguth in *Rosshalde*; Goldmund at the fish market: there is always a mysterious correspondence to life. Fish and moisture—these are related like bird and air, wolf and wood. The fish-motif participates in the water symbolism, and water, as we know, signifies the unconscious in the language of dreams. Water is allurement and peril at the same time. The book that made Hesse famous, *Peter Camenzind* (1904), begins and ends by the Lake of Lucerne. The lake plays a prominent role in *Rosshalde*. Joseph Knecht will meet his death in an Alpine lake. Peter Camenzind's best friend drowns while bathing "in a ridiculously small South German stream." The monastery school pupil Hans Giebenrath (*Unterm Rad*) finds his death in the waves. Death by water—one of Hesse's basic themes.

Giebenrath and Heilner: a friendship that is tragically severed. Siddhartha and Govinda: a friendship that dissolves because the worthy Govinda runs out of breath. In *Demian* friendship ceases to be conflict, parallelism, or interrelation and becomes psychagogy. This pattern is repeated on a higher plane in *Narziss und Goldmund*. Here friendship mirrors the polarity of mind and life. The poet has embodied two dominant traits of his own character in the two figures. We are close to Novalis' theory of the "truly synthetic person": "Each person, though divided into several, is also capable of being one. The genuine analysis of the person as such brings forth persons...."

These would be some examples of Hesse's themes, suggestions toward an analysis that could be carried much further. Thematic and technical analysis—that rarely practiced art—is the only adequate method for interpreting an author. As such, it is the preparatory course for all criticism that wishes to rise above verbiage, circumlocution, and inconsequentiality. Years ago I tried to explore Proust and Joyce by this method. The incentive was especially strong because both authors were using new techniques to render new aspects of life. They were artists in a sense of the word that can hardly be applied to Hesse. The epic writer makes a new aspect of the world visible. He constructs an objective reality. The opening sentence of *Ulysses* places us *in medias res*. Not personal experience but a series of images and characters detached from the writer is communicated. With Hesse this occurs only in *Narziss und Goldmund*. All the rest of his works are autobiographical ectoplasms, transposed life histories. The writer remains trapped in his own subjective sphere. He cannot contrive to set down an objective world and gain a footing in it. The conventions of art are as repugnant to him as those of society. In constantly renewed departures and variations he makes the reader privy to a development that begins in failure to master the tasks of life (*Peter Camenzind, Unterm Rad,* the novel of marriage *Rosshalde*), and then registers the attempts at a cure (psychoanalysis, India-cycle). Sometimes he will deviate into lyrical prose jottings (*Wanderung*), sometimes into diary-like reportage (*Kurgast, Nürnberger Reise*), occasionally into "magic theater" (*Steppenwolf*). Epic presentation is not one of his native gifts. It can happen that the form will grow brittle in his hand (as in the passage cited above from *Die Morgenlandfahrt*). He has a "mistrust of literature in general." "I can only consider the endeavors of contemporary German writers (my own included, naturally) to produce really articulated forms, genuine works of art, as somehow always inadequate and epigone." Literature having lost its certainty, he can grant it value only "insofar as it confessedly expresses its own poverty and the poverty of its age with the greatest possible candor" (all in *Nürnberger Reise*). The dichotomy in this evaluation is reflected by the slack diction, with its conversational jargon ("somehow"), self-conscious doublets ("real forms," "genuine works"), and turgidity ("confessedly," "with the greatest possible candor"). These sentences have no rhythm, no tautness, and are therefore not compelling. The writer not only mistrusts literature; he has no responsible commitment to the exigencies of his craft, to syntax and style. But is it his craft? In *Gertrud* and in *Das Glasperlenspiel* he is a musician, in *Rosshalde* a painter, in *Narziss und Goldmund* a woodcarver. In *Nürnberger Reise* he toys with the idea "that perhaps I might still manage to run away from literature and take up painting for a living, a craft I find more attractive." Is it unfair to lend weight to these utterances? Are they merely the result of passing moods? But the author did think them worth communicating, and they illuminate the problems of his art. They explain too why we were able to say something about Hesse's themes but very little about his technique. It is variable, often groping; now clumsy, now sedulous. The watercolors that Hesse added to a few of his books are done with a coloring box. His handling of language, too, gives the effect of careful daubing, now childlike, now amateurish. There is never any sparkle to this prose. But once in a while—as in Demian's farewell—a note is sounded that touches the heart with its magic.

The copious stream of Hesse's lyric poetry is also for long stretches nothing but diligent rhyming. I choose a poem from *Das Glasperlenspiel*:

Die ewig Unentwegten und Naiven
Ertragen freilich unsre Zweifel nicht.
Flach sei die Welt, erklären sie uns schlicht,
Und Faselei die Sage von den Tiefen.

Denn sollt' es wirklich andre Dimensionen
Als die zwei guten, altvertrauten geben,
Wie könnte da ein Mensch noch sicher wohnen,
Wie könnte da ein Mensch noch sorglos leben?

Um also einen Frieden zu erreichen,
So lasst uns eine Dimension denn streichen!
Denn sind die Unentwegten wirklich ehrlich,
Und ist das Tiefensehen so gefährlich,
Dann ist die dritte Dimension entbehrlich.

[The eternal die-hards and the naïve cannot, to be sure, bear our doubts. The world is flat, they declare simply, and the legend of depth mere drivel. For if dimensions other than the two good old familiar ones really did exist, how could a man still live without anxiety? So in order to reach a peaceful settlement, let us strike one of the dimensions. For if the die-hards are really sincere, and the view of depth is so dangerous, then the third dimension is dispensable.]

This poem looks like a sonnet and was perhaps on the way to becoming one. For this purpose, unfortunately, a line is missing. The rhyme scheme of the first quatrain is abandoned in the second. The rhymes are more miss than hit. "Die-hard" is the worst sort of newspaper jargon. The whole thing is versified prose with intrusive padding. For that matter, the weakness of Hesse's style generally has always been that he cannot leave anything out. In a preface to a collection of poems, *Die Harfe. Vierundzwanzig Gedichte [The Harp. Twenty-four Poems]*, published in 1917, Alfred Kerr wrote: "Poets fill ten printed volumes. But a few islands finally project above the flood of time. Not to burden the world, I present the islands immediately." A few islands project above the flood of Hesse's lyric poetry too. They could fill one of those thin "Insel" volumes and in such a selection become a German possession.

This essay does not aim at a comprehensive evaluation of Hesse's work. That would be impossible in any case, if for no other reason than that many—and important—books are inaccessible. I have traced only a few of the main lines that conduce to an understanding of *Das Glasperlenspiel* (1943). The appearance of this work, impressive in content and scope, of the poet's old age, came as a happy surprise. When a writer in the seventh decade of life sums up his existence in a broadly-conceived work, it is noteworthy. But when it is a poet who has accompanied us from the days of our youth, whom we encountered in a new shape after the First World War, and who now speaks again across the abyss of calamitous years, we are moved and grateful. Something takes place in us that transcends everything literary: an exchange of greetings by the survivors of a catastrophe; the rediscovery of a familiar voice. Memories of long decades are stirred and give the work a resonance which vibrates with many destinies. The generations that awakened to maturity in the first decade of the twentieth century found their intellectual orientation in the writers born before and after 1870: George (1868), Hofmannsthal (1874), Rilke (1875), Thomas Mann (1875), Rudolf Borchardt (1877) in Germany; Romain Rolland (1866), André Gide (1869), Paul Claudel (1870) in France. Proust and Valéry (both born in 1871) did not achieve prominence till after 1918. Ten proud names radiating from one decade. Lives that intersected, attracting one another, repelling one another. And yet, from the perspective of the present, belonging to the same world. In the eighties a new generation emerges: the "moderns" of 1920: Joyce (1882), Ortega (1883), Eliot (1888). Between the first and the second row stands Hermann Hesse. He stands by himself, in scarcely more than fleeting touch with any of those named. We have referred to the slight contact with Eliot. Romain Rolland is mentioned once in a dedication; the *Nürnberger Reise* records a visit with Thomas Mann. But Hesse was never affected by the works of his great coevals. He shunned the living Europe of the twentieth century. France had nothing to give him. "Paris was ghastly," opines Peter Camenzind. "Nothing but art, politics, literature, and sluttishness, nothing but artists, literary men, politicians, and low women" (tautology as a stylistic device). The *Nürnberger Reise* informs us that the poet has "hitherto succeeded" in avoiding Berlin. Merely the journey to Nuremberg was a hazard. "It was beautiful and mysterious, but to me, as a south German, depressing and frightening as well. I thought to myself, if I should travel on, there would be more and more pines, and then more snow, and then perhaps Leipzig or Berlin and pretty soon Spitzbergen and the North Pole. Good Lord, what if I had gone so far as to accept the invitation to Dresden! It was unthinkable." "Except for my native town in the Black Forest, I have felt really at home only in the region around Locarno."

Fortunately, between the Black Forest and Locarno there is a place called Switzerland—one of those friendly gifts of a durable kind that history has conferred upon our small, tormented portion of the globe. A country and a people secure in themselves; small enough to be protected from the troubles of their neighbors; large and varied enough to be a mirror of Europe. Years ago the Basel philosopher Karl Joël gave a lively description of the "Switzerizing" of Europe in the eighteenth century. Pestalozzi and Rousseau became the educators of the continent. Haller and Gessner transformed the view of nature, Bodmer and Breitinger prepared the ground for the revolt against French Classicism. Voltaire lives near the Swiss border; Gibbon completes his history, conceived in Rome, at Lausanne. Goethe pledges fellowship with Lavater. In the nineteenth and twentieth centuries Switzerland becomes an asylum for those politically persecuted or disaffected in their own countries. Hesse, who had many ties with Basel, adopted Switzerland as his homeland. Transposed into the utopian "Castalia," it becomes the setting of *Das Glasperlenspiel.*

The work has been called a novel of education. That is one of its many aspects, but it does not touch the core of the book. We can approach it more closely by asking ourselves why Hesse picks up the theme of education again, and why he presents Joseph Knecht first as a student, then as a teacher, and finally as "magister ludi," the master of the game. *Unterm Rad* depicts the boy's failure in school. In *Das Glasperlenspiel* the delinquent pupil catches up on his schooling, as it were, and becomes a teacher himself (at a monastery school, like Narcissus). Thus a theme from Hesse's early period is taken up again in his latest, changed in value from negative to positive, and "reconciled on a higher level." Not just this theme alone. All the poet's themes (among which we found conflicts but also attempts at a cure) are taken up again and treated contrapuntally in this work. The *Versuch einer Lebensbeschreibung des Joseph Knecht* [*Essay at a Description of the Life of Joseph Knecht*] is the last and now definitively realized transposition and sublimation of all those personal histories in which Hesse depicted himself as Camenzind, as Giebenrath, as Sinclair, as Siddhartha, as Goldmund. All those personal histories crystallized around conflicts: conflict with the home and its pietistic atmosphere; with the school; with the middle-class world; with society in general. Finally, too, the conflict with the chosen profession— that of literature. As late as 1927 the poet notes: "As for myself, I am certain that no respectable, hard-working person would ever shake my hand again if he knew how little I value my time, how I waste my days and weeks and even months, with what childish games I fritter away my life." A fifty year-old writer who cannot stop playing games and admits it with a bad conscience.

But is the play-instinct something to be ashamed of? Undetected and unanalyzed residue of a bourgeois prejudice! Play and the capacity for play is one of the most important functions of man's relation to the world. A learned historian of culture has meticulously examined American Indian games in order to confront *homo sapiens* with *homo ludens*. Animals and men play, and so do the Gods, in India as in Hellas. Plato views man as an articulated puppet fashioned by the Gods perhaps for the sole purpose of being their plaything. What conclusion shall we draw? The play-instinct is to be affirmed. A negative converted into a positive. To play one's own game with the deep seriousness of a child at play. The highest achievement would be— to invent a game of one's own. This the poet has succeeded in doing. He is the inventor of the glass bead game. He has learned to master it: the game of life, the game of the beads. Thus he has become in two senses of the word *magister ludi* (in Latin *ludus* means both "game" and "school"). The glass bead game is the symbol for the successful completion of the school of life. The discovery of this motif determined the conception: at once inspiration and stroke of luck; the seed from which the golden blossom sprouted.

Motif and theme are two different things, and critics would do well to distinguish between them. The motif is what sets the fable (the "mythos" in Aristotle's *Poetics*) in motion and holds it together. Motif belongs to the objective side. Theme comprises everything that concerns the person's primary orientation toward the world. The thematics of a poet is the scale or register of his typical reactions to certain situations in which life places him. Theme belongs to the subjective side. It is a psychological constant. Motif is given by inspiration, discovered, invented—all of which amounts to the same thing. He who has nothing but themes cannot attain to epic or drama. Or, for that matter, to the great lyric. Here we touch upon a law of aesthetics the best formulation of which I find in T. S. Eliot: "The only way of expressing emotion in the form of art is by finding an 'objective correlative'; in other words, a set of objects, a situation, a chain of events which shall be the formula of that particular emotion; such that when the external facts, which must terminate in sensory experience, are given, the emotion is immediately evoked." By means of the motif, the "objective correlative," the insufficiencies of personal experience are overcome. The motif is an organic, autonomous structure, like a plant. It unfolds, forms nodes, branches out, puts forth leaves, buds, fruit. Once the bead game was in existence, a whole world had to be built up around it. That could only be an imaginary world, i.e., a Utopia, or a Uchronia (Renouvier's concept). But this world had to be transferred to an era which was not too distant in time from our own. For elements of our own culture must still survive in Castalia. Hence a—

somewhat labored—introduction is necessary to serve as a bridge between the twenty-second and twentieth century. This allows for a critique of our age, but, what is more important, it demonstrates that the glass bead game has precursors in every epoch of the European mind. This means, however, the integration of western tradition into Hesse's spiritual universe.

And the Orient? Like all the main themes of the poet it is crystallized on to the new structure. The work is dedicated to the "Travelers to the East." The psychic techniques of Yoga are practiced in Castalia. India reappears in *Indischer Lebenslauf* [*The Indian Life*]. Nevertheless, the role of guide has passed to China. Castalia has a "Chinese House of Studies," it even has, as in a rococo park, a Chinese hermitage called the "Bamboo-grove." There one finds gold-fish ponds, yarrow stalks for consulting the oracle, brushes and water-color bowls: pretty chinoiserie. But when the hermit is invited to Waldzell, there arrives in his stead only a daintily-colored Chinese letter containing the irrefutable assertion: "Movement leads to obstacles." Seneca, Thomas a Kempis, Pascal had stated something similar, if with less preciosity. Thus *Das Glasperlenspiel* also concludes and crowns the poet's Oriental cycle. And yet the world of the East is not the essential core of the book but rather the decorative back-ground. Its effect is "antiquarian," as Demian says of Dr. Pistorius's Abraxas-mythology.

*Das Glasperlenspiel* is a western book. An ancestry is established for the bead game originating with Pythagoras and Gnosticism and continuing through Scholasticism and Humanism to the philosophy of Cusanus, the universal mathematics of Leibniz, and even to the intuitions of Novalis. Two names, however, with which only the fewest readers might be expected to be familiar, are mentioned with especial piety: Johann Albrecht Bengel (1687–1752) and Friedrich Christoph Oetinger (1702–1782), great Swabian theologians, in whom a strict belief in the Bible was united with apocalyptic doctrines, theosophy, chemistry, and Cabbala. They are intermediaries between Böhme, Swedenborg, and Schelling. Oetinger was pastor at Hirsau, near Calw, where Hesse was born. The prominence given these names implies the resolution of the conflict with the Swabian Pietism of his home and, by the same token, a rapprochement with Christianity. This rapprochement is further evidenced by Knecht's intimacy with Pater Jacobus and the Order of St. Benedict.

Castalia, too, is an Order. So Hesse's oldest theme is drawn into the organization of the work: the theme of the monastery. It is most remarkable how this theme too is transformed by a newly-won freedom. As he has invented his own game, so the poet has invented his own order. Psychologically this means: he has become his own master. By his own full power he can impose the authority with which he will comply. What had, as a neurotic conflict, been a stumbling block becomes, through "anagogy," a building block. The revolt against all external authority is now recognized as the passionate search for an authority derived from his own inner law. Joseph Knecht passes through all the degrees of the Order, submitting voluntarily to its regulations. After long service, long mastership, he "awakens" (we recall that Goldmund was "awakened" by Narcissus). Knecht's inner law compels him to quit the Order. His departure takes place in the prescribed ceremonial forms. To be sure, the administration of the Order cannot approve of this step. As he is about to leave, Knecht says to himself: "If only he had been able to explain and prove to the others what seemed so clear to him: that the 'arbitrariness' of his present action was in reality service and obedience; that it was not freedom he was going toward but new, unknown, and uncanny obligations; and that he was going not as a fugitive but as one who is summoned, not willfully but obediently, not as master but as sacrifice." So, after five decades, the boy's flight from the monastery school is repeated, only with its signs reversed from negative to positive; recast and purged of all slag it has come to be understood in its deeper significance: as a level of transcendence. In this work of the poet's old age, all the previous stages of his life have become transparent to him. It was conceived on the level of "illumination."

Where is the awakened teacher of the Order summoned by his inner law? To the "world outside," the ordinary human world beyond Castalia's serene precincts. The "unknown obligation" toward which he is moving is—death. But this departure for the unknown, no longer of a wandering scholar but of a man who is "summoned," is the heroic setting-out of the Nordic man whom Oriental absorption does not restrain. Final confirmation of the return to the West; Protestant nonconformism; Düreresque knight-errantry.

One last point! We found that in Hesse psychoanalysis and Oriental wisdom were attempts at healing neurotic conflicts. In addition, a theme to which we have barely alluded, although it runs through all the books from *Peter Camenzind* on—the escape into alcoholic intoxication. *Das Glasperlenspiel* is the result and testimony of a self-cure, the only cure that is dignified and genuine because it proceeds from the very core of the person. Psychoanalysis, Yoga, Chinese wisdom, were only expedients. He who has been "awakened" no longer needs them. The conflicts are resolved in a blessed new period of creativity. It is brought on by the discovery of the bead game. This functions as the center around which the person and the productivity of the poet are reorganized. The resolution of discords is the great new experience. That is why music is so important in the work. It is a

symbol of euphony and concord, of rhythmically articulated spiritual-
ization—harmony with the All.

A more precise analysis, a more searching appreciation of the rich late
work I must leave to others.

*1947*

## NOTES

1. Literally, examination for one-year volunteers. It enabled the holder
of the certificate to reduce his military service to one year.—TR.

2. Cf. *Demian*, p. 143: "the first fulfillment of my life and my admission
to the Order."

# THOMAS MANN

# *Introduction to* Demian

A full decade has passed since I last shook Hermann Hesse's hand. Indeed the time seems even longer, so much has happened meanwhile—so much has happened in the world of history and, even amid the stress and uproar of this convulsive age, so much has come from the uninterrupted industry of our own hand. The outer events, in particular the inevitable ruin of unhappy Germany, both of us foresaw and both lived to witness—far removed from each other in space, so far that at times no communication was possible, yet always together, always in each other's thoughts. Our paths in general take clearly separate courses through the land of the spirit, at a formal distance one from the other. And yet in some sense the course is the same, in some sense we are indeed fellow pilgrims and brothers, or perhaps I should say, a shade less intimately, confreres; for I like to think of our relationship in the terms of the meeting between his Joseph Knecht and the Benedictine friar Jacobus in *Glasperlenspiel* which cannot take place without the "playful and prolonged ceremony of endless bowings like the salutations between two saints or princes of the church"—a half ironic ceremonial, Chinese in character, which Knecht greatly enjoys and of which, he remarks, Magister Ludi Thomas von der Trave was also past master.

Thus it is only natural that our names should be mentioned together from time to time, and even when this happens in the strangest of ways it is

From *Demian*. © 1948 by Holt, Rinehart and Winston, Incorporated.

agreeable to us. A well-known elderly composer in Munich, obstinately German and bitterly angry, in a recent letter to America called us both, Hesse and me, "wretches" because we do not believe that we Germans are the highest and noblest of peoples, "a canary among a flock of sparrows." The simile itself is peculiarly weak and fatuous quite apart from the ignorance, the incorrigible arrogance which it expresses and which one would think had brought misery enough to this ill-fated people. For my own part, I accept with resignation this verdict of the "German soul." Very likely in my own country I was nothing but a gray sparrow of the intellect among a flock of emotional Harz songsters, and so in 1933 they were heartily glad to be rid of me, though today they make a great show of being deeply injured because I do not return. But Hesse? What ignorance, what lack of culture, to banish this nightingale (for, true enough, he is no middle-class canary) from its German grove, this lyric poet whom Moerike would have embraced with emotion, who has produced from our language images of purest and most delicate form, who created from it songs and aphorisms of the most profound artistic insight—to call him a "wretch" who betrays his German heritage simply because he holds the idea separate from the form which so often debases it, because he tells the people from whom he sprang the truth which the most dreadful experiences still cannot make them understand, and because the misdeeds committed by this race in its self-absorption stirred his conscience.

If today, when national individualism lies dying, when no single problem can any longer be solved from a purely national point of view, when everything connected with the "fatherland" has become stifling provincialism and no spirit that does not represent the European tradition as a whole any longer merits consideration, if today the genuinely national, the specifically popular, still has any value at all—and a picturesque value may it retain—then certainly the essential thing is, as always, not vociferous opinion but actual accomplishment. In Germany especially, those who were least content with things German were always the truest Germans. And who could fail to see that the educational labors alone of Hesse the man of letters—here I am leaving the creative writer completely out of account—the devoted universality of his activities as editor and collector, have a specifically German quality? The concept of "world literature," originated by Goethe, is most natural and native to him. One of his works, which has in fact appeared in America, "published in the public interest by authority of the Alien Property Custodian, 1945," bears just this title: "Library of World Literature"; and is proof of vast and enthusiastic reading, of especial familiarity with the temples of Eastern wisdom, and of a noble humanistic intimacy with the "most ancient and holy testimonials of the human spirit." Special studies of his are the essays on Francis of Assisi and on Boccaccio dated 1904, and his three papers on Dostoevski which he called *Blick ins Chaos (Glance into Chaos)*. Editions of medieval stories, of novelle and tales by old Italian writers, Oriental fairy tales, *Songs of the German Poets*, new editions of Jean Paul, Novalis, and other German romantics bear his name. They represent labor, veneration, selection, editing, reissuing and the writing of informed prefaces—enough to fill the life of many an erudite man of letters. With Hesse it is mere superabundance of love (and energy!), an active hobby in addition to his personal, most extraordinarily personal, work—work which for the many levels of thought it touches and its concern with the problems of the world and the self is without peer among his contemporaries.

Moreover, even as a poet he likes the role of editor and archivist, the game of masquerade behind the guise of one who "brings to light" other people's papers. The greatest example of this is the sublime work of his old age, *Glasperlenspiel*, drawn from all sources of human culture, both East and West, with its subtitle "Attempt at a Description of the Life of Magister Ludi Thomas Knecht, Together with Knecht's Posthumous Writings, Edited by Hermann Hesse." In reading it I very strongly felt (as I wrote to him at that time) how much the element of parody, the fiction and persiflage of a biography based upon learned conjectures, in short the verbal playfulness, help keep within limits this late work, with its dangerously advanced intellectuality, and contribute to its dramatic effectiveness.

German? Well, if that's the question, this late work together with all the earlier work is indeed German, German to an almost impossible degree, German in its blunt refusal to try to please the world, a refusal that in the end will be neutralized, whatever the old man may do, by world fame: for the simple reason that this is Germanic in the old, happy, free, and intellectual sense to which the name of Germany owes its best repute, to which it owes the sympathy of mankind. This chaste and daring work, full of fantasy and at the same time highly intellectual, is full of tradition, loyalty, memory, secrecy—without being in the least derivative. It raises the intimate and familiar to a new intellectual, yes, revolutionary level—revolutionary in no direct political or social sense but rather in a psychic, poetical one: in genuine and honest fashion it is prophetic of the future, sensitive to the future. I do not know how else to describe the special, ambiguous, and unique charm it holds for me. It possesses the romantic timbre, the tenuousness, the complex, hypochondriacal humor of the German soul—organically and personally bound up with elements of a very different and far less emotional nature, elements of a very different and far less emotional nature, elements of

European criticism and of psychoanalysis. The relationship of this Swabian writer of lyrics and idyls to the erotological "depth psychology" of Vienna, as for example it is expressed in *Narziss und Goldmund*, a poetic novel unique in its purity and fascination, is a spiritual paradox of the most appealing kind. It is no less remarkable and characteristic than this author's attraction to the Jewish genius of Prague, Franz Kafka, whom he early called an "uncrowned king of German prose," and to whom he paid critical tribute at every opportunity—long before Kafka's name had become so fashionable in Paris and New York.

If he is "German," there is certainly nothing plain or homely about him. The electrifying influence exercised on a whole generation just after the First World War by *Demian*, from the pen of a certain mysterious Sinclair, is unforgettable. With uncanny accuracy this poetic work struck the nerve of the times and called forth grateful rapture from a whole youthful generation who believed that an interpreter of their innermost life had risen from their own midst—whereas it was a man already forty-two years old who gave them what they sought. And need it be stated that, as an experimental novel, *Steppenwolf* is no less daring than *Ulysses* and *The Counterfeiters?*

For me his lifework, with its roots in native German romanticism, for all its occasional strange individualism, its now humorously petulant and now mystically yearning estrangement from the world and the times, belongs to the highest and purest spiritual aspirations and labors of our epoch. Of the literary generation to which I belong I early chose him, who has now attained the biblical age, as the one nearest and dearest to me and I have followed his growth with a sympathy that sprang as much from our differences as from our similarities. The latter, however, have sometimes astounded me. He has written things—why should I not avow it?—such as *Badegast* and indeed much in *Glasperlenspiel*, especially the great introduction, which I read and feel "as though 'twere part of me."

I also love Hesse the man, his cheerfully thoughtful, roguishly kind ways, the beautiful, deep look of his, alas, ailing eyes, whose blue illuminates the sharp-cut face of an old Swabian peasant. It was only fourteen years ago that I first came to know him intimately when, suffering from the first shock of losing my country, my house and my hearth, I was often with him in his beautiful house and garden in the Ticino. How I envied him in those days!—not alone for his security in a free country, but most of all for the degree of hard-won spiritual freedom by which he surpassed me, for his philosophical detachment from all German politics. There was nothing more comforting, more healing in those confused days than his conversation.

For a decade and more I have been urging that his work be crowned with the Swedish world prize for literature. It would not have come too soon in his sixtieth year, and the choice of a naturalized Swiss citizen would have been a witty way out at a time when Hitler (on account of Ossietzky) had forbidden the acceptance of the prize to all Germans forevermore. But there is much appropriateness in the honor now, too, when the seventy-year-old author has himself crowned his already rich work with something sublime, his great novel of education. This prize carries around the world a name that hitherto has not received proper attention in all countries and it could not fail to enhance the renown of this name in America as well, to arouse the interest of publishers and public. It is a delight for me to write a sympathetic foreword of warm commendation to this American edition of *Demian*, the stirring prose-poem, written in his vigorous middle years. A small volume; but it is often books of small size that exert the greatest dynamic power—take for example *Werther*, to which, in regard to its effectiveness in Germany, *Demian* bears a distant resemblance. The author must have had a very lively sense of the suprapersonal validity of his creation as is proved by the intentional ambiguity of the subtitle "The Story of a Youth" which may be taken to apply to a whole young generation as well as to an individual. This feeling is demonstrated too by the fact that it was this particular book which Hesse did not wish to have appear over his own name which was already known and typed. Instead he had the pseudonym Sinclair—a name selected from the Hölderlin circle—printed on the jacket and for a long time carefully concealed his authorship. I wrote at that time to his publisher, who was also mine, S. Fischer in Berlin, and urgently asked him for particulars about this striking book and who "Sinclair" might be. The old man lied loyally: he had received the manuscript from Switzerland through a third person. Nevertheless, the truth slowly became known, partly through critical analysis of the style, but also through indiscretions. The tenth edition, however, was the first to bear Hesse's name.

Toward the end of the book (the time is 1914) Demian says to his friend Sinclair: "There will be war…. But you will see, Sinclair, that this is just the beginning. Perhaps it will become a great war, a very great war. But even that is just the beginning. The new is beginning and for those who cling to the old the new will be horrible. What will you do?"

The right answer would be: "Assist the new without sacrificing the old." The best servitors of the new—Hesse is an example—may be those who know and love the old and carry it over into the new.

RALPH FREEDMAN

# The Novel as a Disguised Lyric

1

The adoration of young German readers for Hermann Hesse during the nineteen-twenties and early thirties was rooted in a shrewd recognition of a common language. They shared a peculiar rebellion against the industrial civilization they held responsible for the past, which expressed itself in an occasionally strained, often sentimental return to nature and spirit: a revival of romantic values. With the phenomenal success of *Demian* (1919), Hesse had made himself the spokesman of this generation of youth as Thomas Mann had been the spokesman for the immediately preceding one. In a preface to his selected works (whose publication he later prevented), Hesse stated his own sense of his place in the tradition of German letters: "Narrative as a disguised lyric, the novel as a borrowed label for the experimentations of poetic spirits to express their feeling of self and world; this was a specifically German and romantic matter, here I felt immediately a common heritage and guilt." This guilt, Hesse continues, is shared by many of his contemporaries and predecessors, for German prose is an enticing instrument for making music to whose lure many poets have succumbed without realizing that lyricism must be accompanied by a gift for storytelling.[1]

---

From *The Lyrical Novel: Studies in Hermann Hesse, André Gide, and Virginia Woolf.* © 1963 by Princeton University Press.

Although Hesse's awareness of his lyrical conception of narrative was often accompanied by anguish, he felt that in a time of mechanization there is a great need for a survival of romantic values, of which he saw himself as the last standard-bearer. He admired Thomas Mann's ability, in *Doktor Faustus*, to equip his showcases lavishly with characters and scenes, to create a world of profusion against which Leverkühn's organized and transparent inner world stands out in sharp relief.[2] But Hesse's work as a whole seems to invoke Novalis and Hölderlin—or Indian and Chinese thinkers who, it seemed to him, expressed similar ideas—to show that the lively world of experience finds its most subtle reflection in a heightened vision of the self caught by the magic of art. In a preface to an American edition of *Demian*, Mann himself distinguished between his own intellectual and Hesse's lyrical bent: "Very likely in my own country I was nothing but a gray sparrow of the intellect among a flock of emotional Hartz songsters.... But Hesse? What ignorance, what lack of culture, to banish this nightingale...from its German grove, this lyric poet whom Mocrike would have embraced with emotion, who has produced from our language images of purest and most delicate form."[3] It is quite true, as Ernst Robert Curtius has suggested, that this amazingly faithful reproduction of the romantic tradition has placed Hesse outside the main stream of the European novel from Flaubert to Joyce, Gide, and Mann.[4] But Hesse used romanticism as a tool for the development of a unique approach, leading to a sharp analysis of the self, the meaning of personal identity and the conditions of self-consciousness, which he explores in contemporary terms.

2

Hesse's new kind of romanticism is perhaps best expressed in two famous titles: *Blick ins Chaos (1920)* and *Weg nach Innen* (1931).[5] The fashionable romantic form that had been his stock in trade for some time moved in an oddly analytic direction. Hesse's postwar novels are concerned with the inner world turned inside out, yielding not only dreams, memories, or hallucinations *per se* but also the world underlying perception, which is dissolved and recomposed in the self's inner landscape. If Hölderlin's Hyperion and Novalis' Heinrich reflect their encounters directly in expressions of feeling and symbolic images, Hesse's protagonists penetrate further to the conditions of awareness, exhibiting society and nature in an internal perspective.

As it confronts the world, the self seeks to absorb its opponent. In a frightening scene in "Eine Traumfolge," included in *Märchen* (1919), the protagonist seizes society's most offensive exemplar and hammers him to his liking. (III, 329–330) Characters opposing an alien social reality, whether in "Klein und Wagner" or *Der Steppenwolf*, are dissolved either through death or schizophrenia. This alien reality or "world" is variously identified with anything seemingly external to the self, including objects of perception, non-intuitive reasoning, social pressures, or mercantilism; in short, it is a very wide concept and includes the very world of perception as well as contemporary reality. If, then, the self attempts to come to terms with the world by uniting it with its psyche, it can be successful only if the experiences absorbed by the self are not inimical to "nature," that is, to sensuous reality. In *Narziss und Goldmund*, the natural world of *Bilder* within the self (of Goldmund) is easily linked with experiences of nature; only then can the intellect (Narziss) intervene and impose form upon the sensuous-natural material. But if the "world" is immediately identified with a non-intuitive, anti-sensuous, or even dehumanized world, the kind of failure must result which Hesse describes in his *Nürnberger Reise* (1928). As in perception both form and sensuous content are joined in the self, so the tension between a sensuous self and a hostile, desensualized world must also be joined in the self. Hesse is forced to deal with the conflict of self and world, sense and intellect, quite as much in psychological as in social or intellectual terms.[6]

The perennial split between the individual and the world beyond him is portrayed, not in dramatic action, but in symbolic or allegorical self-representation. Echoing Novalis' idea of the artist as a supreme mimic dissolving alien existence in himself, Hesse renders his conflicts as symbolic "self-portraits." In his novels, representative characters mirror their divided selves in drawings, statues, and fictional biographies. As might be expected, these figures also depict their divided condition with sharply psychological implications, evolving schizophrenic distortions far more intense than those envisaged by Novalis. These psychological self-portraits include particularly Hesse's versions of the "eternal self" regulating the "I" of poet and hero. Besides functioning as a Freudian superego, or, more pertinently, as a Jungian collective unconscious, this higher aspect of the self acts as a *daemon* who guards its activities and comments upon them ironically.[7] Hidden faculties of control, as well as possible resolutions of inner conflict between self and world, are revealed externally by teachers and guides like Demian or Leo of *Die Morgenlandfahrt*. Internally, they might appear as the hero's double vision—images of the inner man in which both the ideal and the mortal self are juxtaposed.

Hesse's various interpretations of the artist's relationship with his experience turn primarily on the opposition of sense and intellect, which is associated with that of dark and light, mother and father, sensuality and ascetic control. An analysis of Hesse's use of these categories shows them to be elusive. *Geist*, both spirit and intellect, includes diverse connotations, ranging from the regulating, paternal force of control to the destructive power of a rationalistic culture, although often it also includes the clarity of a divinely rational spirit. Its counterpoint, *Seele*, on the other hand, is both sensuality and soul, associated with sexuality, debauch, sense experience, and the recognition of the mother image or the collective unconscious.[8] There is no doubt about Hesse's primary impulses: in *Narziss und Goldmund* integration was to have taken place chiefly through *Seele*, in *Das Glasperlenspiel* through *Geist*. But intuitively he weighs his evidence on the side of *Seele*. Sexuality, the world of the senses, must be experienced in its wholeness; it must be reflected in the magic vision of the imagination—the lesson of *Der Steppenwolf*. Sensuality makes possible artistic integration, but it must be wedded to the ordering intellect or else chaos will result—the lesson of *Narziss und Goldmund*. Even in *Das Glasperlenspiel*, its hero, Josef Knecht, turns his back on the paradise of *Geist* and reenters sensual nature, there to find his death. Indeed, although Hesse greatly admired *Geist* and thought it indispensable to artistic creation, he nowhere allowed it to triumph in the end: neither in the intuitive vision of harmony in *Siddhartha* nor in the ethereal clarity of *Das Glasperlenspiel*.[9]

A reciprocal tension of *Geist* and *Seele*, then, is woven into the fabric of Hesse's narratives. Continuously requiring and counteracting one another, these opposing poles act like antinomics which recall Fichte's *Weobselwirkung*, the thought underlying Novalis' and Hölderlin's *Fragmente*, and even Schiller's opposition of *Form* and *Stoff* to be reconciled in the *Spiel* of art. In consonance with this analogy, Hesse views the artist's *Stoff*, the material of *Seele*, as the sensual component which entails sexuality. Indeed, Hesse's concept of *Seele* in the double sense of non-intellectual, intuitive vision (*Schau*) and sensuality enables him to move from the opposition of creative sensuality (feminine) and controlling intellectuality (masculine) to their integration, literally, in an over-soul, a transcendental soul. On the way to this union of *Seele* and *Geist* in a heightened self, Hesse's characters often reenact Christian salvation from and through the immersion in sensuality. The search for fulfillment, which for Hesse seems to involve both the Augustinian notion and Nietzschean transcendence, is shown in many different ways: in Klein's and Knecht's deaths by water, or, in *Demian*, in Sinclair's final vision at the moment of his death. On these occasions, *Seele* is raised from a psychological to a metaphysical level of existence as resolution approaches; it is transferred from a sensual to a transcendental plane. But this transcendental *Seele* is not unrelated to the *Seelenwelt* of the artist's material. In her double function of mistress and mother, woman embodies for Hesse the libidinal force which represents the artist's material (the world of nature he must incorporate and merge with his own) and the maternal goal, the *Urgrund*, in which salvation and aesthetic reconciliation are found.[10] "We all," Hesse says in his introduction to *Demian*, "come out of the same abyss." (III, 100) In the womb, the original matrix of experience, whatever its possibilities of chaos may be, integration is reached. By acquiring a vision of this ground, the poet can attain to *Seele* in its transcendental function. He can, with Novalis, become the "transcendental physician."[11]

Hesse appears to use a variety of related concepts to express the relationship between the personal self which absorbs the contradictory flow of experience and some higher or symbolic self in which its oppositions are resolved. These include the unities of Yoga mysticism and Jung's collective unconscious. The obvious indebtedness of this notion to the romantic reconciliation of opposites reminiscent of Schiller and Novalis, however, does not obscure Hesse's peculiarly analytic twist. It is of no small moment that the self and ideal self mirrored in one another correspond to the libidinal self and its universal archetype. The absolute has been derived from psychological experience which is raised to its higher level through the mystic's insight or the artist's imagination.

3

For a contemporary romantic like Hermann Hesse, the novelist projects inner schisms into a hero who ultimately raises his inadequate sensual self to the state of a harmonious or symbolic self. As we have seen, the conflict between self and world is projected into an ego that can unify them only in mystical revelation or in the illusion induced by art. For Hesse, these two realms are interdependent—the mystic's vision encompassing more fully any unity achieved by art, the poet's apprehension sustaining in time the harmonies briefly envisioned in the mystic's trance. Both function through an act of will, which is efficacious in a realm of creative illusion. In *Siddhartha*, Hesse suggests that the soul is ready to achieve unity by being able to think the idea of unity at any given time within the manifold stream of experience. (III, 716, 720) The artist, however, reenacts this vision or *Schau* through his imagination.

Two principles are involved in this concept of the imagination, both of which are reminiscent of Novalis. The relationship between the self in the world of sense and its higher projection suggests Novalis' notion of "romanticising." The dual nature of the aesthetic act as mystical integration and as psychological dissolution and resolution parallels Novalis' use of the term "magic" as a merging of dissonances which may manifest itself as madness in individual experience but which, publicly exhibited and consciously applied according to rules, becomes analogous to art.[12] Hesse's concept of "magic" is quite similar, although it has been enriched by Jungian, Buddhist, and Taoist thought, and is directed more fully toward a penetration of the individual consciousness.

For Hesse, the poet, or his *persona*, apprehends the manifold and refashions it into a form of the imagination. Magic, then, corresponds to the creative will of the imagination. In the slight fantasy "Kindheit des Zauberers" the poet himself is a magician, who, as Hesse puts it elsewhere, "forces reality, through magic, to suit his meaning." (IV, 487) A mature version is the "magic theater" of *Der Steppenwolf*, in which an imaginary stage represents spiritual unity comprising the dissonances of the inner and outer life. The schizophrenic hero, who is projected onto this stage, is shown how to discover such a unity, and to accept with detachment its illusory character.

Magic, so conceived, supersedes temporal sequence and even verbal expression. Jean Paul Richter had demanded that poetry should speak through the objects of nature, transcending the analytic world of philistines and pedants.[13] Hesse's narratives may express the hope for a language which can "say the unsayable" as in *Der Steppenwolf* or show a preference for those characters who communicate through images rather than words as in *Narziss und Goldmund*. They include innumerable examples in which visionary belief or the myth of poetry are held more effective than discourse or reasoning— the tools of *Geist*. A similar prejudice against temporal progression is suggested in the amusing climax of Hesse's whimsical autobiography, "Kurzgefasster Lebenslauf." The author (a modern Socrates waiting for his hemlock in the nightmare of a Kafkaesque bureaucracy) climbs on the train of his own painting and disappears in a cloud of smoke.[14] The "dull consecutiveness" of time has been canceled out in a world of appearance and play. Hesse's narrative and descriptive techniques implement this view of "magic" in peculiarly modern terms.

4

The moment of reconciliation must be frozen in time. To elicit "magic" from the materials of crude experience, Hesse must represent unity within the flow of time. The artist must capture the mystic's vision through his medium of words. This relationship between "dull consecutiveness" and the vision of integrating magic, particularly evident in the novel, had been thoroughly explored in romantic aesthetics.

In practice, Hesse borrows a good deal from romantic sources, notably from Novalis, to portray the relation between the time-bound experiences which his protagonists encounter and their reflections in timeless art. Two motifs or methods, suggestive of *Heinrich von Ofterdingen*, have been used with particular frequency. The first of these is the poetic symbol, the Blue Flower of poetry, through which the ideal above time can be portrayed simultaneously with a movement through time (the quest). The fairy tale "Iris," for example, borrows from Novalis the description of Anselmus' search for a flower which represents mystical vision and, ultimately, art. In Hesse's postwar novels, specific symbols such as the sparrow hawk and "Abraxas" in *Demian* or the flower symbolism of *Der Steppenwolf* portray reconciliations of opposites like light and dark, intellect and soul, unity and manifold beyond the time-bound order of the characters' lives. But for Hesse the object of the quest often represents not only poetry but also a hoped-for or achieved resolution of schizophrenic states through which a torn self is raised to a condition of illusory magic. Even in periods in which Hesse suppressed psychological meanings, he chose aesthetic symbols, such as statues in *Narziss und Goldmund* and *Die Morgenlandfahrt* or the Game of Glass Beads in *Das Glasperlenspiel*, to represent a unification of dissonances frozen in time through sensibly or intuitively accessible representation.

The second method posits a wanderer through space and time who acts as a perceiving eye, that is, as the passive romantic hero, in whom encounters and dreams are mirrored as art. Hesse poignantly utilizes the theme of wandering in *Der Novalis* (1907, published 1940), in which the structure and symbolism of *Heinrich von Ofterdingen* are suggested by a description of the transformations suffered by an old copy of Novalis' works. This story epitomizes the characteristic tension in Hesse's narratives between the world of images experienced in consecutive time and the sensibility of the experiencer which they ultimately portray. Moreover, as Hesse uses this method, perception is turned inward. Like Wilhelm Meister and Heinrich von Ofterdingen, Goldmund and Haller wander through the world of sense and symbolic dream, their sensibilities modified by events and encounters. But Hesse, the twentieth-century novelist, dissects them, more sharply. Unlike Wilhelm and Heinrich, Goldmund and Haller move through worlds which mirror, directly and allegorically, their internal states of mind, that is, disintegrations and resolutions occurring beneath the ordinary level of conscious and even unconscious experience.

Music and painting are likewise effectively employed to portray a union of opposites beyond time. Music functions as a combination of contradictory elements in self and world, either producing the dissonance of their continuous conflict, which it is the artist's hopeless task to resolve, or harmonizing opposites in the "appearance" of art. In the famous passage from *Der Kurgast*, Hesse dramatizes this point in terms of a significant personal longing:

> If I were a musician I could write without difficulty a melody in two voices, a melody which consists of two notes and sequences which correspond to each other, which complement each other, which condition each other, which in any event stand to one another in the closest and liveliest reciprocity and mutual relationship. And anyone who can read music, could read my double melody, could see and hear in each tone its counterpoint, the brother, the enemy, the antipode. Well, and just this double-voiced melody and eternally moving antithesis, this double line I want to express with my own material, with words, and I work myself sore at it, and it doesn't work. (IV, 113)

As a writer, Hesse longs to be a musician, not because he might feel more at home in a non-literary métier,[15] but because music embodies the very concept of harmony within dissonance which in his prevailing theme. The clash of opposites and their reconciliation is not only heard and made visually apparent to the reader of musical notations; it is also dramatized. As each note is accompanied by its antipode, it catches moments of unity in a world where contrasts shift, unite, and separate. In one sense, this view of music takes on a psychological dimension, as an expression of schizophrenia caught by the musical interplay of contrasting motifs. But in another sense, the *Wechselwirkung* of the antipodes is reminiscent of Fichte's *Wissenschaftslehre* and especially of Schiller's dialectic of form and matter and their reconciliation in the *Schein* of art.

In its function of presenting simultaneously the harmony and dissonance of opposing motifs, music seems to solve the conflicts in self and world. It is, in the phrase of Wackenroder and Tieck's *Phantasien über die Kunst*, the only art form which "reduces the most manifold and most contradictory movements of our soul to the *same* beautiful harmonies."[16] As we shall see, music functions as precisely such a symbol in *Das Glasperlenspiel*. It resolves dissonance by organizing experience and directing it toward a total vision rather than toward its consecutive or analytic explication. In this way, music can be seen, with Bettina von Arnim, as the quintessence of imagination. It is "the infinite within the finite, the element of genius present in all forms of art."[17] Its language, composed of magic formulae, is apt to frighten away philistines as new, indefinable worlds are opened up. An example of this view of music is Hesse's famous distinction in *Der Steppenwolf* between *rauschende* and *beitere Musik*. The former is chaotic music, likened to that of Wagner. A deceptive vision of unity is achieved by the massive sound which blurs boundaries between contradictory elements and themes. Its chaos, apparently triumphant, merely reflects diversity in an indistinguishable mass. The latter is clear, detached music likened to that of Mozart. Its ordered harmonies show the interplay of contrasting motifs with precision; its detachment prevents the blurring of boundaries between self and world and so reflects an independent unity.[18]

If music deepens the melody of life and catches it in art, the effect of painting works precisely in the opposite direction: it freezes the fluid manifold of experience in timeless portraiture. Hesse himself was a diligent water colorist and occasionally he even dreamed of turning to painting altogether as one of his major forms of expression. His small landscapes are reminiscent of romantic idylls: a church by a lake, a cluster of trees and houses, a cottage amid mountains with dusk drawing over the darkening water. His pictures are distinguished by an obvious desire to be precise both in the literal rendering of his subject and in the feelings he wished to convey. In his fiction, however, he viewed painting more analytically and metaphorically as a means of enhancing the idea of unity in illusion: the magic painting on the prison wall in "Kurzgefasster Lebenslauf." Diverse experiences, entire inner worlds are gathered in pictures: the statues carved by Goldmund and the peepshow sequences viewed by Haller. In each case, the inner world in which time is not necessarily a factor and the outer world which exists in time are rendered together to lend themselves to instantaneous apprehension.

In Hesse's narratives, pictorial presentation occurs in two important ways. One significant usage is that of the idyll as suggested in Jean Paul Richter's novels and in Friedrich Schlegel's notion of the arabesque. In "Kurzgefasster Lebenslauf," the idyllic picture is humorously treated; in *Nürnberger Reise*, changing landscapes are often portrayed through the author's changing attitudes in the act of painting. Throughout Hesse's novels, stories, and fairy tales, idyllic moments and scenes occur as essential structural elements through which the hero's quest is accentuated and ultimately defined. But in another usage, that of the self-portrait, painting has a further symbolic function. Like Heinrich von Ofterdingen, who reads his own life as a book of pictures in the Hermit's cave, Hesse's protagonists, and occasionally the author himself, depict their experiences so as to unify past, present, and future in a single moment of apprehension. Perhaps the most striking example of this method, extending Novalis' view of the interrelation of the arts, is the self-portrait drawn by the hero in "Klingsors letzter Sommer," which combines the effects of painting and music through a poetic description.[19]

In the context of the narrative, Klingsor draws his self-portrait against a background of the "music of doom," which he hears as an accompaniment to his painting. This music frees Klingsor from a need to represent himself and his inner world naturalistically, because its harmonies and dissonances dissolve spatial forms. It liberates his vision so that the painting he creates is a self-portrait embodying less its object, his own image, than his inner dissolution within the context of a larger world. It leads him to modify the world as he perceives it and to absorb it into his imagination. At the same time that music releases the limitations of his painting, his painting acts to control the chaotic implications of the experience of music, setting spatial limits and distributions into which the musically inspired vision of intoxicated harmony can be placed. As a result, the painting is a double exposure of a limited self and an unlimited universe. It emerges as a work of imagination which expresses Hesse's view of the function of art as the heightened image of the self, in which self and world are imposed upon one another in creative illusion.

> And not only his own features or his own thousand faces did he paint upon this picture, not merely his eyes and lips, the suffering gorge of his mouth, the split rock of his forehead, the root-like hands, the twitching fingers, the contempt of reason, death in his eye. He also painted, in his self-willed, crowded, compressed and twitching signature, his belief, his despair. (III, 611–612)

This painting is not composed of the orderly sequence of pictures that Heinrich von Ofterdingen views in the hermit's cave. It is rather a condensed image of world and man, produced by a kind of "magic," in which seemingly disparate elements, landscapes and features, coalesce. This rationale of Klingsor's self portrait also applies to other works. In *Narziss und Goldmund*, different images are marshaled in the orderly sequence of allegorical progression, yet they are gathered up in the statue carved by Goldmund. In the Game of *Das Glasperlenspiel*, which can be seen simultaneously as musical harmony and abstract representation, distinct elements are condensed into a "picture" denuded of any visualizable aspects. Elsewhere, portraitures abound in Hesse's work, depicting the inner man as he absorbs an alien world and resolving his conflict in timeless images.

In this way, all of Hesse's techniques—from picaresque structures to music and painting—suggest a concept of the imagination which combines the nineteenth-century reconciliation of opposites with a twentieth-century meaning of psychological conflict. His solution in the novel, based on the passive hero of the romantic tradition, is a *lyrical* solution. Three of his postwar works which have determined his reputation—*Demian, Der Steppenwolf,* and *Das Glasperlenspiel*—serve to measure the extent and limitation of Hesse's success in a romantic version of the lyrical novel.

## NOTES

1. "Vorrede eines Dichters zu seinen ausgewählten Werken" (1921). 'Betrachtungen, Gesammelte Dichtungen (Berlin-Zürich: Suhrkamp Verlag, 1957), VII, 252 (hereafter cited as *Dichtungen*; parentheses in the text refer to this edition). Hesse's lyricism is stressed by Ernst Robert Curtius, who points out that Hesse desired neither aesthetic nor social ties but rather sought immediate self-expression. Hence, Curtius concludes, Hesse's works are lyrical rather than epic, for the world implied by the latter is absent in them. "Hermann Hesse," *Kritische Essays zur europäischen Literatur* (Bern: A. Francke, 1950), pp. 212–213. In *Die Nürnberger Reise* (1928), Hesse identifies the romantic spirit with an anti-modern spirit and readily allies himself with it; *Dichtungen*, IV, 128–129. Hesse's authoritative biographer, Hugo Ball, speaks of his subject as the "letzte Ritter aus dem glanzvollen Zuge der Romantik"; *Hermann Hesse: Sein Leben and Werk* (Berlin: S. Fischer, 1927), pp. 26–27. For a fuller study of Hesse's relationship to German romanticism, see the Bern dissertation by Kurt Weibel, *Hermann Hesse and die deutsche Romantik* (Winterthur: P. G. Keller, 1954).

2. Letter to Thomas Mann, 12 Dec. 1947 in *Briefe, Dichtungen*, VII, 668–670.

3. "Foreword," *Demian* (New York: Henry Holt and Company, 1948), p. vi; "Einleitung zu einer amerikanischen Demianausgabe," *Die Neue Rundschau* (1947), p. 246.

4. Curtius, "Hermann Hesse," pp. 215ff.

5. Kurt Weibel identifies the *Weg nach Innen* with Hesse's affinity for German romanticism which finds its apex in *Siddhartha*. Beyond *Siddhartha*, he suggests a new direction, moving toward an affirmation of man's place as

a skilled practitioner of his craft within the universal harmony—an attainment suggesting a Goethean "classicism" of (masculine) *Geist. See Hermann Hesse und die deutsche Romantik*, pp. 7f., 24–28, 76–77, *et passim.*

6. Poetry (an intuitive, sensual apprehension of the world) must lead to "Streit und Zerfall mit der Wirklichkeit"; *Dichtungen*, IV, 149.

This explains the dual conflict which is so often seen in Hesse, that is, the conflict of the self with the external world and the conflict within the self. As the self seeks to absorb the world, the two oppositions coincide. Cf. Peter Heller, "The Creative Unconscious and the Spirit: A Study of Polarities in Hesse's Image of the Writer," *Modern Language Forum*, XXXVIII (March-June, 1953), 28–40.

7. "[Ich] kenne besser als irgendeiner den Zustand, in welchem das ewige Selbst in uns dem sterblichen Ich zuschaut und seine Sprünge und Grimassen begutachtet, voll Mitleid, voll Spott, voll Neutralität." *Die Nürnberger Reise, Dichtungen*, IV, 158–159. In "Kindheit des Zauberers," the universalizing, controlling force of the self, referred to as the "demon," is *der kleine Mann* who compels the child Hesse to follow him and who directs even the activities of Hesse, the older magician and grown artist (IV, 458ff.).

See also Oskar Seidlin, "Hermann Hesse: the Exorcism of the Demon," *Symposium*, IV (Nov. 1950), 327–328, 337, *et passim.*

8. See Seidlin, "Exorcism of the Demon," p. 333. For specific discussions of *Geist*, see Max Schmid, *Hermann Hesse: Weg und Wandlung* (Zürich: Fretz und Wasmuth, 1947), pp. 108, 123–125, 210–217. See also "The Creative Unconscious," pp. 35–36. Heller cautiously suggests that integration through *Geist* does not take place even in *Das Glasperlenspiel* (pp. 39–40).

Max Schmid develops the opposition of *Geist* and *Seele* in his attempt to show Hesse's relationship to Ludwig Klages' *Kosmogenischer Eros* and *Der Geist als Widersacher der Seele; Weg und Wandlung*, pp. 12–14, 94–96, 100–102, 210ff. *et passim.*

9. Intuitive vision or *Schatt* need not be that of *Geist*. For a comparison of the "romantic" vision of harmony in *Siddhartha* and the "classical" vision of harmony in *Das Glasperlenspiel*, see Max Schmid, *Weg und Wandlung*, pp. 210–211. Yet the end of *Das Glasperlenspiel* suggests that the absolute dominion of *Geist* is called into question by Knecht's rejection of Castalia and by his "legendary" death in the mountain lake. See also Hilde Cohn, "The Symbolic End of Herman Hesse's *Glasperlenspiel*," *Modern Language Quarterly*, XI (Sept. 1950), 347–357.

10. In "Eine Traumfolge," the symbol for art is a woman, mysterious but decidedly sexual, who dissolves into a child as the artist carries her into a

different realm; *Dichtungen*, III, 330–331. In "Märchen," the artist's song is made possible by a kiss which from then on inspires his art; *Dichtungen*, III, 296. Indeed, the artist's search is intrinsically sexual; sequences of debauch, in "Augustus" or "Klingsors letzter Sommer," in *Knulp* and "Klein und Wagner," and in *Siddhartha, Demian, Der Steppenwolf* and *Narziss und Goldmund* act as moments of essential experience, as the matter that goes into the making of art.

Max Schmid views Klein's death as a dissolution of the self in the stream of experience, Knecht's death as self-discovery through which the master can pass on his mission to his pupil; *Weg und Wandlung*, pp. 49–50, 189–191.

Miss Cohn views Knecht's death in water as a symbolic act through which the spirit can be passed from teacher to pupil. In her judgment, the maternal archetype of water, a Jungian notion, is combined with the Christian idea of baptism and rebirth. "The Symbolic End," pp. 355–356.

11. "Neue Fragmentensammlungen," 1798, *Schriften*, II, 326.

12. See Novalis' definitions of "magical idealism," "Das allgemeine Brouillon," *Schriften*, III, 227–228; "Neue Fragmentensammlungen," *Schriften*, II, 335–339.

13. *Werke*, Part I, 233.

14. *Dichtungen*, IV, 487–489. "Kurzgefasster Lebenslauf" was written with Jean Paul's "Konjekturalbiographie" in mind. (IV, 469)

15. Cf. Curtius, "Hermann Hesse," pp. 213–214.

16. *Phantasien über die Kunst, für Freunde der Kunst* (1799). Cited in *Kunstanschauung der Frühromantik*, ed. Andreas Müller (Leipzig: Philipp Reclam, 1931), p. 114.

17. *Goethes Briefwechsel mit einem Kinde*, I, 18If.; II, 283f. Cited in *Kunstanschauung der jüngeren Romantik*, ed. Andreas Müller (Leipzig: Philipp Reclam, 1934), pp. 226–227.

18. See *Der Steppenwolf, Dichtungen*, IV, 402–403; *Das Glasperlenspiel, Dichtungen*, VI, 99–100.

19. "Neue Fragmentensammlungen" (1798), *Schriften*, II, 359.

THEODORE ZIOLKOWSKI

# The Glass Bead Game: *Beyond Castalia*

Hesse's last novel forms a bridge from the aestheticism of his own generation to the existential engagement of the next. It not only contains one of the most striking symbols of man's faith in an eternal realm of art and the spirit; it also documents the author's struggle to free himself from this autonomous kingdom of *l'art pour l'art* for the sake of personal commitment to his fellow man. Because Hesse's attitude toward the aesthetic ideal (Castalia) changed during the eleven years of its genesis, the novel is not free of structural flaws. They are not, however, flaws of organization (as some critics have argued), but of point of view. We can approach the problem by comparing *The Glass Bead Game* with two other novels with which it has much in common.

Many critics have pointed out the similarities between Hesse's book and Thomas Mann's *Doctor Faustus* (1947). This is hardly surprising since both authors were struck by the resemblance.[1] Both books deal with the aesthetic sphere of music and offer, in addition to the action of the plot, a thumbnail history and theory of music in the text. Hesse's Tegularius, like Mann's Leverkühn (both of whom have traits borrowed from Nietzsche!), represents the hazards of excessive aestheticism and artistic despair. Both novels, in a certain sense, are *romans à clef*, referring to significant figures from the intellectual and cultural history of Germany; and both make use of a

From *The Novels of Hermann Hesse: A Study in Theme and Structure.* © 1965 by Princeton University Press.

montage technique through which quotations and essayistic passages are built into the texture of the fiction. In both books, finally, a criticism of contemporary society is suspended in a network of tension between irony and seriousness. Many other points might be mentioned; the possibilities of comparison have by no means been exhausted by scholarship. Yet these points represent largely thematic similarities. Structurally the two novels are poles apart.

*Doctor Faustus* is a masterpiece of epic integration; like Joyce's *Ulysses*, which inspired it, the novel is constructed organically from within and forms a tightly knit artistic whole. *The Glass Bead Game*, while likewise highly organized, represents an entirely different structural principle; its balance, if the analogy be permitted, is less organic than architectonic—a fact that can be accounted for by the genesis of the novel. Hesse's structural ideas changed several times during the composition, while Thomas Mann had his general organization in mind from the outset.

Far closer to Hesse's novel, both in genesis and ultimate organization, is another work: the third volume of Hermann Broch's *The Sleepwalkers*, which Hesse read and reviewed shortly after its publication in 1932. In both of these works we find a range of technique that is lacking in *Doctor Faustus:* from the total objectivity of the abstract essay to the absolute subjectivity of lyric poetry. (In Mann's novel the essayistic passages are built organically into the fiction as conversations and reflections; the point of view of the narrator is consistent throughout.) Both eschew organic integration in order to broaden the horizons and implications of the central story by means of parallel plots and interpolated essays. Both revolve around a theoretical tract on the decline of values that culminates in the vision of an aesthetic ideal existing autonomously apart from reality. And both, finally, achieve their artistic integration through a narrator who—in contrast to the narrator of *Doctor Faustus*, who is unable to understand the full implications of his story and, at the same time, represents a dialectical antithesis to the hero—stands above his material, viewing it, so to speak, *sub specie aeternitatis*. This does not imply that Hesse was "influenced" by Broch's novel. Many of these devices were anticipated to a certain extent in *The Steppenwolf* and *The Journey to the East*. It merely demonstrates that Hesse and Broch were striving for integration of a different sort than Thomas Mann. *The Glass Bead Game*, structurally, must be judged according to different criteria from *Doctor Faustus*.

It is in this connection, I believe, that Hesse's novel can most fruitfully be compared with *Wilhelm Meister's Travels (Wanderjahre)*. The innumerable scholarly discussions concerning the similarity of the two novels goes back, again, to Hesse's own hints. In the course of the book he explicitly refers, on several occasions, to Castalia as "the pedagogical province"—a term borrowed from Goethe's last novel; it has often been pointed out that his hero's name (*Knecht*, or "servant") is used in direct and conscious contrast to Goethe's Meister ("master"). Although a great deal has been written about these matters, in general the results have shown that the resemblances are often superficial.[2] Goethe's conception of "Doing and Thinking," for instance, turns out to be quite different from Hesse's idea of "vita activa and vita contemplativa."[3] Likewise, the more pragmatic goal of Goethe's pedagogical province is far removed from the aesthetic ideal of Castalia. Moreover, in Goethe's novel the pedagogical province is only one of the various areas of activity while in Hesse's work it is the center of interest throughout. The conception of Castalia as an aesthetic ideal emerged organically, as we shall see, from ideas that Hesse had been developing since *Narziss and Goldmund*. Goethe's pedagogical province unquestionably contributed certain motifs, but it would be a mistake to assume that there exists any close parallel in theme or intention.

Structurally, however, there are undeniable similarities. Both Hesse and Broch have revealed an interest in Goethe's late novel, in contrast to most writers who have been concerned primarily with *Wilhelm Meister's Apprenticeship*. The *Apprenticeship* has long and rightfully been regarded as the founder of a tradition of *Bildungsroman* that reaches from the early Romantic novel right down to contemporary works such as Thomas Mann's *The Magic Mountain*. It can be argued with equal persuasiveness, however, that the *Travels* inaugurated a completely different tradition—one that did not really make its impact until the beginning of the experimental novel of the twenties and thirties. In the *Travels* we find anticipated many of the features that strike us, in *The Sleepwalkers* and *The Glass Bead Game*, as radical and modern: the depiction of a collective society with a corresponding reduction in the role of the individual hero; an internalization of plot with emphasis not on the action itself, but rather on reflection about the action; interpolation of reflection into the novel as pure essay, which is not integrated by means of conversations; a questioning of the efficacy of language and traditional form with a corresponding breakdown of narrative structure in favor of a looser additive form; the development of an anonymous narrator who is sensitive to the problematic nature of his undertaking. These are but a few of the more conspicuous points of similarity, but they represent what I consider to be a more fruitful direction of inquiry into the influence of Goethe on Hesse's novel. An undue preoccupation with details of theme and plot only leads us further away from an understanding of *The Glass Bead Game* in its aims and implications.

For the same reason I should not like to insist too much on the novel's indebtedness to the tradition of the *Bildungsroman*. Although the central section—Knecht's life—has definite points in common with the *Bildungsroman*, the book as a whole has a different structure altogether; and even within the central section the emphasis is split between the hero and the institution to a degree that properly exceeds the limits of the traditional *Bildungsroman*. Although at a certain stage of the composition Hesse may have conceived of the work as a *Bildungsroman*, the shifting focus soon forced him, as we shall see, to shatter the limits of the conventional form.

The long novel—it was originally published in two volumes of 450 pages each—is ostensibly a historical study written around the year 2400 by an anonymous narrator, and it falls into three main sections. A lengthy introduction outlines the history, theory, and practice of the institution known as the Glass Bead Game. The central narrative relates the life of Joseph Knecht, a famous Magister Ludi (i.e. Master of the Glass Bead Game) who lived at about the time when the introduction discontinues, some years prior to the generation of the narrator. A full appendix contains the writings of Joseph Knecht: thirteen poems written surreptitiously while Knecht was in school, and three fictitious "Lives" composed by Knecht during his student years as exercises in history.

The twelve chapters of Knecht's biography proceed chronologically, relating the outstanding periods in his life from his selection, at age twelve or thirteen, into Castalia as a pupil, to his defection from the pedagogic province some thirty-five years later. We see Knecht progress smoothly through his studies at Eschholz and Waldzell (the school for students who wish to devote themselves specifically to the Glass Bead Game). We witness his friendship with Plinio Designori, the "auditor" who returns to the outside world when his studies are ended; with Fritz Tegularius, the hyperintellectual who caricatures, by exaggeration, the principles and values of Castalia; the old Magister Musicae, who represents beatific bliss and harmony achieved in life itself; the Older Brother, a Castalian who has devoted himself so one-sidedly to oriental studies that he has become almost Chinese himself; and Thomas von der Trave (a subtle tribute to Thomas Mann), the polished and urbane Magister Ludi. For two chapters we follow Knecht to the Benedictine monastery of Mariafels, where, as an official emissary of Castalia, he establishes diplomatic relations between the two orders and, from Pater Jacobus, learns basic lessons in history. For eight years, after the death of Thomas von der Trave, Knecht is in office as Magister Ludi, a position in which he attains great renown. After five or six years, however, grave doubts begin to assail him, and they are intensified by conversations with his old friend Plinio Designori. Knecht decides to defect from his position. He sends a long letter of justification to the authorities and then goes to Plinio's house, where he expects to take up a position as tutor to Plinio's son, Tito. On the second day of his liberty Knecht accompanies his pupil to a mountain lodge where, unexpectedly, he drowns while following Tito in a swim across the icy lake at sunrise.

## An Exercise in Symbolic Logic

For an age in which electronic music has combined music and physics, in which sculptures and paintings are plotted according to the table of logarithms, in which philosophy has fused with mathematics to create the new language of symbolic logic, an age in which "literary" and sociological research is carried on by IBM machines—for such an age it is difficult to conceive of a more appropriate symbol than the Glass Bead Game. The name itself, Hesse's narrator assures us, is misleading. When it was originally invented by a group of musicians shortly after 1900, the game was indeed played with beads arranged on a device much like an abacus. By means of the abacus the theme could be modified, transposed, set in counterpoint—in other words, manipulated completely without the aid of musical sound itself. It permitted, in a still primitive form, the total abstraction of the intellectual elements of music. Very rapidly, however, two developments took place: the exercise outgrew the relatively naïve form of the original abacus and developed a symbolic sign system of its own; but it retained the original name although it was no longer played with glass beads on an abacus frame. The technique was gradually adopted by other disciplines in which values could be expressed by a set of mathematical notations: mathematics itself, classical philology, logic, the visual arts, and so forth. For a time the techniques of the Glass Bead Game were developed independently within the various disciplines, but finally it became apparent that cross-references were possible. The abstract notation of a musical theme, for instance, might be identical with the abstracted formula of an architectural edifice (one thinks in this connection of recent scholarship in medieval literature!), a process in physics, or an astronomical configuration. The initiates gradually developed a set of symbols in which it was possible to express graphically the interrelationship of all intellectual disciplines. When this new technique was combined with meditation on the meaning of the symbols, the Glass Bead Game in its supreme form was born.

We shall not make the mistake of some readers who wrote to Hesse that they had invented the Glass Bead Game long before he described it in his novel. (In Hesse's letters one can read his amusing answers to some of these humorless aficionados.) It is fruitless to attempt any description of the rules and techniques of the game, for nowhere is it outlined in detail. By way of analogy: Thomas Mann never intended Adrian Leverkühn's compositions, which he describes with such professional detail and precision in *Doctor Faustus*, to be performed. The modern novelist is not satisfied to state merely that his hero wrote a book, composed a symphony, constructed a perfect game; he wants to depict the act of writing, composing, constructing; and to do this he must describe the work with persuasive realism. But it would be as futile to attempt to set up a game as it would be to reconstruct the score of Leverkühn's *Apocalipsis cum figuris*. As a matter of fact, it would be a decided artistic flaw if the game were described with such precision that a table of rules could be drawn up. Though there are many examples, the Glass Bead Game is intended purely as a symbol, and any symbol must transcend its specific application or else it degenerates into allegory. In the novel the Glass Bead Game symbolizes the universal longing for what Hesse calls the "unio mystica of all disparate elements of the Universitas Litterarum."[4] It is "a refined, symbolic form of the search for perfection, a sublime alchemy, an approach to the spirit that is unified in itself above all images and quantities, an approach to God."[5] Much space is devoted in the novel to descriptions of various games that are played and combinations that are achieved; but it is pedantic to regard these as more than symbolic. As we know from Hesse's poems and letters, he himself was fond of playing the Glass Bead Game. In his private life, however, it was not the elaborate ritual depicted in the novel, but rather the quiet reflection on permanent values that exist eternally in the works of art and intellectual life from different periods of history. The game as it is described in the novel is a successful symbol precisely because it can be identified with so many aspects of contemporary thought and art. It is a common denominator, as it were, for the many attempts in modern times to achieve a new unity, a unified field, from the disintegrated values of our civilization. One could do far worse than to imagine the game as an exercise in symbolic logic.

The mechanics of the game, however, is only one aspect of the problem. "For like every great idea," the narrator tells us, "it actually has no beginning but, as an idea, has always existed."[6] The game, in the terms of this novel, is another symbolic representation of the longing for simultaneity and totality that we have seen in every one of Hesse's later books, and as such it fits organically into the development of his thought following *The Journey to the*

*East.* In his introduction the narrator reminds us that the basic idea can be found in Pythagoras, in late classical civilization, in Hellenistic-Gnostic circles, and among the ancient Chinese. Abelard, Leibniz, and Hegel were likewise striving "to capture the spiritual universe in concentric systems and to unite the living beauty of the spiritual world and art with the magical power of formulization of the exact disciplines."[7] It was not until our own time—the era that Hesse disparagingly calls "the feuilletonistic age"—that the Glass Bead Game was actually precipitated.

Hesse's outline of the development of civilization leading to the invention of the Glass Bead Game shortly after 1900 is remarkable in its similarity to Hermann Broch's essay on "The Disintegration of Values" in *The Sleepwalkers*. He notes two main tendencies in European intellectual life after the Middle Ages: "the freeing of thought and faith from any sort of authoritarian influence...and, on the other hand, the secret but passionate search for the legitimization of this freedom, for a new authority that, emerging from itself, would be adequate."[8] This can be very easily translated into the language that Broch employs. After human intellect freed itself from the bonds of the Roman Catholic Church, it was no longer responsible to any central and authoritative set of values. As liberated intellect applied itself to various areas of activity, it developed new, often conflicting sets of values. There eventually emerged from this chaos the longing for a common center that would once again give meaning to life. During the "feuilletonistic age" the dilemma became particularly acute. Technological developments had advanced at a rapid pace while moral consciousness had remained at a standstill: "they stood, almost defenseless, facing death, anxiety, pain, hunger, no longer consolable by the churches, uncounseled by the spirit." Hesse's narrator explains the frenetic activity of the age—the many popular lectures, card games, cross-word puzzles, as well as the consuming interest in light articles on cultural topics in the feuilleton—as the attempt of an entire generation "to flee in the face of unsolved problems and fearful premonitions of destruction into a harmless world of make-believe."[9]

It was at this time, among various groups determined to remain true to the values of the spirit (the narrator mentions the Eastern Wayfarers of *The Journey to the East* in this connection), that the Glass Bead Game tentatively emerged. As it developed, incorporating first all branches of learning and then the process of meditation, it was formalized into an institution of rigid hierarchical organization with a world commission to govern the archive of symbols, elite schools for the training of initiates, and—at the top—the Magister Ludi or Master Player. In his own mind Hesse clearly regarded this organization as another variation of the ideal as he had represented it in

*Narziss and Goldmund* and *The Journey to the East*. "The creation of a purified atmosphere was necessary to me," he wrote in 1933. "This time I did not go into the past or into a fairy-tale timeless realm, but constructed the fiction of a dated future."[10]

## The Shifting Focus

What we have outlined above is the theory of the Glass Bead Game as it appears in the introduction that was published, in fourth draft, as early as 1934. There, as in the final version of 1943, the introduction presents a utopian dream of synthesized totality that fits smoothly into the development of Hesse's thought as we know it from previous works. The introduction is dedicated to "The Eastern Wayfarers," and the motto—which Hesse wrote himself and had translated into Latin by two friends[11]—indicates that he is concerned principally with representing an ideal vision of his aesthetic realm as persuasively as possible in order to further its realization (*enti nascendique facultati paululum appropinquant*).

It is primarily this introduction, along with the motto, that has given rise to the mistaken notion that *The Glass Bead Game* is a utopian novel. To be sure, the introduction of 1934 is utopian. We can detect there not a single hint of the problematic nature of Castalia as it is revealed in the text of the narrative itself. That is the most serious structural flaw of the book. After his own view of the Glass Bead Game changed, after his own defection from the aestheticism that it represents, Hesse did not adapt the introduction to correspond to the new tone of the later passages. Hesse himself was aware of this defect. "During the first three years my perspective was slightly altered several times. In the beginning I was concerned above all—almost exclusively—with rendering Castalia visible.... Then it became clear to me that the inner reality of Castalia could be rendered plausibly visible only in a dominating person...and so Knecht stepped into the center of the narrative."[12] In the introduction Knecht is briefly mentioned in passing, but the author's interest is focused above all on the game itself. Its importance is highlighted by the fact that the novel gets its title in the German version from the game—not from the man! At this early stage (1933) the theme of defection has not yet appeared. "I intend simply to write the story of a magister ludi," Hesse wrote to a friend. "His name is Knecht, and he lives approximately at the time when the preface ends. I know no more than that.... There will be a spiritual culture that is worth living in and serving—this is the wish-dream that I should like to depict."[13] At this time the Glass

Bead Game and the institution of Castalia represent an ideal vision that, *mutatis mutandis*, corresponds to the League in *The Journey to the East* or the realm of the Immortals in *The Steppenwolf.* There is not the least indication that Joseph Knecht will ultimately question the value of the aesthetic realm. His whole function is merely that of a representative figure in whom the ideal realm can be exemplified.

For several years, however, nothing was done about Joseph Knecht. He is mentioned from time to time in letters and poems, but not until 1938 did Hesse actually begin writing the chapters of his biography. During the intervening years he was concerned with the poems and the "Lives," which were published separately in *Die neue Rundschau* as they were completed: in 1934 "The Rainmaker"; in 1936 "The Father Confessor"; and in 1937 "An Indian Life." In the final version of the novel these stories are introduced as fictitious autobiographies that Knecht wrote as part of his studies—exercises in projecting oneself into the historical past as were required of all students in Castalia. In the novel the narrator also speaks of a fourth "Life" that Knecht never wrote: one dealing with Pietism in eighteenth-century Swabia. There is some indication that Hesse wrote at least a preliminary version of that story, which he did not include in the final work.[14] In any event, the novel outlines the contents of this fourth "Life" and Hesse's letters in 1933 and 1934 demonstrate his extensive reading in the period.

There is reason to believe, however, that these "Lives" were originally intended to fulfill a different function. Toward the end of 1933 Hesse reported to Thomas Mann on his work in progress, mentioning his wide background readings. "My plan of the past two years (concerning the mathematical-musical game) is growing into the conception of a multi-volume work—indeed, of an entire library—all the more lovely and complete in my imagination, the more remote it is from any possibility of realization."[15] Apart from Hesse's other remark to the effect that his perspective shifted several times in the course of composition, there is no documentary evidence to support my conjecture. But it does not seem unreasonable, in the light of textual evidence, to assume that Hesse at this time—from 1933 to 1937—was planning to write something like a history of the aesthetic realm by means of parallel representative lives from various periods, culminating in the figure of Joseph Knecht in Castalia. After all, if the course of Knecht's own life was still not clear to Hesse at this time, then how could he have foreseen that Knecht would be required to write the fictional "Lives" as part of his studies? It seems more logical to assume that the "Lives" were written independently according to a different structural conception: a series of parallel stories illustrating devotion to the spiritual ideal and the gradual emergence, especially in the fourth unwritten "Life," of the idea of a Glass Bead Game. This assumption would explain two problems. First, it would account for the lapse of time before Hesse began writing, in 1938, the central part of the novel; originally it was supposed to be not the *center*, but the *last* in a series. And, more important, it would justify the fact that the three published "Lives" portray a rejection of life and a devotion to the autonomous spiritual realm from which Joseph Knecht defects.

It is rather a surprise for the reader of the novel, when he comes to the three appended "Lives," to ascertain that they do not anticipate in any way the defection toward which the central part of the book builds so steadily.[16] Thematically they are related to Knecht's life by the ideal of service—a theme indicated by the variations on the names of the heroes, all of which mean "servant": Knecht, Famulus, Dasa. But it is service restricted exclusively to the spiritual ideal as we found in *The Journey to the East*.

This is particularly conspicuous in the earliest of the "Lives," which portrays the career of a rainmaker in a primitive matriarchal society. There are striking parallels in theme and vocabulary between this story and the theoretical introduction to the Glass Bead Game, both of which appeared in 1934. Briefly, the story tells of Knecht's apprenticeship to the rainmaker Turu, his own investiture as rainmaker and finally his self-immolation for the sake of his spiritual office. It must be stressed that his sacrifice is *not* for the sake of the tribe; the tribe, as Knecht knows, is in no further danger. He sacrifices himself in order to retain the faith of the tribe in the spiritual powers that he represents. His sacrifice represents, in other words, an act of allegiance to the realm of spirit and not of commitment to his fellow man. The rainmaker embodies, in this primitive society, the forces of spirit and intellect; society as a whole is regarded with the same feeling of distrust and hostility that characterizes the Introduction as well as Hesse's other writings up to this point. When he is first introduced to the mysteries of astrology, young Knecht "felt in the first shudder of premonition that everything was a whole and that he himself was ordered into and related to this totality."[17] He regards his tutelage as "his reception into a League and Cult, into a subservient yet honorable relationship to the Ineffable, to the mystery of the world."[18] The magical signs that he learns represent "a reduction of the infinite and the multiform into the Simple, into a system, into a concept."[19] This entire conception of the role of the intellectual corresponds precisely to the definition of the Glass Bead Game and Castalia in the Introduction: the striving for unification and totality, the idea of a cult, and the symbolic function of signs.

The second "Life" has fewer outstanding parallels. It deals with two patristic fathers, Joseph Famulus and Dion Pugil, both of whom have devoted their lives to service of the spirit as personified—in the context of the story—by the Christian God. At an advanced age, however, both of them are overtaken by doubts as to the validity of their function as confessors. The story relates how each, by his example, comforts the other and leads him back into service of the spiritual ideal. In both cases we have a temporary impulsive doubt, but it leads back to a renewed and intensified devotion to the spirit—not, like Joseph Knecht's defection, out of the spiritual realm and into the world.

"An Indian Life," finally, focuses even more sharply on the life of the spirit than the other two. Although Dasa undergoes what appear to be highly sensual adventures in the world of the flesh—a logical inconsistency, by the way, when the inexperienced and unworldly scholar Knecht is later purported to be the author of these "Lives"—these events are subsequently revealed to have been nothing but an illusion, the veil of Maya. Dasa ends his days in the forests in the company of an aged yogin, forsaking the temptations of the world. Again: the ideal of service is a theme, but it is service specifically isolated from the realm of life and consecrated to the eternal spirit.

The most interesting of the "Lives" is the fourth, unwritten one. According to the narrator, the school authorities urged Knecht to turn his attention to a period that offered more documentary evidence and to concern himself more with historical detail—a subtle indication that Hesse was not unaware of criticisms made of *Siddhartha* and *Narziss and Goldmund*. So he turned to the eighteenth century. "He intended to appear there as a Swabian theologian who later gave up the church for music, who was a pupil of Johann Albrecht Bengel, a friend of Oetinger, and for a time a guest of the Zinzendorf congregation."[20] All of these names occur frequently in Hesse's letters and essays; they belong to the cultural period in which, as we have seen, he felt most at home: the Swabian eighteenth century. In the present connection, however, it is the theologian Bengel who concerns us most. Later in the novel he is mentioned again, specifically as a precursor of the Glass Bead Game. "In his early years, before the great Bible work took up his time, Bengel once told his friends of his plan to encompass all the knowledge of his day in an encyclopedic work organized symmetrically and synoptically around a central idea. That is exactly what the Glass Bead Game does.... Bengel was striving not only for a parallelism of the areas of knowledge and research, but for an interrelationship, an organic order; he was searching for the common denominator. And that is one of the basic concepts of the Glass

Bead Game."[21] It is impossible to determine why Hesse never completed this "Life," which in many respects should have meant most to him. But it should be pointed out that he was working on it most intensively in the years 1933 and 1934, precisely at the time when he wrote the theoretical introduction to the novel. It requires no great insight to ascertain the striking parallels between the two projects. The "Life" of the Swabian theologian, had it been written, would have represented a pre-stage of the Glass Bead Game. Even in the few hints we can see the main principles: the idea of unification of all knowledge, the element of music, and the religious impulse. Like the other "Lives," this one glorifies the aesthetic and spiritual ideal at the expense of life itself.

Although Hesse wrote these "Lives" before the theme of Knecht's defection had emerged in his mind—and probably, as I have suggested, in accordance with an originally different structural plan—they still fit organically into the work as it was finally published. For the narrator carefully points out that they were written at a time in Knecht's life when his doubts concerning the validity of a purely aesthetic realm like Castalia had not yet assailed him. Secondly, they were written as official studies, and so Knecht would have been careful to suppress any doubts that he may have had from the authorities. As they appear in the work now, they represent young Knecht's faith in the realm of the spirit and in the ideal of service to the hierarchy, in which the personality of the individual is effaced and subjugated to the needs of the whole. This ideal of selflessness conforms, in turn, to the biographical principles of the narrator, who tells us in his introduction that the Castalian conception of biography differs from that of the "feuilletonistic age," which was fascinated less by the typical than by the aberrant characteristics of individuals. "For us only those men are heroes and worthy of special interest, who by nature and training are put into a position in which their persons are subsumed almost totally in their hierarchic function."[22] Joseph Knecht of the early chapters fulfills this ideal almost completely.


## THREE CASTALIAS

Hesse himself has pointed out that Knecht in his early years "represents the inner meaning and value of this world, whereas the older Knecht, who has been trained in history, embodies the thought of the relativity and transitoriness of even the most ideal world."[23] This ambivalency must be stressed. Up to now we have discussed those parts of the novel (introduction and the "Lives") in which all concerned—Hesse, the fictitious narrator, and Knecht—are convinced of the utopian value of the spiritual realm represented by Castalia. In the central text of the novel, however—the twelve chapters of the biography—the perspective has shifted considerably: Castalia is no longer a utopian ideal, but rather a dialectical antithesis to the forces of life that Knecht encounters in the course of his career. Knecht himself, as we shall see, becomes aware of the problematic nature of Castalia only gradually. The fictitious narrator, however, who is in a position to survey Knecht's life from beginning to end, perceives the dangers inherent in a purely aesthetic realm even while Knecht is still basking in the euphorious bliss of the Glass Bead Game. We must not forget that the narrator, who according to Hesse's fiction is living some years after Knecht's death, has profited from Knecht's experience. His Castalia has benefited from Knecht's defection and death.

Some readers have tended to interpret the ending of the novel solely from the viewpoint of Tito, the young boy whose tutor Knecht becomes after his departure from Castalia. The narrator repeatedly makes it clear, however, that Knecht's sacrifice had profound implications for Castalia itself, which underwent a revaluation of its principles after the abrupt defection of the renowned Magister Ludi. At one point the narrator interjects a personal remark to condone Knecht, who recognized "long before the rest of us that the complicated and sensitive apparatus of our republic was an aging organism that was in need of rejuvenation in certain respects."[24] Later, after relating that Castalia was temporarily split into two factions over the validity of Knecht's criticism, the narrator points out that it is no longer necessary to take sides in the argument, for "the synthesis from that conflict of verdicts and opinions concerning Joseph Knecht's person and life has long since been in process of formation."[25] Finally, the changed attitude of the authorities is evidenced by the very fact that the narrator, a Castalian himself, is allowed to undertake a biography of the great renegade Knecht; that he has at his disposal not only more or less public documents like the "Legend" relating Knecht's last days but also letters by Knecht as well as many addressed to him, conversations jotted down by friends both in Castalia and in the world outside, copies of Knecht's own lectures, and—finally—official reports from the archives of Castalia. Without belaboring the textual details we can state that the fiction of the narrator is maintained consistently throughout the novel; he reports only those incidents, conversations, and thoughts for which he has an acknowledged and legitimate source. Far more important is the mere fact that the biography was written. To state the case most radically: the true beneficiary of Knecht's sacrifice is neither Knecht nor Tito, but the narrator himself, who represents a Castalia tempered by the criticisms made by Knecht during his lifetime. The novel actually depicts, implicitly or explicitly, *three* visions of Castalia: the utopian spiritual realm portrayed in the introduction and *only* there; the Alexandrine republic of aestheticism, sharply attacked by Knecht and the narrator alike in the text of the novel; and finally a more balanced synthesis of life and spirit represented by the narrator himself. It is necessary to make sharp distinctions between these three stages.

Now what Hesse and most of his critics mean when they speak of Castalia is the realm portrayed in the central section of the novel—the "pedagogical province" from which Knecht defects. It is obvious that this Castalia is no utopia except in the etymological sense of the word. Hesse has carefully denied its idealistically utopian nature. The only time he used the word "utopia" without any qualifying restrictions to apply to his novel was in the explanatory note accompanying the publication of the introduction in *Die neue Rundschau* in 1934: "This treatise is the preface to a utopian work; one should think of it as having been written approximately around 2400." As we have seen, only that introduction is genuinely utopian in the sense, say, of *The Journey to the East*. All of Hesse's later remarks qualify the expression "utopia" when it is used. "I am glad that you recognized so correctly the structure of my utopia and formulated it so well: it shows merely one possibility of spiritual life, a Platonic dream—not an ideal that should be considered eternally valid, but a potential world that is conscious of its own relativity."[26]

A more fruitful approach, and one that permits us to fit the novel into the tendencies of modern literature in general, is to regard Castalia not as a utopia, but rather as what might be called—to borrow a term from art criticism—a realistic abstraction.[27] It is necessary, in order to discuss this novel, to be able to distinguish between the abstractionism of the game itself and the abstract nature of the structure. The rejection of aesthetic abstractionism is the principal theme of the novel, culminating in Knecht's defection. Yet the structure remains abstract throughout. To indicate a similar dilemma in painting, Piet Mondrian spoke of neo-plasticism and "peinture abstraite réelle." In 1930 Theo van Doesburg introduced a new name for the same concept in the title of his journal *Art concret*. All of these terms were an attempt to avoid the implications popularly associated with the word "abstract" as it was used after 1910 by Kandinsky and others in order to designate a wholly non-objective art. The new art of the twenties marked a return to real and concrete objects, even though the objects were portrayed in their ideal essence rather than in their naturalistic manifestation.[28] Now precisely this distinction can be useful to us. The Glass Bead Game is wholly abstract, as we have seen; it operates with symbols abstracted from the original object or thing. The novel as a structure, on the other hand, is a realistic or concrete abstraction.

Utopias, along with their negative counterpart, the apocalyptic novel, are by no means absent from recent literature. In postwar German literature one thinks—to take only the most conspicuous examples—of Franz Werfel's *Star of the Unborn* (1946), Hermann Kasack's *City beyond the River* (1947), and Ernst Jünger's *Heliopolis* (1949). It is noteworthy, however, that most utopias are conceived by writers of the older aesthetic generation. The authors of the postwar era no longer have the faith implicit in any utopia, whether it be aesthetic, social, political, or otherwise. The general tendency in their writings has been toward the realistic abstraction. Superficially this type of abstraction has certain features in common with the utopia—specifically the qualities of timelessness and placelessness. The utopia traditionally and typically represents the envisaged realm as an ideal to be achieved; it has no time or place because it has not been realized here and now. The realistic abstraction, on the other hand, exploits the techniques of utopism and uchronism for diametrically opposed reasons. The abstraction assumes that the situation it renders is so typical and so omnipresent that it would be misleading to pin it down to a specific time or place. These writers are dealing with problems—say, the question of human guilt or freedom—that are equally valid whether the scene be France, Germany, or America, whether the time be the present, the future, or the remote past. This is conspicuously the case in many contemporary dramas; one thinks of Thornton Wilder, Max Frisch, and various young German playwrights such as Tankred Dorst or Richard Hey. The German *Hörspiel* (radio drama), whenever it has attained the status of a genuine and unique art form, has exploited precisely this built-in placelessness of its medium. Although the novel tends to cling more closely to its roots in realism, the realistic abstraction has a distinguished forerunner in the fiction of Franz Kafka, and it has found contemporary exponents in writers such as Albert Camus, Alfred Andersch, or William Golding. None of their works could be called utopias; none, on the other hand, could be termed realistic depictions. What they have in common is a concern with immediate and recognizable human problems, abstracted to the extent that the situations transcend the specific and become general or universal; yet they maintain a freedom of characterization that distinguishes them in turn from simple allegory.

A definition of this sort seems to be implicit in all the utterances in which Hesse seeks to explain the implications of his novel. "Actually, in the book I was thinking neither of a utopia (in the sense of a dogmatic program) nor of a prophecy; rather, I tried to portray something that I consider to be one of the genuine and legitimate ideas, the realization of which one can sense at many points of world history."[29] In another letter he emphasizes the fact that Castalia is merely the representation of a mode of life that already exists. "In connection with Castalia one must consider that it is not only— not even primarily—a utopia, a dream, and a future, but also reality. For orders, Platonic academies, yoga schools—all of these have existed often and for a long time."[30] In a letter to Thomas Mann, Hesse praises in *Doctor Faustus* precisely the qualities that he had striven to achieve in his own novel: "…the way in which this set of problems is transferred into the realm of music and analyzed there with the calmness and objectivity that are possible only in the abstract. What I find most astonishing and surprising is the fact that you do not allow this pure extract, this ideal abstraction to soar out into an ideal realm, but that you locate it in the midst of a realistically visualized world and time…"[31] This analysis amounts to a definition of the realistic abstraction and might well be the structural principle underlying Hesse's own book.

Hesse was not trying to represent an ideal or utopian society. Instead, after his devastating satire of the "feuilletonistic age" in the introduction, he goes on to lay bare the dangers of its antithesis: a purely intellectually or aesthetically oriented existence that lives without commitment to the world around it. This exposé is accomplished in an abstracted vision of society, but it is no less a plea for engagement and commitment than other more naturalistic works of our own generation. The reasons for Knecht's defection are made quite clear in the course of the novel; it is more difficult to account for Hesse's own swing from the aestheticism attained in *The Journey to the East* to the commitment to life and to fellow man symbolized by the ending of *The Glass Bead Game*. However, in 1932 it was far easier to maintain an attitude of detached aestheticism than was the case during the succeeding decade of world history. The first signs of disenchantment with the aesthetic ideal can be detected in the poems that Hesse wrote in the middle thirties, a selection of which was later included in the novel as Knecht's own work.


## THE UNTENABLE IDEAL

The "Lives," as we saw, were written from a positive attitude toward Castalia and their inclusion was subsequently justified on the grounds that they represented official studies of Knecht as a student. Hesse obviously realized the self-contradiction implicit in the poems, which, for the most part, reject that same ideal. As a result, they are explained by the narrator as being surreptitious products of Knecht's first doubts—poems written expressly in opposition to the rules of the institution and preserved secretly in manuscript form. The narrator is aware of the crisis manifested in the poems. "In certain lines there resounds a deep sense of disquiet, a basic doubt in himself and in the meaning of his existence, until in the poem 'The Glass Bead Game' the devout submission seems to have been achieved."[32] From the vantage point of our knowledge concerning the genesis of the novel, this explanation is not lacking in a certain irony. The poem that the narrator mentions as expressing the resolution of Knecht's conflicts—the one printed last in the collection— was actually written in 1934 *before* all the other poems. "The Glass Bead Game," which does indeed reveal full approval of the aesthetic ideal, dates from the same year as the introduction. The other more skeptical poems were written later—mainly in 1935 and 1936, during the crucial transitional period—but in order to satisfy the fiction of the novel the early poem was arranged as the final one. According to the plot Knecht's early doubts had to be resolved for a time! This is another example of the careful structuring through which Hesse sought to integrate the diverse materials of his novel as it changed in conception and perspective. By and large, I believe that the attempt was successful, for few readers, without a knowledge of the genesis, would guess the true order of composition.

To return to the earlier question: other poems, written at a later date, reveal Hesse's own doubts regarding the validity of his original ideal. "The Last Magister Ludi," written in 1938, is typical in this connection, for it shows that the imminent war in Europe was making a travesty of his aesthetic realm. The poem depicts the last magister, an old man, sitting alone in a land devastated by battle. At one time he had been a famous man, surrounded by eager hordes of students and admirers. Now he is antiquated, useless in a changed world:

> Jetzt blieb er übrig, alt, verbraucht, allein,
> Es wirbt kein Jünger mehr um seinen Segen,
> Es lädt ihn kein Magister zum Disput;
> Sie sind dahin, und auch die Tempel, Büchereien,
> Schulen Kastaliens sind nicht mehr....

> (Now he was left, old, exhausted, alone.
> No longer do disciples seek his blessing,
> No magister invites him to debate.
> They are gone, and also the temples, libraries,
> Schools of Castalia are no longer....)

Even the beads, which once symbolized the total synthesis of knowledge in his aesthetic realm, have lost their meaning and roll noiselessly into the sand.

It does not require much imagination to realize that the vision of an aesthetic kingdom had to pale before the harsh reality of the war that threatened, in 1938, to engulf and destroy Europe. Hesse realized that his ideal, which had sufficed for a time, must give way to another view of reality. Castalia was but one transitory stage in his own development and not the permanent utopia that he had conceived in 1933 and 1934. The latest poem in the group, "Steps" (1941), best expresses the idea that constant progress—Gide's *disponibilité*—is necessary, that every ideal must be transcended:

> Wir sollen heiter Raum um Raum durchschreiten,
> An keinem wie an einer Heimat hängen,
> Der Weltgeist will nicht fesseln uns und engen,
> Er will uns Stuf' um Stufe heben, weiten.

> (We must cheerfully pass through one area
> after the other,
> Clinging to none as though it were home;
> The world spirit does not wish to fetter and hem
> us in;
> It wishes to raise and enlarge us, step by step.)

The last lines, finally, imply the new commitment to life that ultimately motivates Knecht's defection:

> Des Lebens Ruf an uns wird niemals enden...
> Wohlan denn, Herz, nimm Abschied und gesunde!

> (Life's call to us will never end...
> Very well, then, heart—take leave and recover!)

The structure of Castalia can most easily be grasped as a realistic abstraction based upon other hierarchical organizations of world history—most notably the Roman Catholic Church. Castalia is a concept that emerged only *after* the introduction was written. In the introduction the word "Castalia" does not occur; the narrator speaks of "the order," "the hierarchy," "the academy"; but it is described in only the most general terms. The description, moreover, does not correspond in every detail to the elaborate hierarchy developed in the body of the book. Like the idealized conception of the Glass Bead Game, this is a structural inconsistency that was not obviated in the final version. In the introduction the (nameless) institution is centered exclusively on the game itself, and the Magister Ludi is the supreme head of the order. In Hesse's subsequent relativized conception the Magister Ludi is only one member of a commission that embraces all areas of intellectual endeavor. It is methodologically false to consider remarks on these two different stages of the Castalian idea as though they represented the same institution.

Castalia is a rigidly hierarchical institution that branches down from the directorate of twenty members to the elite schools in which the members of the order are trained. In this hierarchy more than the Glass Bead Game is represented; there are altogether thirteen disciplines in the College of Masters. In addition to the Magister Ludi we hear of a Magister Musicae, Magister Philologiae, as well as masters of meditation, mathematics, philosophy, physics, pedagogy, astronomy, and other fields. In this system the Magister Ludi is substantially reduced in importance, and he distinguishes himself principally by the fact that his discipline is most remote from the world of everyday life. Physics, mathematics, and the other subjects have a useful function in the world outside. The Glass Bead Game, practiced only within the province, is the most endangered area of Castalia since it will be the first to disappear if once the purely aesthetic values represented by the province should be questioned and outside support withdrawn. The other disciplines could conceivably justify and support themselves—not the game.

More significant than the details of the organization is the fact that it is consciously patterned after the Roman Catholic Church. (In the chapter on *Narziss and Goldmund* we considered Hesse's attitude toward the Church as an institution.) Superficially the hierarchy from the elite schools upward to the College of Masters resembles the ladder from the Catholic seminaries up to the College of Cardinals. The rules of the order stipulate poverty and celibacy. The narrator employs phrases like *ad maiorem gloriam Castaliae*, which are overtly based upon the liturgy. And the annual *ludus sollennis* is described in terms that might equally well be applied to the Pope's Easter message. Hesse has not, of course, written a Catholic novel any more than he copied Goethe's pedagogical province. It is stated repeatedly in the course of the book that the Church maintained an attitude of hostility or reserve toward Castalia and its principles. Yet in constructing his spiritual realm, Hesse turned to the hierarchical institution whose organization he most admired.

It belongs to the nature of the realistic abstraction that it enriches the texture of its abstract construct with details instantly identifiable as realistic.

The Church, in this sense, contributes texturally rather than structurally or contextually to the novel. The same may be said of the various Chinese elements that give the novel its unique tone.[33] To take a specific example: on several occasions Knecht consults the book of wisdom *I Ging* in order to confirm his decisions or to plan his course. These prophetic utterances fit so naturally into the development of plot and them that they seem almost, like the motto, to have been written by Hesse himself. Actually, they are taken verbatim from Richard Wilhelm's translation of the Chinese classic and thus contribute richly to the realistic texture of the fiction. This is but another example of the careful montage technique that Hesse, like Thomas Mann in *Doctor Faustus*, uses here with such virtuosity. But montage is not essentially a structural principle, but rather a device used, as we observed, to give a realistic texture to the basically abstract structure.

### PATER JACOBUS BURCKHARDT

Knecht's rejection of the aesthetic realm is the result of a gradual process that he calls "awakening," but it is precipitated consciously by his conversations with the brilliant Benedictine historian, Pater Jacobus. Like so many of the names in the novel, Pater Jacobus is a hidden tribute to a figure from real life. Thomas von der Trave has been identified as a reference to Thomas Mann, born in Lübeck on the Trave; Carlo Ferromonte is a Latinization of the name of Hesse's nephew Karl Isenberg; and practically every other name has some association—more or less private—in Hesse's own life.[34] In the case of the Benedictine father, Hesse has made an explicit reference: "...for my ability to see Castalia, my utopia, in its relativity, I am indebted to the Jacobus from whom the Pater got his name: Jacob Burckhardt."[35] Burckhardt belongs, along with Nietzsche and Bachofen, to the triumvirate of Swiss thinkers who decisively affected Hesse's ideas, and his interest in the Basel historian is well documented. In 1951 Hesse published a newspaper account of his early years in Basel (1899–1903), while he was still a young bookdealer: "Here everything was saturated by the spirit, the influence and the example of the man who for several decades had served intellectual Basel as a teacher and, in cultural affairs, as *arbiter elegantiarum*. His name was Jacob Burckhardt, and he had died only a few years earlier. Even at that time I read him, of course. In Tübingen I had read *The Culture of the Renaissance* and, in Basel, *Constantine*. But I was still too deeply enchanted by Nietzsche to be completely susceptible to his direct influence. The indirect influence was all the more powerful. I lived, a receptive young man eager to learn, in the midst of a circle of people whose knowledge and interests, whose reading and travels, whose way of thinking, conception of history and conversation were influenced and shaped by no one so much as Jacob Burckhardt."[36] In 1946, in the preface to his essays on *War and Peace*, Hesse mentions three great influences that shaped his thinking: the Christian and non-nationalistic spirit of his parental home, the great Chinese writers, and "the only historian to whom I was ever devoted in trust, reverence and grateful discipleship: Jacob Burckhardt."[37] This last testimonial must be read with a grain of salt: it was written in 1946 by a man no longer young, who chose to forget the immense impact that more romantic spirits such as Nietzsche and Jung, Dostoevsky and Bachofen had exerted upon him at crucial stages in his career. Yet in the present connection the date is relevant, for the remark was written shortly after the completion of *The Glass Bead Game*. In general, the references to Burckhardt are far more frequent in the letters and essays of the thirties and forties than was the case earlier, and the influence of Burckhardt on the novel is unmistakable.

In addition to his name Pater Jacobus owes at least one of his remarks, literally, to Burckhardt. Knecht closes his circular letter to the officials at Castalia with a quotation from the Pater: "Times of terror and of deepest misery may come. If, however, there is to be any happiness in the midst of the misery, it can be only a spiritual happiness: facing backward for the preservation of the achievements of the past and facing forward toward the serene and undismayed representation of the spirit in a time that might otherwise capitulate wholly to material concerns."[38] With the exception of the first sentence, this paragraph is taken word for word from Burckhardt's study of "The Revolutionary Age"[39] and built into the texture of the novel like other passages from *I Ging*, Novalis, and Nietzsche—a use of the quotation strikingly similar to that of Thomas Mann in *Doctor Faustus*.

We are concerned here, however, with the deeper implications of Burckhardt's thought for Hesse's novel, and in this connection the series of lectures published posthumously as *Observation on World History* are of central importance. Here Burckhardt expressed the principles according to which his great historical studies were carried out. Three main ideas seem to have made the most profound impression on Hesse. The first is Burckhardt's categorical rejection of all philosophy of history, which he called "a centaur, a *contradictio in adjecto*."[40] According to Burckhardt the study of history is the coordination of facts, not the subordination of facts to a system, as is the goal of all philosophy. He refused to view history as a dialectical process, but sought in the past the constant and typical elements: in a word, the exemplary facts that repeat themselves unceasingly. Hand in hand with this goes the second point, namely Burckhardt's insistence on the relativity of human institutions. He sees permanency in the human spirit and regards history as a "spiritual continuum."[41] But the temporal manifestation of this spirit in institutions is highly relative: "The spirit is mutable, but not transitory."[42] Finally, Burckhardt regards civilization and history as the interaction of three powers or forces upon one another: the state, religion, and culture. We shall take up the third of these points in a later section. The first two belong together as the basis for Knecht's defection from Castalia, for they summarize, in brief, his rejection of the aesthetic abstraction of the Glass Bead Game and his realization that Castalia, as an institution, can claim no eternal validity.

Although Hesse, by his own acknowledgment, derived his thoughts largely from Burckhardt, Joseph Knecht's process of "awakening" is portrayed as a gradual one that simply was precipitated in his conversations with Pater Jacobus. "Awakening" is the name that Knecht applies to the existential experience of reality in contrast to the abstract view of life that is practiced in Castalia; it is a form of the epiphany that Siddhartha experienced in his development. This "awakening" impels Knecht ultimately to forsake the exclusive *vita contemplativa* of Castalia for a tentative *vita activa* of commitment in the world. "In the state of awakening one did not penetrate more closely to the core of things, to the truth; one grasped, carried out or suffered only the relationship of one's own Self to the momentary state of affairs. One did not discover laws, but made decisions."[43] Instead of standing at a distance and analyzing a situation intellectually, one felt involved and committed to the moment.

One result of this "awakening" is the serene bliss characterized by the smile and gaze of certain Castalians, a serenity that the narrator defines as "the affirmation of all reality, the state of awakeness on the brink of all depths and abysses."[44] Another implication is the phenomenon of ineffability that we have observed earlier in connection with such epiphany-like awakenings. On several occasions Knecht relates that the experience of these moments is essentially inexpressible, that it is impossible "to make rational what is obviously extra-rational."[45] These moments take him into an area beyond the periphery of experience that can be reduced to the abstractions current in Castalia. "Communication from this realm of life seemed not to be among the functions of language"[46]—that is, rational expression as it is known to the Castalians. It is worth noting that even the vocabulary of these passages— though not technically existentialist—would not be unfamiliar to philosophers such as Karl Jaspers or Sartre. The almost overwhelming sensation of the reality of things, the necessity for decision and action, the

*Grenzsituation* on the brink of despair—these belong to the lingua franca of existentialism in its various forms. This existential attitude, of course, implies a criticism of the very foundations of the Glass Bead Game, which is based upon the assumption that a situation or process can be grasped in its abstracted essence, which can in turn be compared with other abstractions so as to construct an elaborate aesthetic structure.

Knecht's inner doubts are first stirred during his years at the school in Waldzell, when he engages regularly in debates with Plinio Designori. (It was these early misgivings that ostensibly produced the poems appended to the biography.) In these debates Plinio advocates the role of Life as opposed to pure, disengaged intellect. "I have to remind you again and again," he argues, "how daring, dangerous and, in the last analysis, unfruitful a life is if it is directed exclusively toward the mind."[47] Though Knecht distinguishes himself by a skillful justification of Castalia and its form of existence, he is persuaded inwardly that his own realm does not embrace all life, as he had supposed before. "The whole of life, physical as well as mental, is a dynamic phenomenon, of which the Glass Bead Game encompasses only the aesthetic aspect."[48] Already here the keynote is sounded: the Glass Bead Game and Castalia are identified as aesthetic views of life rather than as points of view that can be totally satisfying and all-embracing.

The most conspicuous personification of the dangers inherent in pure aestheticism is Knecht's friend Fritz Tegularius, who has been persuasively identified by Joseph Mileck as a characterization of Friedrich Nietzsche.[49] Tegularius, like Nietzsche a classical philologist, is a brilliant adept at the Glass Bead Game. He is unequalled in his capacity for sharp analysis, but his physical frailty and emotional lability make him unfit for any position of authority or responsibility. Characteristically, Pater Jacobus reacts against Tegularius just as Burckhardt recoiled from Nietzsche. Like Nietzsche, Tegularius has a strong aversion to the study of history as such, conceding only that the *philosophy* of history can be an amusing pastime. In one of his conversations with Tegularius, Knecht objects to the excessive abstractionism represented by his friend's attitude. "Not everybody can breathe, eat and drink abstractions exclusively for a whole lifetime. History has one advantage over those things that a tutor at Waldzell deems worthy of his attention: it deals with reality. Abstractions are delightful, but I support the view that one must also breathe air and eat bread."[50] In the novel Tegularius embodies the extremes that pure aestheticism can attain, and he serves as a living warning to Knecht, who understands him so well. At the same time, he represents a stage in Hesse's own development—an attitude of anti-historism expressed most forcefully in an essay on "World History"

(1918) written during the period when Hesse was most directly under the influence of Nietzsche. In that essay Hesse polemicizes specifically against the historical opportunism of intellectuals and others who adapt their view of history to the political exigencies of the moment. But he lets himself be carried away, maintaining that true poets and religious thinkers can never succeed in thinking historically. He anticipates reproaches of the sort to be made twenty years later by Pater Jacobus: "I hear the voices of those who see in our unhistorical and apolitical thinking nothing but the blasé indifference of 'intellectuals.'"[51] Probably no quotation better illustrates Hesse's remark that, in those early days, he was too much under the influence of Nietzsche to be responsive to Burckhardt's ideas.

Most Castalians live in complete ignorance of the dangers inherent in the system and of the threat from an outside world that might one day weary of supporting an institution that was becoming more and more autonomous in its disengagement from reality. Only a few political officials are alert to these dangers, and it is Dubois, the chief of the political bureau, who indoctrinates Knecht before his mission to Mariafels. Dubois points out that Castalia, contrary to the widespread fancy of most Castalians, is indeed dependent upon the world outside and not an autotelic aesthetic realm that can exist indefinitely by itself.

Despite all earlier premonitions, however, it is Pater Jacobus who articulates the suspicions that had up to now remained more or less inchoate in Knecht's mind. Knecht's reaction to Plinio Designori was instinctive. Dubois' comments dealt with practical matters. Pater Jacobus is the first person who appeals to Knecht's mind. He criticizes the illusory nature of an "intellectual-aesthetic spirituality" that exists without any real foundation in life. "You treat world history as a mathematician treats mathematics, where there are only laws and formulas, but no reality, no good and evil, no time, no yesterday, no tomorrow—only an eternal, flat, mathematical present."[52] Pater Jacobus intensifies Knecht's reservations about a purely aesthetic culture and then adds to this the new ingredient of historism. The Castalians, he says, are great scholars and aestheticians, but their total concern is only a game. "Your supreme mystery and symbol is nothing but a game—the Glass Bead Game."[53] He makes no attempt to convert Knecht, remarking disparagingly that Castalia is too remote from life even to comprehend theological questions. He is concerned above all because Castalia has cut itself off from the world. "You don't know what men are like, their bestiality and their likeness unto God. You know only the Castalian—a specialty, a caste, a rare experiment in breeding."[54] Gradually, through his conversations with the Pater, Knecht comes to realize that the greatest deficiency in his own education and the greatest threat to Castalia is the total lack of political awareness in the broad sense of the word: a knowledge of human relations. He was even, to his own dismay, uninformed about the historical circumstances that had attended the establishment of Castalia. From this time on the conversations between the two revolve more and more about contemporary political issues, dealing specifically with Knecht's own potential role in history. Knecht begins to think of himself no longer as an aesthete dwelling apart in an absolute and timeless realm, but as a man engaged in life and swept along by the tide of history.

## THE SYMBOLS OF RESOLUTION

Shortly after Knecht's return from Mariafels he is elected to the position of Magister Ludi, an office that he fills with honor and devotion for eight years. Up to the very day of his defection he carries out his duties so meticulously that of his closest associates only Tegularius is aware of his inner turmoil. The theme of inner conflict is paralleled by the motif of outer representation (a motif often strong in the works of Thomas Mann). This produces the frequently incongruous situation that Knecht, after performing a brilliant public Glass Bead Game, is able in the next instant to warn his students of the dangers that lie in store for Castalia. The years spent with Pater Jacobus produce two practical effects in Knecht's life during his tenure as Magister Ludi. First, he begins to concern himself deeply with the history of Castalia and the Glass Bead Game, seeking to determine its function and position in the history of the world. Secondly, he begins to think of his office—as Magister Ludi—less in an abstract sense and more in literal terms: that is, as a schoolmaster engaged in practical teaching, rather than as a mandarin of the aesthetic game. Since he recognizes now the dangers of excessive abstraction, he hopes to eradicate these evils at a basic level by giving a proper introduction to pupils in the most elementary principles. If it is too late to heal types like Tegularius, at least—he hopes—he can prevent the growth of others. Both of the teachings of Pater Jacobus have left their mark on Knecht. At the same time, he is aware of his own limitations. He does not urge an abrupt turn from aesthetics into the world of politics and action— there is too much of Castalia in him. "We should not flee from the *vita activa* into a *vita contemplativa*, nor vice-versa; rather, we should be alternately in both, at home in both, participating in both."[55]

By the end of his eighth year in office Knecht is still dissatisfied. His efforts to reconstruct Castalia from within have had some success, but only relatively so. In the first place, he realizes that the institution is too vast to be changed in the lifetime of one man, no matter how strenuous his efforts may be. Secondly, all his action has been within the aesthetic province, with no effect whatsoever on the wide world outside. His failure is brought home to him vividly when he sees Plinio Designori again after many years. Plinio had left the province originally with the intention of bridging the gap between Castalia and the world, of injecting the spirit of Castalia into his functions as a statesman in the world outside. But he failed, and his failure has embittered him toward Castalia. His struggles have left their mark upon him, for his face shows lines of character unaccustomed among Castalians, whose lives are spent in a serene, unabrasive atmosphere. When Knecht sees Plinio, he realizes how futile his own attempts at reform had been. Confined as he was to Castalia, he had been spared all contact with the world of life. Knecht resolves, after careful deliberation, to give up his position in Castalia and to fulfill his function—that of a teacher, not a man of affairs—in the world outside. He outlines his reasons in detail in a letter to the authorities of Castalia, but basically they are variations on the two themes that we have been considering: the dangers of isolated aestheticism and the historical relativity of Castalia.

Knecht's "awakening," a gradual process that takes place over a period of some thirty years, is the central theme of the novel. The ultimate resolution of Knecht's inner doubts in the synthesis of *vita activa* and *vita contemplativa*, however, is anticipated throughout the novel in the symbol of music. In *The Glass Bead Game* music does not have the structural function that it had in *The Steppenwolf*, but it is equally important in other respects. It supplies much of the texture of the story and forms the substance of many essayistic passages in which the history and theory of music are discussed. Most of all, music as a symbol provides the counterpole to the game itself. If aestheticism as exemplified by the game marks the outset of the novel, a synthesis of life and spirit as manifested in music anticipates the finish. Music, as we have seen, provided the original basis for the game and has remained, throughout its history, a central discipline in Castalia—a branch represented by Knecht's friend Carlo Ferromonte. Symbolically, however, music embodies the synthesis of aesthetics and actions that Knecht finds at the end of the book. This chord is struck in the introduction when the narrator quotes a passage from *Spring and Fall* by the Chinese philosopher Lu Bu We, to the effect that music arises from the harmony of Yin and Yang, the two poles of life. If either pole—intellectuality or sensuality—prevails, then music degenerates, marking a decline in the civilization that produces it. Precisely this conception of music is advanced by the most harmonious figure in the novel, the man who more than anyone else embodies an ideal vision of Castalia: the old Magister Musicae. Even before Knecht's admission to Waldzell, the master warns him of the dangers inherent in the game, which tends to deal only with the cerebral aspects of music, ignoring its sensual elements. The Magister Musicae is the only figure in the novel, apart from Knecht himself, who experiences life existentially rather than abstractly, and his warning to Knecht early in the novel anticipates the ending. "Divinity is in you, not in concepts and books. Truth is lived, not taught."[56] In his own lectures as Magister Ludi, after his awakening through Pater Jacobus, Knecht repeats this message. He warns his students that music is made with the hands and the fingers, the mouth and the lungs—not with the brain alone. A man who can read music but not play an instrument cannot claim to be a competent musician, for music more than all other arts demands a synthesis of the abstract and the concrete. This view determines Knecht's attitude toward the history of music. He regards the music of the nineteenth and twentieth centuries as degenerate since there the sensuous elements outweigh the intellectual. In the Glass Bead Game, on the other hand, the opposite danger prevails: too often the purely intellectual is abstracted from the full substance. For Knecht perfection in music is achieved in the period 1500–1800 (specifically by Bach), in which a delicate balance of the intellectual and the sensual is maintained. Just as the Glass Bead Game is an adequate symbol of pure aestheticism, this conception of music as the synthesis of the poles of life corresponds admirably to the theme that it symbolizes.[57]

## THE THREE POWERS

Joseph Knecht's life differs markedly from that of almost all other Castalians—whether they are typical members, extremists like Tegularius, representative like Thomas von der Trave, or idealized like the old Magister Musicae—because their lives are spent within the confines of Castalia while his carries him, on the one hand, into the monastery of Mariafels and, on the other, into the world and the home of Plinio Designori. If we ask why Hesse chose to deal specifically with these areas of life—after all, it is a step beyond the customary duality of nature and spirit that we have encountered in the earlier works—it seems reasonable to assume that the influence of Burckhardt has again made itself felt. Here the influence is not restricted as in the preceding considerations to questions of theme, but it actually determines the structure of the work.

Burckhardt devotes the two central chapters of his *Observations on World History* to a definition of the three powers—state, religion, culture—and to a discussion of their interaction.[58] State and religion are expressions of the political and metaphysical needs of mankind that he regards as universal. Culture, on the other hand, is the sum of mankind's intellectual achievements—technical, artistic, poetic, scientific—and varies or adapts itself from age to age. In these areas he sees an expression of three basic needs of mankind, and he insists that the most fruitful approach to history is through the study of these areas in their interaction.

*The Glass Bead Game* deals with the three powers that Burckhardt outlines. They may constitute an arbitrary division of human activity— Burckhardt anticipates the objection. Yet they are the three areas that he chooses to define and that Hesse employs in his novel. This is especially striking in view of Hesse's earlier novels in which theme played an important structural role. In *Siddhartha*, for instance, we found theme projected into landscape: the two sides of the river, symbolizing nature and spirit. The same polarity was exploited, in a different way, in *Narziss and Goldmund*, where the monastery and the world outside again represented life and spirit, where actual geographical location could express thematic tension. Beyond these two works, what we have seen in every case—the "two worlds" of *Demian* as well as the contrast between Haller's library and Pablo's jazz den in *The Steppenwolf*—is a basic *duality*. So it is instantly striking to find in the last novel *three* symbolic areas of activity. Pater Jacobus is explicitly a representative of the Church and the authority of religion. Plinio Designori is a statesman involved deeply in the political affairs of the world. And Castalia can almost be described by Burckhardt's definition of culture: "We call culture the entire sum of those developments of the mind that occur spontaneously and make no claim upon universal or compulsory validity.... Furthermore, it is that multiform process by means of which naïve and impulsive action is transformed into reflective ability—yes, in its last and highest stage (science and especially philosophy) into pure reflection."[59] The last phrase even expands the definition to embrace an implicit criticism of the hyperintellectual abstractionism of Castalia.

The narrative chapters of the novel constitute an architectonically structured work. In the first three chapters—"The Call," "Waldzell," "Years of Study"—the development of incidents is determined almost programmatically by the hierarchic organization of Castalia. Knecht's early life, and, to outside observers, even his later years are in many respects exemplary. "Undisturbed by sudden disclosures and indiscretions the noble process took place—the typical boyhood and early history of every noble mind.

Harmoniously and evenly inner world and outer world worked and grew toward each other."[60] In no other work of German literature besides Adalbert Stifter's *Indian Summer* (*Der Nachsommer*) and Novalis' *Heinrich von Ofterdingen* (both of which Hesse admired immensely) is the development of a young man depicted with such classical evenness and with such a total absence of abrasive conflict as in these early chapters. In this world even death has lost its sting. The few deaths mentioned are so tranquil and ethereal that they fit unobtrusively into the pattern of Castalian existence, providing no shock for those concerned. Characteristic of this invalidation of death is the portrayal of the last days of the old Magister Musicae. "He was not sick, and his death was not actually an act of dying; it was a progressive dematerialization, a disappearance of the bodily substance and the bodily functions."[61] The old man vanishes, almost like the Cheshire Cat, behind the glow of his serene smile. In the absolute aesthetic realm of Castalia—the timeless, mathematical present that Pater Jacobus decried—the threat of death has been annulled. To this extent the novel, as a *Bildungsroman*, differs from traditional representatives of the genre from Goethe's *Wilhelm Meister's Apprenticeship* or Gottfried Keller's *Green Henry* down to Thomas Mann's *The Magic Mountain*, in all of which death—and in general the abrasive conflict between the hero and reality—plays an important role. As Hesse has pointed out, young Knecht was intended to symbolize the inner meaning of Castalia in its loftiest manifestation, and in these three opening chapters theory and practice of Castalia merge into a smooth, flowing development.

These chapters are followed by two that describe Knecht's mission to Mariafels and his conversations with Pater Jacobus. From this point on the tension between theory and actuality provides the narrative impulse. After Mariafels, another group of three chapters depicts Knecht's return to Castalia and his years as Magister Ludi. On the surface the harmony of the early years is maintained by Knecht's sense of responsibility and his conception of his representative function. The two chapters defining the area of religion are paralleled by two that introduce the area of the state: Plinio's return for a visit in Castalia and Knecht's conversations with him as well as his visit to Plinio's home in the world outside. These four groups of parallel chapters—idealized culture, religion, relativized culture, state—complete the development of the novel. In the last two the logical conclusions are drawn. In "The Circular Letter," Knecht outlines to the authorities the reasons for his defection, but no new arguments are advanced; the chapter is a summation of what has preceded. "The Legend" relates the story of Knecht's brief excursion into the world and his death. The rigid structuring of the chapters indicates beyond a doubt that Hesse, whether he consciously

followed Burckhardt or not, was interested in defining precisely the same
three areas of human activity with which the historian was concerned. In
view of his own acknowledgment of indebtedness to the Swiss historian, we
are probably justified in assuming that this structure is consciously patterned
after Burckhardt's three powers.

The question of the interaction of these areas is far more interesting
and, I believe, equally plausible. Here lies the key to the meaning of the
novel. The much discussed relationship Knecht-Tito, namely, represents
merely one of the four possibilities of interaction that concerned Hesse in
the novel. As we anticipated in our discussion of the narrator, the true
beneficiary of Knecht's sacrifice is neither Knecht nor Tito nor Plinio nor
any of the other figures of the novel; but rather, the later generation
represented by the anonymous narrator. Some critics have asserted that the
narrator lives in an age of decline, that he is an epigonal figure. This claim
cannot be documented by the text. From the point of view of the
introduction, to be sure, some such interpretation might be made. But the
narrator of Knecht's life is not writing from the same point of view—an
inconsistency that we have already noted. This narrator represents the
Castalia of which Knecht dreamed. The game is no longer played so
brilliantly, but from the standpoint of the mature Knecht, that is an
improvement rather than a decline. As the narrator points out, "there exists
in recent times in the directorate of the order a tendency to discard certain
specialties in the pursuit of knowledge, which were felt to be over-refined,
and to compensate for this by an intensification in the practice of
meditation."[62] The abstract aestheticism symbolized by the game has given
way to a Castalia more fully attuned to the other two areas of life: religion
and the state. Knecht was dismayed, for instance, by the historical ignorance
and political naïveté of Castalia when he returned from his mission to
Mariafels. The narrator is fully aware of the historical circumstances
surrounding the origins of Castalia and of the position that Castalia occupies
with relation to the other powers. Knecht dies before he is able to see any of
his hopes realized; Plinio is already an old and weary man; Knecht's
contemporaries in Castalia are unmoved by his eloquent pleas for reform;
and Tito, though the ending of the novel suggests that his life will be
changed by Knecht's death, is just one person. Only the processes of history,
directed by the actions of Knecht's life, can bring about the changes for
which he hoped—no single individual. The nameless narrator, writing years
after Knecht's death, is the living voice of a Castalia that has achieved what
Knecht was striving to bring about. The processes that made possible this
new and ideal Castalia were catalyzed by Knecht's symbolic interaction with

Pater Jacobus and Plinio. His death is a moving symbol of his commitment to life and fellow man, of his rejection of Castalian aestheticism and abstraction.

But it would be romantic to interpret the entire long novel simply from the standpoint of Knecht's death, which comes so suddenly in the last few pages of the book—so suddenly, indeed, that it has struck some critics as an arbitrary ending.[63] His life, which was devoted to an instigation of the interactions of which Burckhardt spoke, is vastly more meaningful than his death. Hesse himself has indicated something of the sort in a remark of Pater Jacobus that Knecht passes on to his friends. "Great men are, for youth, the raisins in the pastry of world history."[64] But the Pater (and by implication Hesse) goes on to say that the mature mind is interested, rather, in the history and development of great institutions. This observation, applied to the novel, means that the significance of Knecht's life in any but an exemplary sense must not be overstressed; it is the development of Castalia and its relations with the other two powers that are of true significance— even *after* Knecht's spectacular death, which is so dramatic that it threatens to overshadow the meaning of his life!

We have seen how Knecht's development was affected by Pater Jacobus. It has not so frequently been observed what an impact Knecht, in turn, made upon the Pater and what vast implications their friendship had for the future of Castalia. Knecht is sent to Mariafels ostensibly to give instruction in the art of the Glass Bead Game to a few interested monks. He soon observes, however, that he has been sent as much to learn as to teach. After two years his stay in the monastery is given a more specific direction. At the time of the story there exists an attitude of cool suspicion on the part of the Church toward Castalia. The Castalian authorities hope that Knecht, by capitalizing on the favorable impression that he had made on Pater Jacobus, can persuade that influential personage to give his approval to an official diplomatic exchange between the two powers. The Pater, who begins with vociferous criticism of Castalia's aestheticism and anti-historism, gradually begins to perceive the merits of a pedagogical province that could produce a man like Knecht. He agrees to the proposed establishment of diplomatic relations. One of the narrator's remarks indicates that a strong bond of interaction did actually develop as a result of the friendship between Knecht and the Pater. "How attentively the Pater followed Knecht's elucidations and how extensively, through them, he came to know and to acknowledge Castalia, is revealed by his subsequent attitude. To these two men we owe the understanding between Rome and Castalia that reaches down to the present day. It began with benevolent neutrality and occasional scholarly exchange and has developed with each subsequent contact into true collaboration and confederation."[65] As this statement proves, the major effect of the friendship and initial interaction took place later—that is, only after Knecht's death, as a historical process.

We observed, on the other hand, how Knecht's friendship with Plinio Designori, from the date of their early disputes at Waldzell, made Knecht aware of the claims of life and the state upon Castalia. Plinio's own ambitions, in turn, reveal how anxious he is to bring about a synthesis of Castalia and the state—an attempt in which he failed. In his debates with Plinio as well as the Pater, the narrator reminds us, Knecht "succeeded in compelling them to acknowledge honorably his person as well as the principle and ideal that he represented."[66] Previously the relationship between these foreign areas had been marked by an almost total inability to communicate. In one of his discussions with Plinio, Knecht concedes that absolute communication among men is probably impossible. "Yet if we are of good will, then we can still communicate very much to each other and can guess or surmise much that transcends what is exactly communicable."[67] The alienation between Castalia and the state is another problem that, implicitly, is solved by the time of the narrator of the biography. In contrast to the perspective in the introduction, he is able to assume that his readers are well informed about circumstances in Castalia. The very fact that Castalia still exists, despite its perilous state during Knecht's lifetime, is proof in itself that a fruitful interaction took place in that area as well.

All of these factors—the historism of Pater Jacobus and its impact on Knecht's thinking, the three areas of activity and the careful structuring of the novel, the repeated implication that the Castalia of the narrator represents an advance beyond the endangered Castalia of Knecht's lifetime—convince me that the meaning of Knecht's life and defection must be sought in his life, not in his death. To put it most radically, what happens to Knecht after his defection is totally irrelevant as far as the central theme is concerned: the role of spirit in the modern world. That question is answered by the narrator, not by Knecht's death. It is necessary for the area of intellect and spirit to interact fruitfully with the realms of state and religion. In other words, spirit must be given meaning by religion; and it must be given direction by the state (practical life). As far as the fiction of the novel is concerned, the historical processes that bring about this interaction are set in motion before Knecht's death, and their action is inevitable regardless of his own fate. When he departs from Castalia, Knecht has completed his function as an exemplary figure. Since his mission to Mariafels and his circular letter to the authorities have activated the gears of history, nothing that he now does will affect Castalia one way or the other. His representative life is over. He is now free to live or to die as an individual.

## THE EXISTENTIAL ACT

Knecht's death is his only act in the entire novel which has no exemplary significance, but a purely personal and existential meaning for him as an individual. It is motivated by his sense of commitment and responsibility: commitment not in a narrow political sense, but with the broader meaning of involvement in the general human condition; and responsibility (Hesse uses the two expressions *mitverantwortlich* and *mitschuldig*) as the explicit opposite of the disengagement traditionally characteristic of Castalia. In his circular letter he singles out this lack of responsibility as one of his principal objections to the aestheticism of Castalia. "The average Castalian may regard the man of the world, the non-scholar, without contempt, without envy, without animosity; but he does not regard him as a brother, he does not see in him his employer; nor does he feel in the least responsible for what happens in the world outside."[68] Knecht's own defection stems from his feeling of responsibility to the world at large. But more specifically: he feels that Castalia failed in its education of Plinio Designori because it did not prepare him adequately to cope with the problems arising from his efforts to bring about an interpenetration of the ideals of Castalia and the world. Instead of dismissing as too impersonal and abstract this responsibility of the entire province to Designori, Knecht decides to take it upon himself. He discards the disengagement of abstraction for the responsibility of action. As in the process of awakening, he feels unable to keep himself sufficiently remote from the problem to analyze it intellectually. Instead he plunges in to rectify it by deed.[69]

It is useful to make a distinction between the ideal of service, which has so often been discussed in connection with the novel, and the sense of commitment and responsibility as defined above. Service (*Dienst*) is, of course, an important theme in the novel. But one should keep in mind that service emerged as a theme in *The Journey to the East* and that it is most meaningful within the framework of the aesthetic realm defined in that book and in the early parts of *The Glass Bead Game* before the ideal of Castalia is questioned. As the possibility of interaction between the three powers becomes more and more evident, the narrator uses words for "commitment" and "responsibility" more frequently. Service to the ideal and to the hierarchy is one of the cardinal principles of life in Castalia. While Knecht never forsakes the ideal of spirit consecrated to life, he does, by his defection, reject the tenet of service to the hierarchy. I believe that the shift from "service" to "commitment" characterizes in diction the shift of emphasis that takes place in the course of the novel from detached aestheticism to engagement. It can be easily ascertained that the ideal of "service" occurs more regularly in the introduction, the "Lives," and the first three chapters than it does later as increasing doubts cause Knecht to reexamine his values. During the crucial years as Magister Ludi when Knecht must serve the very hierarchy whose meaning he seriously questions, the theme of representation, significantly, begins to replace the ideal of absolute service. From service through representation to rejection—that is the development of Knecht's attitude toward the hierarchy of aestheticism. The counterpoint is supplied by his progression from disengagement through interest to commitment to life.

As a sign of his sense of commitment he undertakes the tutelage of Plinio's son Tito. Ironically, this same impulsive sense of "awakening" leads him, on the third morning of his freedom, to his death. For had Knecht, instead of plunging suddenly into the icy lake, paused to consider the situation coolly and rationally, he would never have drowned. Having once committed himself to a course of action instead of reflection, he has no choice. To renege at this point, to disappoint his pupil in this first crucial trial, this first plea for commitment, would mean total failure and would travesty his defection. So Knecht plunges to his death. His unhesitating willingness to commit himself summons up a new sense of responsibility in Tito. "Oh, he thought in horror, now I'm responsible for his death.... And as he felt, despite all objections, a sense of guilt in the master's death, he was overcome in a solemn tremor by the premonition that this responsibility would reshape him and his life, requiring far greater things of him than he had previously ever demanded of himself."[70] Hesse himself has interpreted the ending of the novel in a similar way.

> "He could have refrained, finely and intelligently, from leaping into the mountain water despite his illness. Yet he does it all the same, because there is in him something stronger than intelligence, because he cannot disappoint this boy who is so difficult to win over. And he leaves behind a Tito for whom this sacrificial death of a man vastly superior to him will remain forever an admonition and example, which will teach him more than all the preachments of the wise."[71]

This is almost a recapitulation of the words of the old Magister Musicae that we quoted earlier: "Truth is lived, not taught."

The concluding words of the novel seem clearly to imply a symbolic commitment of the world and state to Castalia, for Tito assumes his responsibility for Knecht's death just as unhesitatingly as Knecht took upon himself the duty of Castalia toward Plinio and the world. Structurally and thematically the novel is closed. It would be pointless for Knecht's life to go on; he could hope to accomplish no more than has been accomplished. By his deeds he has succeeded in bringing about the interaction of Castalia with religion and the state, and he dies at peace with himself. Knecht's defection, of course, does not imply a repudiation of the realm of culture. It is only a rejection of the stage of ineffectual aestheticism to which Castalia had degenerated in the course of its historical development. The Castalia represented by the narrator, as I have argued, is the spiritual realm that Hesse and Knecht envisage: not a realm of abstract aestheticism, but of spirit and intellect committed to the service of mankind.

Hesse has not, of course, written an existentialistic novel in any programmatic sense. Yet I do suggest, at the risk of exaggerating the parallels, that the changes in the theme of the novel during the long years of composition mirror in no small measure contemporary developments in the world and in literature. The differences between the beginning and the end of the novel seem to reflect what R. W. B. Lewis has in mind when, distinguishing between the concerns of Proust, Mann, Joyce, and those of the generation that followed, he speaks of an "aesthetic" and of a "human" world.[72] Knecht starts out in an aesthetic world, but he dies because of his commitment to a human world and because of his new sense of an almost existential intersubjectivity.

This shift in emphasis left its mark on the structure of the novel, for despite the external integration of the parts, there remains, as we have noted, a certain internal inconsistency in the role of the narrator and the conception of Castalia. But if we esteem personal integrity more than artistic virtuosity, then we can only conclude that the value of the novel, at least as a human document, is enhanced by these flaws. It is perhaps the final irony of the work that its shift of allegiance away from aestheticism to human commitment is reflected by artistic shortcomings in the form. Because of his intense sensitivity to changes in the world Hesse was able, in his last novel, to achieve a rejuvenation similar to that which produced *Demian*. Here again he has succeeded in anticipating the feelings of a new era, which has little patience with the aesthetic—"calligraphic" is the pejorative expression favored by many postwar writers—literature of the twenties and thirties, and in bridging, in one work, the chasm between generations. To this extent there exists, despite all differences, a remarkable similarity between the first and the last of the major novels—a parallel that lends to Hesse's later career a pattern of consistency and unity. Through the evolution of themes and the variety of structures there emerges one constant factor in Hesse's work that we must value above all: absolute honesty to himself and to the world, even at the expense of treasured ideals that must be transcended.

## NOTES

1. Hesse in a letter to Thomas Mann on December 12, 1947; GS, VII, 669–70. Thomas Mann in *Die Entstehung des Doktor Faustus* (Berman-Fischer, 1949), p. 68. Among the numerous comparative studies see: Joseph Müller-Blattau, "Sinn und Sendung der Musik in Thomas Manns *Doktor Faustus* und Hermann Hesses *Glasperlenspiel*," *Geistige Welt*, 4 (1949), 29–34; Anni Carlsson, "Gingo Biloba," *Neue Schweizer Rundschau*, Neue Folge 15 (1947–48), 79–87; Karl Schmid, *Hermann Hesse und Thomas Mann: Zwei Möglichkeiten europäischer Humanität* (Olten, 1950).

2. Discussed by Joseph Mileck, *Hermann Hesse and His Critics*, pp. 97–100.

3. Inge D. Halpert, "Vita activa and vita contemplativa," *Monatshefte*, 53 (1961), 159–66.

4. GD, VI, 109.

5. GD, VI, 112.

6. GD, VI, 85.

7. GD, VI, 85.

8. GD, VI, 88.

9. GD, VI, 92.

10. Letter of January 28, 1933; GS, VII, 541.

11. The motto was translated into monastic Latin by Hesse's former schoolmate Franz Schall and later revised by another friend, Feinhals. Hesse acknowledged the help in his whimsical textual note: *ed. Clangor et Collof[ino]*.

12. Letter of 1949–50; GS, VII, 701–02.

13. Letter of January 28, 1933; GS, VII, 540–41.

14. Richard B. Matzig, *Hermann Hesse in Montagnola* (Basel, 1947), p. 7.

15. GS, VII, 562.

16. See Sidney M. Johnson, "The Autobiographies in Hermann Hesse's *Glasperlenspiel*," *German Quarterly*, 29 (1956), 160–71.

17. GD, VI, 569.

18. GD, VI, 571.

19. GD, VI, 583.

20. GD, VI, 192–93.

21. GD, VI, 249.

22. GD, VI, 82.

23. Letter of November 1, 1943; GS, VII, 637.

24. GD, VI, 374.

25. GD, VI, 386.

26. Letter of November 1, 1943; GS, VII, 637.

27. Oskar Seidlin, "Hermann Hesses *Glasperlenspiel*," *Germanic Review*, 23 (1948), 263–73, has most articulately opposed the utopian interpretation: "Aber um eine Utopie, d.h. eine Zukunftsvision einer höheren individuellen oder gesellschaftlichen Existenz, handelt es sich durchaus nicht. Kastalien ist nicht Utopie, sondern Mythos: d.h. Konkretisierung eines Ewigen, eines Etwas, das war, das ist und das sein wird" (p. 264). Although I agree completely with Seidlin's analysis and definition, I prefer the term "realistic abstraction" for two reasons: it serves more easily to link Hesse with other modern artists; and it avoids certain ambiguities associated with the term "myth." One might say that a realistic abstraction can in time, if it is accepted as valid, become a myth.

28. See Werner Haftmann, *Malerei im 20. Jahrhundert, Textband*, p. 279.

29. Letter of January, 1944; GS, VII, 637.

30. Letter of February 22, 1944; GS, VII, 640.

31. Letter of December 12, 1947; GS, VII, 669.

32. GD, VI, 182.

33. See Gottfried Koller, "Kastalien und China," *Annales Universitatis Saraviensis*, 1 (1952), 5–18.

34. See Joseph Mileck, "Names and the Creative Process," *Monatshefte*, 53 (1961), 167–80.

35. Letter of November 1, 1943; GS, VII, 637.

36. "Ein paar Basler Erinnerungen"; quoted in *Hermann Hesse: Eine Chronik in Bildern*, ed. Bernard Zeller (Suhrkamp, 1960), p. 36.

37. "Geleitwort zur Ausgabe *Krieg und Frieden* 1946"; GS, VII, 435.

38. GD, VI, 472.

39. "Das Revolutionszeitalter," in Jacob Burckhardt, *Historische Fragmente aus dem Nachlass. Gesamtausgabe* (Berlin & Leipzig, 1929), VII, 426. The passage was originally identified by G. F. Hering, "Burckhardts Worte im Glasperlenspiel," *Die Zeit*, Nr. 28 (July 10, 1947), p. 6.

40. *Weltgeschichtliche Betrachtungen*, ed. Rudolf Marx (7th ed Stuttgart, 1949), p. 4.

41. *Ibid.*, p. 9.

42. *Ibid*, p. 7.

43. GD, VI, 490–91.

44. GD, VI, 419.

45. GD, VI, 508.

46. GD, VI, 491.

47. GD, VI, 184.

48. GD, VI, 186.

49. "Names and the Creative Process," p. 175.

50. GD, VI, 377.

51. "Weltgeschichte"; GS, VII, 121–26.

52. GD, VI, 251.

53. GD, VI, 273.

54. GD, VI, 274.

55. GD, VI, 329.

56. GD, VI, 157.

57. This conception of music as resolution is identical with the function of music in Hermann Broch's novels (especially *Der Versucher*), but quite different from the more Romantic and demonic conception of Thomas Mann in *Doctor Faustus* and earlier works, in which music is regarded as a symbol of irrationality.

58. *Weltgeschichtliche Betrachtungen*: Chapter 2, "Von den drei Potenzen"; Chapter 3, "Die Betrachtung der sechs Bedingtheiten."

59. *Ibid.*, p. 57.

60. GD, VI, 130–31.

61. GD, VI, 377.

62. GD, VI, 374.

63. See Curt von Faber du Faur, "Zu Hermann Hesses *Glasperlenspiel*," *Monatshefte*, 40 (1948), 177–194.

64. GD, VI, 252.

65. GD, VI, 281.

66. GD, VI, 364.

67. GD, VI, 394.

68. GD, VI, 455.

69. In connection with the ending see especially Oskar Seidlin, "Hermann Hesse's *Glasperlenspiel*," *Germanic Review*, 23 (1948), 263–273; Hilde Cohn, "The Symbolic End of Hermann Hesse's *Glasperlenspiel*," *Modern Language Quarterly*, 11 (1950), 347–57; and Kenneth Negus, "On the

Death of Joseph Knecht in Hermann Hesse's *Glasperlenspiel,*" *Monatshefte*, 53 (1961), 181–89.

70. GD, VI, 543.

71. Letter of November, 1947; "Ein Briefwechsel," *Die Neue Rundschau* (1948), 244–45.

72. *The Picaresque Saint*, p. 9.

MARK BOULBY

# Narziss and Goldmund

In the "Preface of a Writer to His Selected Works" (1921) Hesse compares
the great novelists and narrative artists of the nineteenth century, such as
Dickens, Turgeniev, and Keller, with himself, concluding that he is not really
a novelist at all. In this situation he finds that he is not alone: "Modern
German literature, for the last hundred years, has been full of novels which
are not novels, and of writers who behave as though they were storytellers
but are not" (VII, 251). He cites Josef von Eichendorff, who wrote
"ostensible novellas"; he feels at one with writers such as this, in their sins of
commission: "The story as disguised lyric poetry, the novel as a borrowed
label for the attempts of poetic personalities to express their experience of
themselves and the world, this was a specifically German and Romantic
matter, in this I at once realized myself to be involved and to share
responsibility" (VII, 252). Poets such as Eichendorff, Hölderlin, and
Nietzsche wrote prose because German prose can indeed provide a superb
outlet for that musical impulse which is the true source of the lyrical. "But
few, extremely few were strong or sensitive enough to deprive themselves of
the advantages which derived from using the story form on loan (and one of
these advantages was that of a larger public).... And so I also, without being
fully aware of it, had played the role of the storyteller as a deceiver who was
himself deceived.... Of my tales—there was no longer any doubt about

From *Hermann Hesse: His Mind and Art.* © 1967 by Cornell University.

this—not a single one was pure enough as a work of art still to deserve mention" (VII, 252).

Such self-doubt, first coming to the surface in "Klingsor," becomes a recurrent theme of Hesse's writings in the twenties. To obtain a public by stealth, by disguising lyric poetry in the form of novels, is seen as an impermissible procedure which revenges itself by the impure sediment which it deposits in the works themselves. Hesse perceived that his monologues were not novels at all, any more than the prose productions of Hölderlin and Novalis had been, but he found that the company he kept was still no excuse. In *The Nuremberg Journey* a related issue is aired: "I do not believe in the value of the literature of our age.... Invariably I can only feel that the attempts of contemporary German writers (naturally including my own) at real creation, at genuine works, are somehow the inadequate efforts of epigones, everywhere I imagine I can see a glimmer of routine, of models which have lost their living qualities" (IV, 156).[1] Feeling the dead hand of tradition upon him, he thoroughly approved of much of the extremism and the conscious and crude iconoclasm of the younger generation who desperately strove to escape the clammy hold. He himself was caught in a conflict which had first become manifest at the time of *Demian*, the conflict between uninhibited confession and fine writing: "Between the demand for honesty, for confession, for the ultimate in self-revelation, and that other requirement—with us since our youth—for beautiful expression...the entire literature of my generation oscillates desperately back and forth" (IV, 157).

The conventional Neo-Romantic style cannot, by definition, cope with the demands of the *Expressionist* will, for Expressionism is the laying bare of the archetypal. The style that can do this has not yet been found and perhaps will never be; psychoanalysis, on which great hopes were set, has proved too academic a tool to liberate the poets. Side by side with thoughts and implications such as these, it is characteristic that we should find in Hesse a certain readiness to approve and applaud his own Neo-Romantic heritage: "I have, I think, always been a traditionalist as a writer, with few exceptions I was content to use a conventional form, a current routine style, a schema, I never cared about producing anything that was formally new, about being in the avant-garde and an originator. That harmed quite a number of my works, and it was equally beneficial to others, and I am happy to admit to it."[2] He knew very well what the psychological basis of the epigone in fact was, and also that many of those who threw stones at such targets themselves dwelt unwittingly in glass houses. A lyricist disguised as a novelist, Hesse might be defined as a self-confessed Romantic epigone who yearns for raw truth, for the purity of absolute self-disclosure, but who knows that artistic advantage may sometimes lie in the very failure to attain this end; for the struggle for confession at all costs leads even further "out and beyond the good and fine tradition of storytelling"[3] and eventually into a formless world.

Highly relevant is the contrast which Hesse has drawn between the *Confessions* of Rousseau and those of Augustine: Augustine surrenders himself openly and completely and becomes a saint; Rousseau succumbs to some degree of self-justification and becomes a poet. The confession of the artist is never an unsullied one, for he always values it in the wrong way: "Confession is overrated by the artist, he devotes to it more love and care than to anything else in the world, and the more honest, the more careful and complete, the more ruthless his confession is the more is it in danger of once more becoming wholly art, wholly work, wholly an end it itself."[4] One may guess that Hesse had in mind not only Rousseau but also Strindberg when he wrote these words. The artist remains trapped in the magic circle of the self, inevitably exaggerating the importance of his work, since in this alone does he find the justification of his life, entranced—as for instance was Marcel Proust—by the beauty of his own confession.

Hesse called both *Peter Camenzind* and *Beneath the Wheel* a "novel"; *Demian* was subtitled "The Story of a Youth" and *Siddhartha* "An Indian Poetic Fiction" (*Dichtung*); while *The Steppenwolf*, that most unconventional of Hesse's works, had no sub-designation at all. *Narziss and Goldmund*, however, is called a "tale" (*Erzäblung*). This might suggest a conscious attempt to find a home within a tradition, to turn away from whatever experimentation there may have been in *The Steppenwolf*, and furthermore an effort to overcome the supremacy of the lyrical impulse. Indeed, certain features of the novel, its narrative breadth and the technique of the good raconteur which distinguishes it, support such a view, and there are good reasons why it has become perhaps the most permanently popular work of Hesse's later period; the public which had recoiled in aversion from *The Steppenwolf* showed itself receptive, once more, to *Narziss and Goldmund*. But this may not have been altogether a good sign, and Hesse himself seems to have preferred the earlier work, perceiving that it probably represents a much higher level of artistic achievement, although its content is evidently too disturbing for the average reader. Even in the case of *Narziss and Goldmund* there was no lack of those who found it "unheroic...soft...erotic and shameless."[5]

On rereading the novel after twenty-five years, the author discerned a number of faults in it; in particular he found it longwinded. His limitations as a formal artist seemed linked with what was perceived to be a repetitiousness of motifs and characters—"Thus my Goldmund was prefigured not only in Klingsor, but already even in Knulp, as were Castalia and Joseph Knecht in Mariabronn and Narziss."[6] (These are only a few, of course, of the comparisons that might be drawn.) After twenty-five years what Hesse felt closest to in *Narziss and Goldmund* was, most significantly, "the cadences of this writing, its melody."[7] All these ponderings over the limitations of his art are surely rather more than merely that pathetic honesty of self-depreciation which a hostile critic of Hesse, K. H. Deschner, would see and applaud in them;[8] they pose the whole issue of tradition in literature, of the modern gulf between language and experience, the Nietzschean antinomies of truth and art, and in a narrower sphere, in the history of styles, the problems involved in the transition from the new Romanticism to Expressionism and beyond, as they may be seen reflected in the work of so many writers, for instance Hofmannsthal.

No appreciation of *Narziss and Goldmund*—indeed no study of Hermann Hesse—can really avoid this issue. Deschner seeks to compare this author (unfavorably) with Hermann Broch and Hans Henny Jahnn, a critical procedure which might be questioned; he picks Hesse out, in fact, as perhaps his most eminent example of an inflated reputation, finding in him little but the meretricious, the imitativeness of the epigone. The obvious weaknesses in Deschner's logical arguments do not,  however, dispose entirely of this polemicist's strictures. One might feel inclined to deny outright that the novel in question is merely *Goldschnittsirup*;[9] however, *Narziss and Goldmund* is by no means free of sentimentality—for instance the unfortunate episode of Marie, the lame girl who vainly adores Goldmund, which is, frankly, reminiscent of Paul Heyse. In point of composition, the novel is inferior to *The Steppenwolf*, while its language, which resembles that  of *Siddhartha*, fails to achieve the same smooth, ritualistic perfection. The repetitiousness of theme and imagery, which the author himself regarded as a flaw, goes so far that it suggests a certain weariness of the artistic imagination, a degree  of carelessness, which last criticism is further attested by an actual narrative error.[10] The objection that the book lacks depth, however, derives from a misunderstanding of the function in it of the reflective element and poses a fundamental issue, relevant to Hesse's work as a whole, to which we shall return. Suffice it to note at the outset that *Narziss and Goldmund* is a "tale" by a writer who has denied that he is a storyteller in the true sense—a "tale" by a lyricist in  whom the religious yearning for truth at all costs has for more than a decade been in bitter and ambiguous contest with the will to form, and in whom the drive to uncover the fundamental and the new conflicts with a passionate sense of tradition and  of historical affinity. It is a work composed by an artist who is devoted to play, but whose deepest necessity was not to play but to confess.

It is a *Künstlerroman* with religious sources; its forming energy derives from the friction between the religious and the aesthetic impulses. When Goldmund, after his life of dissipation, returns to the monastery, the abbot, Narziss, hears his confession and awards him a penance, which is a conscious and meticulous repetition of prayers and hymns. Narziss adds the admonition that he must not speculate about these exercises: they are to be performed "in the same way as for instance when you are singing and playing the lute you do not pursue any clever ideas or speculations but try to produce each note and pressure of the fingers one after another as purely and perfectly as possible" (V, 296). Music is—as Pablo made clear to Harry Haller—not synonymous with musicology nor with passive appreciation; it belongs neither to the feelings nor to the intellect, but to the will; it is really valid only as active performance, "*Handwerk*"; and so it is with the exercises of the Spirit.

The *tertium comparationis* is, of course, artistic technique in general, or rather form, that in which inspiration is sublimated, as Goldmund's is in the exercises of penance. It is good, says Narziss, that Goldmund went out into the world, that he did not remain within the monastery walls and try to become a thinker; for had he done this, he would inevitably have turned into a mystic; and mystics are, one and all, "secret artists...all without exception unhappy people" (V, 287). Unacceptable, no doubt, as a diagnosis of the mystic, the remark yet sheds great light upon the sources of *Narziss and Goldmund*; if the mystic is secretly an unhappy artist so is the artist secretly an unhappy mystic—though false in logic, this was psychologically true for Hesse, at least. "Artists," says a priest to Goldmund, "are not in the habit of being saints" (V, 154), and Hesse had certainly found that the Way of the artist and the Way of the saint were very different in practice, although the former ought ideally to lead into the latter through depersonalization, through "de-becoming" (*Entwerden*), the surrender of the tormented ego. And yet Hesse finds this Way of depersonalization, which Augustine followed but which eluded Rousseau, impossible for him too, even though he declares "the saint" to be his chosen model. He attributes his incapacity to the debilitating consequences of his Pietistic upbringing, to the fact that he has never belonged to a "genuine" religious tradition (such as the Roman). The tradition to which he did belong was essentially an aesthetic one. Thus *Narziss and Goldmund* should primarily be understood as the conversion of confession into music, into cadences, and as the refuge-seeking of the disappointed mystic in art.

In its ritual repetitions, its "triple impulses,"[11] the prose of *Narziss and Goldmund* harks back to that of *Siddhartha*. In structure the novel is of course "contrapuntal" (always bearing in mind that musical terminology as such adds little to the understanding of literary forms); it is the most obvious example in Hesse's work of "the two-voicedness of the melody of life,"[12] a study of the life of the artist in its mobile relationship with the hieratic life. In *Siddhartha* already, as perhaps even in *Demian*, there was the counterpoint between the wanderer, the "world-traveler," the Faustian figure, and the rationalist (Gide's "*frère aîné*") who remained within the grove, practicing his methods, his rational mysticism. In *Narziss and Goldmund*, Govinda has become dignified as Narziss and is even given a temporary primacy of place—Goldmund begins by being (and in a sense always remains) *his* "shadow." In Harry Haller both extremes, Wagner the famulus and Faust himself, were blended in uncomfortable company; thus Anni Carlsson's observation that Goldmund, had Narziss not liberated him by analysis, was set fair to turn into a Steppenwolf[13] is capped by Max Schmid's perception that it is in fact in combination that the twain would form (or *do* form) a Haller[14] (and since this is clearly right, any interpretation of the novel based upon the view that some sort of "harmony" of Narziss and Goldmund is ultimately achieved is transparently absurd).

Contrapuntal though it is, *Narziss and Goldmund* lacks the relatively strict conditioning by musical prototype which has been noticed in the case of *The Steppenwolf*. On the other hand, it has just that interleaving of nodal incident and interpretative conversation which is to be found in all the major novels, especially *Demian*; it resembles *Demian* also in the pattern of its action—a pupil, in whose early life a spiritual teacher makes a radical intervention, who then goes out into the world, and returns in the end to a tryst with his teacher and friend. In its external realism (which has been compared with Stifter's),[15] its panoramic breadth so unusual in Hesse, the novel is apparently more extraverted than either *Demian* or *Siddhartha*; but in no sense could it be deemed a realistic novel in the classical nineteenth-century sense. It remains a lyrical "tale," a species of *Bildungsroman*, in which the external world stays distinctly subordinate to the exposition of the pivotal moments of the *vita*. Like Eichendorff's *Taugenichts*, with which it has a good deal in common, it makes great use of the technique of summary to bridge gaps and form links in what is essentially a lyrical fantasy; it too—were it not so long—might well be designated an "ostensible novella."

Very material to any discussion of *Narziss and Goldmund* is the fragment *Berthold*,[16] the beginnings of a historical novel set in the period of the Thirty Years' War. The hero, Berthold, is educated in a monastery for the priesthood; his powerful instincts, however, conflict with his vocation, lead him to dissipations and eventually, in an act of wild jealousy, to the murder of his friend, the sceptical intellectual Johannes, his "teacher." The fragment then breaks off with Berthold's flight to the wars.

The analogies between his case and that of Goldmund force themselves upon us. Like Goldmund, Berthold cannot remember his childhood. His erotic awakening contests, as was conventional in the school novel, with the embattled academic self, as it does with all the external criteria of social success and worldly acceptance. But of course this is an awakening not only of the sexual instincts, but also of the whole soul, and characteristic figures are employed: "In blissfully drifting dreams his depression was transformed into the smiling release of winged happiness, which took away all the hardness and dissatisfaction of his haughty soul and turned it into a child playing in the grass and a little bird rejoicing in the air" (I, 858). The haughty soul of the would-be priest becomes that of a child again, and the bird is born. Love is a "garden of Venus" (I, 858), a closed garden,[17] the opulent warmth of which contrasts sharply with the cold of early Mass in the dark church. On the amused advice of Johannes, Berthold addresses himself to a servant girl, Barbara, unaware in his innocence of the freedom with which she casts her favors,[18] shows some enterprise, then discovers the truth, and eventually becomes disgusted at his own degradation. A period of abstinence parallels the onset of academic decline (in this resembling several school novels). Finally Berthold falls in love with Agnes, a blond merchant's daughter, several times observed in Cologne cathedral; and when Johannes, half selfishly, intervenes with her, Berthold kills him.

It is a small matter that Goldmund's last lover is also Agnes, "the blond lioness" (V, 245). More interesting is the murder itself. For Johannes, though in his worldliness and his taste for lubricious anecdotes very unlike Narziss, is still the teacher and awakener, the father-figure whom Berthold slays— entirely appropriately—out of sexual jealousy; what is more, "Johannes" is Narziss' name in religion. Goldmund himself commits a couple of murders (and in error almost kills Narziss!). Various other murderers or would-be murderers populate Hesse's tales, such as schoolmaster Wagner, Friedrich Klein, and Harry Haller; there is also a rumor of this kind about Quorm. Thus it has been observed that, in the figure of Berthold, Harry and Goldmund are both contained, both living together tolerably until the moment when homicide splits them apart.[19]

One may even suspect that the novel remained a fragment partly because, for the Hesse of Gaienhofen, Berthold's behavior has already gone a shade too far; he has committed that crime from which much later characters shrink back, of which they only dream. *Berthold* has several features which betray the style of the Gaienhofen years, especially the gnomic reflections; a certain tendency to conscious breadth of portrayal, to the accumulation of thematically irrelevant material, points to the intention to write a wholly naturalistic, historical novel. Such a style was not really natural to Hesse; it is questionable whether it was ever in his capacity to create a broad canvas in this mode, and for this reason also the novel remained unfinished.

Berthold bursts forth into the wide world, the world of the Thirty Years' War; a fugitive, he has murder on his hands. Goldmund's flight takes place in somewhat less dramatic circumstances. He is brought by his father, a stern, unsympathetic official, to the monastery of Mariabronn to be educated for the priesthood; his life, as it turns out, is conceived of by his father as a penance for the sins of his mother. He is named after St. John Chrysostomos, the most eloquent preacher of the Greek church.[20] "He had a golden mouth and with his golden mouth he spoke words, and the words were little swarming birds, they flew away in fluttering crowds" (V, 66). The color gold is again primarily that of iconography, and the birds are the eloquence of the soul. Here, at Mariabronn, Goldmund comes under the influence of the brilliant novice Narziss, so exceptional a Greek scholar that he is allowed to teach during his novitiate.

Narziss is intended as far more than a mere foil to Goldmund, though Hesse's assertion that they are equally significant[21] is not quite true in terms of the novel; and it is to some extent counter-balanced by the impression given in "An Evening of Work" where Goldmund is arrayed after Camenzind, Knulp, Veraguth, Klingsor, and Haller as "a new incarnation, a somewhat differently blended incorporation of my own nature in words."[22] If it be allowed that Goldmund is the central personage of the action, that whole action yet remains meaningless and indeed inconceivable without its starting and finishing point, Narziss. Goldmund's *vita* begins with the artist's aspiration after sainthood, the striving to emulate Narziss, the exercise of the will. As for Narziss, the very name of course suggests introversion; his poise, his remarkable self-containment, his deliberate stunting of his own self-expression, his search for realization within, all these are classical features of the type as described by Jung. He is "awake" (V, 50); a scintillating teacher of Greek, he is contrasted with the simple, pious, humble abbot Daniel as well as with Goldmund, who vainly attempts to combine as the goal of his existence these two irreconcilable ideals. Narziss has one destiny, Goldmund another; if the former is St. John, then the latter is Judas[23]—and the implication of this analogy shows that Narziss is indeed "awakened" in his understanding of the Christian drama, to have been able to make it! In Narziss we have the "handsome youth with the elegant Greek, with the chivalrously immaculate bearing" (V, II), a nobility of appearance reminiscent of Siddhartha's. He incarnates both intellect and will. This is Mariabronn, not Maulbronn, and thus Narziss is no mere stuffy academic. In that he is not a committed pedagogue, Narziss has the chance (and the ambition) to become a teacher in the deeper sense; he is aware of the similarity between himself and Goldmund, and also of their extreme polarity. Between them arise magical connections, "a language of the soul and of signs," and Narziss would have liked to "lead him...to help him bloom" (V, 46). Narziss has the gift of insight into others; he perceives that Goldmund was never intended by fate for the tonsure, and that a false personality is being forced upon the boy. The analogy with Hans Giebenrath is rather close: "He saw this boy's nature as encased in a hard shell, consisting of false fancies, pedagogical errors, paternal decrees.... His task was clear...to liberate him from the shell" (V, 36). The image of the kernel which must be extracted from the shell recurs in this novel; Narziss finds in service of the Spirit the "kernel and sense of life" (V, 25), and then, in conversation, Narziss and Goldmund approach the "kernel and sense of their friendship" (V, 47).

Goldmund, the antithesis of Narziss in everything, suffers from his inability to make himself the same. On his first visit to the Greek class he falls asleep, and is deeply disturbed by his failure to concentrate for long. He even has emotions of revolt "against the Latin teacher" (V, 24). In this world of paternal discipline, guilt feelings are unavoidable. And yet Mariabronn is by no means paternity unalloyed. The very name suggests all that is feminine in the Christian system, and the water of the soul. Abbot Daniel—and later Goldmund himself—is particularly devoted to Mary.

At the gate of the monastery, at the very opening of the book, stands the chestnut tree: "In front of the archway of the entrance to the monastery of Mariabronn with its twin pillars, close by the wayside there stood a chestnut tree, an isolated son of the South, brought back many years ago by a pilgrim to Rome, a noble chestnut with a strong trunk; tenderly its rounded treetop hung over the path" (V, 9). This stranger from the South is the maternal sign over the entrance to Mariabronn,[24] which Goldmund notices at once; moreover, with the old Romantic parallelism, the tree is "related in concealed affinity with the slender sandstone twin pillars of the portal and the stone carving of the window arches" (V, 9), for what is the sculpture of men but a reflection of the patterns of nature? The full significance of the art of the monastery is revealed to Goldmund only many years later after his return from his wanderings, when he finds that all of it—and all Mariabronn's thinking and teaching besides—"was of one stem, one spirit, and fitted together the way the branches of a tree do" (V, 285).

Many generations of seminarians had studied at Mariabronn before Goldmund came, and were divided into those who remained to become monks and those who returned in due course to the world. Goldmund is to fall into neither category, for he breaks out. The "exemplary event," the flight over the wall, is approached gradually and carefully motivated. Goldmund has aspirations to be a "model pupil" (V, 22), but after a year at the monastery, like his prototypes in the school novels, he suffers from headaches and feels constantly sick. His comrade Adolf, with whom he had fought an *affaire d'honneur* on his first day at the school, now suggests that he join in the traditional sportive defiance of monastery rules, described as "going into the village" (V, 27); they slip through a window in the wall, then over a stream, Siddhartha's Rubicon; they are in search of adventure, "something in which you could forget headaches and apathy and every kind of misery" (V, 27).

For Goldmund this is to be the first overt contact with sensual passion, which for him will be the characteristic form of love. But love has many forms and levels; love of God is perhaps rather close to love of the body, an issue adumbrated in *Demian*, and the line between *caritas* and *concupiscentia* is thinner than may be thought.[25] Narziss, basing his life on the former, is not wholly free of the latter, whereas Goldmund later discovers the transfiguration of the latter in his feelings for Lydia, his Donna Anna. When he goes "into the village," however, he experiences simply, and traumatically, the magical effect of woman upon him and of him upon woman. The kiss he receives, reluctantly, from the village girl arouses a desperate conflict within him, and in struggling to forget and to repress he becomes really ill.

Narziss takes personal care of him, and their friendship flowers; learning of the escapade, he discusses it with Goldmund, points out to him that he is no monk, and endeavors to exorcise the other's crippling sense of failure and guilt. In their relationship Narziss is the leader, the clear-sighted analyst, and upon him Goldmund duly transfers his repressed urges. Carried away, in one of their conversations, by his own enthusiasm, Narziss touches the secret spring of Goldmund's being: "You have forgotten your childhood, it woos you from the depths of your soul" (V, 50); he himself is a thinker, Goldmund an artist: "Your peril is drowning in the world of the senses, ours is suffocation in airless space" (V, 51). Drowning is of course the lurking threat outside the wall, as we know from *Peter Camenzind* and above all from *Beneath the Wheel*; airless space, on the other hand, points to *The Steppenwolf*, to the principal disadvantage of the sphere of Harry Haller's Immortals—the fact that one cannot breathe there. Goldmund is shocked, he staggers into the cloisters, and in this novel in which all things are explained an analysis of the situation is duly offered: Narziss "had called the name of the demon which possessed his friend, he had confronted him" (V, 52–53). In the cloisters, stone faces of dogs or wolves seem to swoop down into Goldmund and tear at his bowels. Narziss has already suspected the boy's secret; his obsessive devotion to the path of asceticism, his inability—despite his powerful plastic imagination—to evoke for Narziss his father, this "empty idol" (V, 43): these facts point to the total repression of the world of the mother in him. His love of church music, of Marian hymns, of his horse Bless, and of all the things of nature are symptoms which seep through the shell; but his father had conscientiously filled the boy's soul with dreams "which were so foreign to the kernel of this soul" (V, 43).

Fainting in the cloisters, Goldmund remains a long time unconscious. This, once more, unlikely though the occasion may appear, is the *Tiefschlaf* of the Vedanta, slept before by Siddhartha and by the Steppenwolf. Returning to himself, he captures again a little of the ebbing dream world, what he has now at last *seen:* "He saw Her. He saw the Great One, the Radiant One, with the full flowering mouth, with the gleaming hair. He saw his mother...unspeakably beloved" (V, 59–60). The face of his mother, the wild dancer of heathen origins who had brought shame into his father's life by her desertion, is later to modify gradually in Goldmund's imagination, to take on the quality of archetype, to become "Eva, the primal mother" (V, 40). To him so far his mother has been only a legend, a "terrible legend" (V, 63)— the legendary is again the sphere of the free, the "feminine" and the soul. By the resurgence of this memory Goldmund is liberated from the clutches of the father-world, so foreign to his real nature: it seemed as if "that touch of playfulness, of premature wisdom, of falseness in Goldmund's nature had melted away, that somewhat precocious monkishness" (V, 63). The Way of the monk, as Hesse conceives of it, must always remain in some sense a game, for it depends on will. Goldmund will escape the fate of the priesthood, for him a misshapen destiny in any case (and we recall "In Pressel's Summerhouse"). The kernel stands revealed, and Narziss now feels himself "like a discarded shell" (V, 64); his superiority is gone; he and Goldmund are now full equals. For Goldmund the path is clear; the mother leads him in one direction only: "Into the uncertain, into involvement, need, perhaps death. She did not lead to tranquillity, softness, security, the monk's cell and the lifelong community of the monastery" (V, 64–65).

As suddenly as did Siddhartha, Goldmund realizes that on leaving the monks behind he will not return to his father. The way over the wall leads into the vast feminine Without, and a whole array of symbols now comes to life: there is Goldmund's singing tone of voice, bewitching like that of

Chrysostomos. There are Goldmund's dreams—"these many-threaded webs of senses suffused with soul" (V, 65)—he dreams of a paradise like Pictor's. There are the flowers, birds, and above all the fish which people his imagination; then there is the tree with the hair beneath the branch as in the depths of an armpit—hair is, throughout *Narziss and Goldmund*, the supreme figure for the sensual. And there is still ambiguity, hermaphroditism; "tranquillity, softness, security"—these scarcely seem very masculine characteristics. The great Without is also Janus-faced: it contains "childhood and maternal love, the radiantly golden morning of life" but also "everything that was terrifying and dark" (V, 65). The escape over the wall is a flight into purposelessness, into sin. Goldmund encounters the gypsy girl, Lise, when he is sent by Pater Anselm to look for herbs in the woods; this encounter teaches him that in sex experience, and perhaps in that alone, there lies for him "the path to life and the path to the meaning of life" (V, 85)—it is, however, perhaps worth noticing that this is still explicitly only the way and not the goal. He goes out again to spend the night with Lise in a haystack, after apologizing to Narziss for the shame of his act. Goldmund's escape, unlike the first trip "into the village," is this time effected without any fear; he walks naked through the deep, tugging waters of the stream. On the bank behind him he leaves his "false home" (V, 87), Mariabronn.

Lise had first come upon Goldmund asleep and had approached him "with a little burning-red wood-pink in her mouth" (V, 79). The image is evocative. And yet the language which describes their first lovemaking does not have this vivid sensuality at all: "The lovely, short bliss of love arched above him, flared up golden and burning, subsided and died away" (V, 80). In characteristic rhythm and delicately toned, this sentence still has a curious emptiness; there is a *vault* above them, the red flower has given place to the color gold; the "lovely short bliss" and the sacramental fire which burns here in fact suggest religious ecstasy. In particular the word *"glühen"* has this *double-entendre* in Hesse, and we may recall the euphemism "to ordain" (*die Weihen geben*) as used in *Berthold*; the sensual is subsumed in the religious; erotic and divine love are indeed close in Hesse; and very frequently the language which tells of Goldmund's seductions disguises the spiritual passion of the mystic. The night with Lise passes almost wordlessly, and when they awake it is to sadness; for she must return to her husband.

Goldmund is left alone in the great wide world, in the forest. His senses always were alive to the fascinating beauty of natural things, the art of God; he had peered amazed at the "minute, starry heaven" (V, 77) embroidered in the leaves of the St. John's wort, at the miraculously formed spiral in the empty snail's shell. Like Siddhartha after his first moment of illumination,

Goldmund *sees;* all around him is color and rapid animal movement: "He met many a hare, they shot suddenly out of the undergrowth when he approached, stared at him, turned and fled, their ears flattened, bright hued beneath their tails" (V, 95). Then the forest is transformed in Goldmund's fancy, and he wishes himself metamorphosed into a woodpecker. He recalls how at school he had often drawn flowers, leaves, trees, animals and human heads upon his slate, blending the forms of the species indiscriminately. These illustrations to *Pictor's Transformations* (V, 94–95) evoke paradise and confirm that the Pictor *Märchen* is, on one of its levels at least, an allegory for the processes of art, of play.[26] Nature responds to Goldmund's urge for life, and the imagery of "Iris" reappears gently sensualized: "He picked a little violet flower in the grass, held it close to his eye, peered into the narrow little calices, there were veins there and tiny organs as thin as hairs" (V, 103). Goldmund spends in the forest (exactly as Hermann Heilner did) two nights and two days; then he arrives at a village, where he addresses himself to a farmer's wife—he as wordlessly as before, though she makes feline noises in her throat.

Goldmund's wanderings commence, and the central narrative of the novel opens out. His adventures are arranged in five main sections, of which the first (Lydia and Julie), the third (Meister Niklaus and Lisbeth), and the fifth (Agnes and Narziss) take place within the walls of a castle or a city and are moments of pause (or in the last case the culmination and conclusion) in the years of vagrancy which are evoked in the second (Viktor) and the fourth (Robert, Lene, and the plague). Goldmund is Don Juan, all things to all women, although they almost all hasten back to their security after a night or two spent with him; and true to type he prefers his freedom. In the calyx of the violet flower Goldmund had seen "how in the bosom of a woman or the brain of a thinker life moved, pleasure trembled" (V, 103); equally revelatory of the parallelism upon which this novel is constructed is the analogy between the development of Goldmund's powers of sensual discrimination— between various kinds of skin and hair, "this capacity for recognition and discrimination" (V, 107), and Narziss' definition of the work of the intellect, of scholarship as "the obsession with the discovery of differences" (V, 47).

Tramping through his medieval world, Goldmund first comes to rest at the castle of a knight for whom he works for some months as a secretary. With the elder daughter, Lydia, he has a melancholic and all but chaste affair and learns that desire is not the whole of love. Then he is put to the test in extraordinary fashion by the younger sister, Julie, who threatens to wake her father unless he admits her to the bed he is sharing with Lydia. Goldmund of course yields, and caresses them both with either hand; he has a gay abandon no other lover in Hesse's novels ever remotely approaches, and there is piquancy and comedy in many of his exploits.

Expelled by the indignant knight, he sets off again through "strange parts" (V, 132), "distant and arid places" (V, 224), and, as he comes to learn, the kingdom of "the great fear" (V, 141). He has much in him of the eternal vagrant. Lying in the wood beside the sleeping vagabond Viktor, Goldmund feels "more strongly than ever before the feelings of the homeless one who has built no house or castle or monastery walls between himself and the great fear" (V, 141). It takes him only a short time to discover what really lies in wait outside the wall, a secret which, though some may have suspected its nature, none of Hesse's previous protagonists ever clearly formulated for himself. What is beyond the wall is simply death: "Are you afraid, Narziss,' he talked to him, 'do you shudder, have you noticed something? Yes, honored friend, the world is full of death, full of death, he sits in every hedge, he stands behind every tree, and it is useless to build walls and dormitories and chapels and churches, he peeps through the window!'" (V, 145). The sexual act and death, intimately linked, dominate Goldmund's world. Perhaps the central section of *Narziss and Goldmund* may be seen in some degree as a parody of the *Abenteurerroman*, the picaresque novel. Goldmund is the vagabond, the wandering scholar, and also the *picaro;* certain of his adventures have something of the picaresque outtrumping of the secure and the great. Hesse several times noted the possible relationship between vagabondage, or indeed the pursuit of travel experiences nowadays called tourism, and the erotic impulse.[27] *Narziss and Goldmund* contains a reflective discourse on the life of the vagabond and perpetual wayfarer: these are the sons of Adam, "who was expelled from Paradise" (V, 199), loathed by the possessing classes because they remind them of transience and death, of "the ice of space," "the remorseless icy death which fills the universe all around us" (V, 200). How different, how much more negative is the use of this frigid imagery here from that in *The Steppenwolf!*

At heart the vagabond is a child (as Knulp was), "his maternal origins, his deviation from law and the mind, his exposure and secret perpetual proximity to death had long ago taken deep possession of Goldmund's soul and had shaped it" (V, 200). Eichendorff's Taugenichts was also only a child, and Goldmund, like Taugenichts, remains perpetually attached to his starting point as it were by the tails of his coat. But proximity to the Eichendorffian model is refuted by the overt eroticism and above all the violence of life as portrayed in this novel. Tough-minded beggars are not uncommon in Hesse's works, and for their rascality and rapacity the author betrays a certain sympathy.[28] The thieving Viktor, with whom Goldmund journeys for a while and whom he has to kill in self-defense, is a more genuine vagabond type than Goldmund is himself; Viktor predicts that one day Goldmund will creep back "in some walls or other" (V, 141), and the latter knows that this is probably true, though it does not imply that he will ever feel secure and at rest.

Goldmund's slaying of Viktor teaches him the need to fight tooth and nail for survival, a thing he is physically well equipped to do. Alone in the savage winter, he defends himself against death "with lust" (V, 147), and all but succumbs. True sympathy with death he aquires only when he comes upon the first signs of the plague. The expansive account of the ravages of the Black Death is in the best Romantic tradition, and one might well think of the wanderings of Renzo and presume the influence of *I Promessi Sposi*. In the peasants' hut, where Goldmund finds five corpses, is an appalling stench of death; his eager eyes are caught by curious details, for instance the dead wife's hair, which seems to refuse to submit to its demise—a far cry, perhaps, from the hair in Julie's armpits. Goldmund is relentlessly attracted by these new sights; understanding the inevitability of death and corruption, he remains gripped but unafraid. Filled with a bitter *amor fati*, Goldmund has come to understand the intimate connection of pleasure and pain, while looking at the expression on the face of a woman in labor; now he grasps the link between the life-urge and the death-wish. The pilgrim Robert—exiled to the highways and byways because his family failed to welcome him back from his Rome pilgrimage "like the Prodigal Son" (V, 202)—teams up with Goldmund, is terrified, however, by the risks he takes and by his monstrous curiosity. There is a short idyll in a hut in the forest with a new paramour, Lene, until she dies of the plague, having been bitten in the breast by a rapist whom Goldmund slays. Life with Lene desperately affirms the generative against a back cloth of decay, though Goldmund is inclined to dismiss the whole episode, with sad irony, as "playing at homes" (V, 221).

The wayfarer continues his dreadful peregrination through the land of death, the land of the mother; he studies a fresco of the dance of death, which captures the ruthlessness and the harshness of it, but Goldmund "would have wished for another picture of it, the wild song of death had a quite different music for him, not bony and severe, but rather sweet and seductive, enticing homeward, maternal" (V, 228). For him death is no stern masculine judge, no executioner, but a motherly embrace, an invitation to incest. Goldmund's journey through the countryside of the plague is his "passage through hell" (V, 227), but his is not the hell of Harry Haller, it is the hell of Klingsor, the *bomme sensuel*, the artist.

The Way of the body, of "wide open senses" (V, 228), teaches first and foremost the lesson of transience. Lydia sees in the depths of Goldmund's eyes "nothing but mourning; as if your eyes knew that there is no happiness and that all beautiful and beloved things do not stay with us long" (V, 120). Goldmund's eyes linger constantly upon the signs of transience: in the fish market there are the gaping, expiring fish, while the fishmongers all-oblivious loudly call their wares; there is the question of Viktor's hair—does any still remain upon his buried skull? And above all there is Goldmund's particular pastime, gazing at a certain moment into his lover's eyes, Lise's eyes (V, 104) and Agnes' eyes (V, 250). The flicker of the woman's eyes at the moment of orgasm is like the shudder of the dying fish and reminds Goldmund also of one of his deepest moments of insight into the soul. Lovemaking has its paradigm in music, Goldmund being the minstrel, the player: "I am a minstrel, if you like and you are my sweet lute" (V, 250). In him culminates the Don Juan motif which first appeared in Hesse's work in "Klingsor's Last Summer" and "Klein and Wagner," as Goldmund moves from lover to lover in search of that permanence which is never to be found.[29] That he can—or must—stand back from his entrancement and make his observations points to the artist in him.

The episode with the Jewess Rebecca, whose family have just lost their lives in a pogrom and who rejects his advances with scorn, stresses the need for a man to see and accept his fate, especially when that be imminent death. It stresses also the invincibility of evil, the inevitable working out of original sin.[30] Goldmund's "Hail Marys," his veneration of the Immaculate Conception, speak of his sense of sin; but step by step his faith declines and is lost in the very excess of evil.

Before the onset of the plague year, he had already found his vocation. The thought that Goldmund may be a born artist first comes to Narziss and is expressed with the undisguised directness typical of this novel. Some years after the flight from Mariabronn, the wanderer first suspects his goal. The motivation of this development is interesting—it begins with a Mass he attends in a monastery which stirs his memories, and he feels a vague impulse to be rid of his past, to change his life, to confess. He goes to confession, and receives gentle treatment from the priest. Just then, in his absolved state, he finds his destiny: his gaze lights upon "a Virgin carved in wood…more living, more beautiful and intense and soulful than he thought he had ever seen before" (V, 153). The priest, observing his wonder, refers him to Meister Niklaus in the city, the sculptor of the Madonna. Goldmund is "transformed" (V, 154), in his purposeless life he now has an aim. To Niklaus he relates how the face of the sculptured Virgin held the same secret he had himself once found, the identity, the simultaneity of suffering and serenity in a single smile. Rather unwillingly the master, having tested his skill as a draughtsman, agrees to accept him as a pupil, though not as an official apprentice, for he is too old.

As he begins to learn, Goldmund also observes Meister Niklaus and perceives his inner contradictions. Niklaus is not as Goldmund had imagined the author of that statue must be; he is "older, more modest, more sober, much less radiant and attractive and not at all happy" (V, 159); his face contrasts with his hands, which have a life of their own. The hands indeed are the hands of the artist, the face is the face of the bourgeois. Goldmund's years in the city, rich as they are in learning, in experience of art and sex and fighting (he acquires the reputation of a dangerous customer on the streets), are rewarding and yet frustrating, for he cannot acclimatize himself to his master's outlook or way of life. He is not an industrious pupil, wastes time, plays truant and sleeps; for which waywardness, however, in Niklaus' eyes, his extraordinary natural talent compensates. The born outsider, Goldmund cannot admire the great sculptor's "tranquil, moderate, extremely orderly and respectable life" (V, 168). Niklaus lives a solitary existence, keeping a jealous eye upon his daughter, Lisbeth, the challenging innocence of whose chaste beauty makes Goldmund long to see her face distorted in ecstasy or in pain. Niklaus, his pupil notes, represses drives which are still powerful, and occasionally on a journey can be temporarily rejuvenated and transformed. He accepts commissions for reasons which Goldmund regards as shabby— money and fame. *Gelegenheitskunst* means nothing to Goldmund, it is a "trivial game" (V, 172); he has no use for "the fat bourgeois" (V, 194), nor for compromise of any kind in the sphere of art. While he waits, on the first day, for the master's decision in his case, Goldmund has a moment of self-contemplation, gazing into the well in the yard: "In the dark surface of the well he saw his own reflection and thought...that he and every human being flowed away and constantly changed and ultimately dissolved, while his image, created by the artist, always remained unchangeably the same. Perhaps, he thought, the root of all art and perhaps of all the things of the spirit is the fear of death" (V, 162).

Again and again the novel returns to the motif of the inner image, the vision in the soul which is the root of the work of art. In his subsequent wanderings Goldmund stores up a hoard of such images, to pour them out later in his drawing and his wood carving. Memory—"this entire picture book" (V, 254)—is to be rescued from death. These "genuine images of the soul" (V, 172) are free of will, of purpose, and of function; the "original image of a good work of art," as Goldmund later tells Narziss, "is not flesh and blood, it is mental" (V, 278–279), which the latter finds to be "exactly what the old philosophers call an 'idea.'" In practice, Goldmund's theory of art is Schopenhauerian rather than Platonic, just as Goldmund's world is characteristically Schopenhauer's "world as will," his Sansara.

As he advances in art, so Goldmund surrenders more and more completely to the hegemony of the senses. We recall one of his earlier dreams: "Once he dreamed: he was big and grown, but sat like a child on the floor, had clay before him and like a child was kneading figures out of the clay. The kneading amused him, and he gave the animals and men absurdly large sexual organs, in his dream this appeared very witty to him" (V, 67). He becomes totally at the mercy of women, even those who are no longer young and beautiful; they are all that gives warmth to life, and the transience of their love is the source of his hidden but changeless melancholia. Pleasure gives place to melancholy, which in its turn gives way to desire. Life is seen as a function of tumescence and detumescence, death and delight are one, the mother of life is love and lust, or else corruption and the grave. The eternal Eva perpetually gives birth and destroys. With the wisdom of his blood Goldmund knows that he belongs to her and not to the father.

Yet he defines art as the unity of father and mother, spirit and flesh: "it could begin in the sensual and lead to the most abstract, or it could originate in a pure world of ideas and end in the bloodiest flesh" (V, 176–177). At this point there is a curious, and highly significant, equivocation: art may offer Goldmund the possibility of the reconciliation of his deepest conflicts, or failing this only the possibility "of a magnificent, perpetually fresh analogy for the schism of his nature" (V, 177). Art is hermaphroditic; this does not mean, however, that it is necessarily a true *coincidentia oppositorum*; it may be, it is here admitted, but the simulacrum of the perpetually unresolved polarity of the self. Here lies the reservation of a writer who knew a great deal about sham harmonies; the whole of *The Steppenwolf*, indeed, is just such a simulacrum. Inspiration is one thing, essentially erotic in its origins, as is the sense of transience, as is despair; form is quite another thing and it belongs, as *The Steppenwolf* showed, not merely to the father, but to faith, the divine, to God. Thus we hear of Goldmund's spiritual exercises, which, properly performed, have the austerity of musical technique: "Often during his work smoking with anger and impatience or else in a trance of lustful bliss he ducked down in the pious exercises as in a deep, cool pool of water, which washed from him the arrogance of inspiration just as it did the arrogance of despair" (V, 295). These are cleansing moments, recurrent baptism; at the same time they provide the form which, apparently and always temporarily, resolves the chaos of the soul. Temporarily, for form, like faith, may decay.

Art is, as Narziss ponders, surveying Goldmund's work, "perhaps a game, but certainly no inferior game to that with logic, grammar, and theology" (V, 299). For *Narziss and Goldmund* is by no means, as has occasionally been thought, merely a paean to the mother; it is an affirmation also of the formal, the aesthetic will, both in Narziss' life and in Goldmund's art. Both in himself and in Goldmund, Narziss finds the working of the same "spirit"— "it is this that will show you the way out of the gloomy confusion of the sensual world" (V, 279). And at the same time the inadequacy, the temporariness of the achievements of "spirit" *in life* are deeply felt. Goldmund's art is an act of faith *par excellence*—"Credo, quia absurdum est." In this lies the tragic undertone of the novel.

The Way of the artist, then, has much in common with the Way of the monk; both depend on will and also on unsevered contact with the spring of the soul; the work of art itself is a simulacrum of the perfected life, and it alone does not decay. The practice of art, as we learn, is connected with a state which is almost a kind of nonattachment. Goldmund experiences this as he works upon his figure of St. John the Evangelist, whose features are those of Narziss.[31]

Art is also similar to the religious path in that in the end it requires great sacrifice, the sacrifice of life; Goldmund yearns to avoid the price which Meister Niklaus has had to pay: "To create without having to pay the price of life for this! To live without having to renounce the nobility of being creative! Was that impossible?" (V, 255). Goldmund now finds that art is a harder task-master than Niklaus: "To it he had sacrificed the wild freedom of the forests, the ecstasy of the wide world, the bitter lustful pleasure of danger, the pride of misery" (V, 177)—once again there is a wall around him, the intolerable wall of the artist's ivory tower, to be bolstered—as Niklaus hopes—by the wall of marriage. For art, too, is will. But the harsh ecstasy outside the wall, an orgasm which has the savor of death, is Goldmund's indispensable nourishment, without which, for him at least, there would also be no art. At death's door he talks once more to Narziss about what he thinks are the origins of art: "And I have also had the good fortune to experience the fact that sensuality can be suffused with soul. Out of that arises art" (V, —317–318). However, the artist—unfortunately—rarely finds peace and harmony in his art (Goldmund venerates and envies the peace of Narziss, without realizing that this too is in reality a condition of perpetual tension). The artist relapses constantly into a sensuality which is not "suffused with soul" (*beseelt*), he finds himself again and again returning to a situation which is an agony of transience, and of hypnotization by the specter of death, upon the very floor of his being. The transience of orgasm is the "kernel of all experience" (V, 175), and it is the germ also of the "kernel of his frequent tendency to sadness and disgust" (V, 175); for the difficulty of the Way of the artist is that the completed work of art fails to resolve the polarity in the artist's soul: "Nowhere was there inhaling and exhaling, being male and female at once" (V, 255).

This distinction between the nature of art and the nature of the artist is central to a deeper understanding of *Narziss and Goldmund*. In the insight it has into the fate of the artist lies the real theme of this essentially tragic novel. Of course all his art fails to save Goldmund from choking fear as eventually, caught red-handed in his escapade with Agnes, the governor's mistress, he sits in his dungeon, awaiting dawn and the coming of the hangman. He is confronted by the end of the Romantic pursuit of experience, just as the cosmic pessimists of the Romantic era had envisioned it, "the abyss, the end, death" (V, 261), the horror of the corruption of the body: "Tomorrow he will no longer be alive. He will hang, he will be a thing that birds sit on and at which they peck" (V, 261). What Goldmund cannot endure, besides, is the thought of the loss of sense experience *per se;* and in a torment of nostalgic grief he surrenders his life "into the maternal hands" (V, 263). Long before this he had come to understand that for him art was *not* the end and purpose of existence (an understanding which also came to his closest relative, Klingsor): "Art was a fine thing, but it was no goddess and no end and purpose, not for him; he did not have to follow art, but only the call of the mother" (V, 192).

*Narziss and Goldmund* is, then, a *Künstlerroman* in which dark doubts shadow the redemptive validity of art. Goldmund broods over the relationship between the sphere of art and that of the soul. He sits gazing into the river, deeply attracted, of course, by water: he gazes "at the dark, vague bottom," at the unrecognizable, gold-glinting things below, refuse or fish, "this cursory subdued flicker of sunken golden treasure in the wet black ground. It seemed to him that all genuine mysteries were just like this little mystery of the water, all real, genuine images of the soul: they had no outline, they had no form, they merely suggested it as a distant, lovely possibility, they were veiled and ambiguous" (V, 188–189). The color gold alerts us—it is a numinous experience which is being described. Goldmund stares down into the deep of the soul, where the fish swim, borrows come crumbs of bread from a passing youth and, like little Hans Giebenrath, throws them food. What Goldmund sees is mystery, the sparkling of the formless ultimate ground. It is not the god of Narziss that Goldmund perceives here, the god of Calw, of form, to whom music and exercises may appear to lead. This trembling, fertile mystery, "inexpressibly golden and silvery," this may be caught also in the magic stuff of which dreams are woven, Jungian dreams, "a pool in whose crystal the forms of all human beings, animals, angels, and demons lived as perpetually wakeful possibilities" (V, 189). Goldmund recalls how once at Mariabronn he had seen the letters of the Latin and Greek alphabets undergo "similar dreams of form and magical transformations" (V, 189). He is puzzled that the formless beauty of the river of the soul conveys an experience like that obtained from the perfectly formed work of art. He concludes that in both cases the essential is mystery; art at its highest can express the mystery of the soul. But form is, therefore, not primary; both art and spiritual work are secondary to the mystery of the mother. This vision of the Great Mother, in which his memory of his own mother is enclosed "like the kernel in a cherry" (V, 191), remains inexpressible; and the ultimate destiny of the would-be artist-saint is evidently not form, not self-realization, but its opposite, the embrace of Nothingness, of the dissolute, random world. Thus an issue which was already essentially posed in the antithesis of Demian and Frau Eva becomes perhaps the central problem of Hesse's later novels, both of their message and of their form.

*Narziss and Goldmund*, it has been noted, has its analogies with the *Abenteurerroman* of the seventeenth century (*Berthold* is set in that period), a type of novel in which the Way of the profligate hangs suspended, as that of Grimmelshausen's Simplicissimus does, between hermitage and hermitage, the innocence of the child and the illumination of the saint. In Grimmelshausen's novel every worldly event is seen *sub specie aeternitatis*, and stands therefore under judgment. So it is with Harry Haller, whose judges— except perhaps for the bourgeois narrator—are all projections of that fiercely cruel judge he carries within himself. Goldmund's way—between the flight over the wall and the return to Mariabronn—is never long free of the thought of home and the memory of Narziss. In this he is not unlike Eichendorff's Taugenichts, whom he resembles also in that extreme oscillation of feeling, between exultancy and melancholic depression, upon which Narziss is drawn to comment.

The motif of male friendship, in this novel, discloses its undeniable erotic quality; Hesse commented: "First of all, as far as the friendships Goldmund-Narziss, Veraguth-Burckhardt, Hesse-Knulp, etc., are concerned. That these friendships...are totally free of eroticism seems an erroneous view.... In the case of Narziss it is especially clear. Goldmund means for Narziss not only the friend and not only art, he also means love, the warmth of the senses, what is desired and forbidden."[32] As much as this, in fact, Narziss actually says himself; he is in any case a monk for whom love in the sense of *caritas*, the ideal of service, is the principal goal; in his rejection of purely intellectual, scholarly purposes he differs from many of his brethren (as does Joseph Knecht in *The Glass Bead Game*). That Goldmund represents a certain peril for him, this Narziss well knows; he is, as he says, merely repelled by those not-infrequent cases of monks and teachers who fall in love with novices and students. Goldmund transfers his repressed physical longings to Narziss; he even goes so far as to stroke his friend's hair. Narziss is fully awake and aware: "You are an artist, I am a thinker. You sleep at the mother's breast, I watch in the desert. The sun shines on me, moon and stars on you, your dreams are of girls, mine of boys" (V, 51). The course of Goldmund's love-life, as is the case with earlier heroes, goes from man through woman and back again to man. Agnes, the last stage before the return, has evidently in her something of Hermine, the sister, the *anima*: "At the basin of a well he paused and looked for his reflection. The picture bore a brotherly resemblance to that of the blond woman" (V, 246). In the figures of Narziss and Goldmund are caught many contrasts, that between the priest and thinker, and the artist and Don Juan; that between the homosexual and the heterosexual; the hermetic opposition between *animus* and *anima*, and, further, two contrasting attitudes toward the "exemplary event." In his carving of St. John Goldmund portrays his friend, a figure in whose hands is expressed total serenity, free of all "despair, disorder, and revolt" (V, 179); Narziss lives wholly within the Order: "He had committed himself" (*sich verschrieben*) (V, 74). The phrase "*er hatte sich verschrieben*" has, however, curious overtones, even sinister ones; to commit oneself, this may be of God, but it may also be of the Devil—and one thinks here of Hesse's ambivalent attitude to the Roman Catholic church. Unlike Narziss, Goldmund must leave behind him, just as his mother did, "house and home, husband and child, community and order" (V, 74), following his inner drives alone. He quits "la Maison,"[33] he leaves the "father" behind. When these two meet again, many years have passed;[34] as though by chance the new abbot's opportunity to intervene with the outraged governor then saves the seducer's life. Here Narziss appears as the polished diplomat, finely combining his spiritual empathy with the exercise of political influence, as Joseph Knecht is also called upon to do. The scene of reunion and recognition is a strange one: ostensibly it is to be a moment of confession. Confession is the river bed of the entire novel; moments of confession form turning points (*Wendepunkte*) in the story. Goldmund goes to confession before he first notices Niklaus' Madonna in the side chapel; then on his exhausted return to his master's city years later, through the plague-ridden countryside, he also seeks to confess. This time, however, he finds only empty confessionals, for all the priests have died or fled, and he confesses in the end in one of these, confesses his total loss of faith: "I have lost my confidence in you, Almighty Father, you have made the world badly, you keep it in order ill" (V, 234). Cast into the dungeon, Goldmund awaits the dawn and the priest who will come with it, formulating a desperate plan of escape: to kill the monk and flee in his robes. Thus he plans, albeit unwittingly, the murder of his "father," Johannes, Narziss.

This dreadful, perhaps ultimate, crime is not perpetrated. Pardoned by the governor, Goldmund returns with his friend to Mariabronn, for the last years, for the elucidations of the final conversations, which have a tractlike function.[35] The Prodigal Son, as Viktor predicted he would, crawls back between the walls and confesses to his "father," who is now both priest and abbott. (Of significance here is Goldmund's expressed desire at the beginning of the novel to confess only to Narziss and not to his official confessor.) As Narziss remarks: "You have led the usual worldly life, like the Prodigal Son you have kept the swine, no longer do you know what law and order mean" (V, 280). But as Hesse observed of the act of return: "He who returns home is not the same as he who has never left it."[36] Goldmund, indeed, comes back in triumph, and not as the abject capitulant. Thus the "exemplary event" is transformed; there is a total reversal of the fundamental movement of the old novel of redemption (such as *Simplicissimus*). "Do you not know," Narziss had once asked Goldmund in the words of Demian, "that one of the shortest ways to the life of a saint can be the life of a profligate?" (V, 38). This *Siddhartha* also comes to understand and to live out. But not Goldmund. The vagrant peregrinates in sin, but he does not find the error of his ways.

The novel is not cyclic, it is not the occult spiral; it is by no means the case that Goldmund returns at the end to the state in which he began though on a higher level of insight; he does not progress from *tumb* to *wîs* in the traditional manner. Goldmund does not even, in returning to the world of the father, contrive to blend this with the world of the mother in a lofty synthesis; for what synthesis there is for him really lies only in the achievements of his crayon and his chisel, and not in his life. Though his Way hangs suspended between the Alpha and the Omega of Mariabronn, yet he is not judged against, and forced to submit to, some supreme standard outside himself; on the contrary, his several confessions point in quite a different direction. In the first of these, to the priest in the church where he finds the Madonna, he is astonished by the mildness of his reception: "But the confessor seemed to know the life of the vagrants, he was not horror-struck, he listened calmly, he censured and admonished in a grave and friendly manner without a thought of condemnation" (V, 153). In the second, to the empty confessional, what should be confession turns into a grumbling remonstration with God. In the third, to Narziss, Goldmund is definitely disappointed: "To Goldmund's amazement, indeed disappointment, the confessor did not take his real sins too seriously, but admonished and chastised him unsparingly for his neglect of prayer, confession, and Communion" (V, 294). Here the penance awarded is a set of exercises which will draw off some of the dross from Goldmund's soul and give a little form to his spiritual life. Worldly sin, however, as Dion Pugil in *The Glass Bead Game* later pronounces, is *Childish*; it is not real sin, which is reserved for those with insight. The actual course of Goldmund's worldly life, therefore, all that he felt obliged to confess, is simply not judged against the standard of Mariabronn and Narziss. In fact the opposite is the case; in a very real sense it is Goldmund who is the presiding judge at the end of the novel, sitting in judgment over Narziss. As instinctive man, and as the artist, he carries the justification of his way of life into the very citadel of the will.

In one of their last conversations, Narziss and Goldmund discuss the idea of self-realization (*sich verwirklichen*), which is the approach, step by step, to the unattainable condition of perfect being that is God. The analogy, fundamental to this novel, between the creation of the work of art and spiritual work upon the self is specifically drawn: "If you have freed the image of a person from accidental elements and converted it to pure form—then, as an artist, you have realized this image" (V, 288). Narziss remarks that Goldmund's way of self-realization has been much harder than his, but that he has found it, all the same—the Way of the artist. The conversation is then sidetracked into an argument about the possibility of thinking without images, in which Narziss undertakes a rather naïve defense of pure mathematics, and old resonances of the school novel sound again.

A superficial reading of the book's conclusion might indeed give the impression that Goldmund has realized himself, whereas Narziss has not. But such a view overlooks the deeper tide of the novel. It may well be that the key to an understanding of the place of *Narziss and Goldmund* in its author's development is to be found in a letter dated August 9, 1929, that is, in the period when Hesse was composing the novel:

> In my case it has always been, as you know, a matter of longing for life, for a real, personal, intensive life which has not been mechanized and reduced to norms. Like everyone else I had to pay for the plus in personal freedom which I took for myself partly by renunciations and privations, partly, however, by increased achievement. So with time my profession as a writer became not merely an aid in approaching my ideal of life more

closely, but almost an end in itself. I have become a writer, but I have not become a human being. I have reached a partial goal, but not the main one. I have failed. With respectable remnants and smaller concessions, maybe, than other idealists, but I have failed. My writing is personal, intensive, for myself often a source of joy, but my life is not, my life is nothing else but readiness to work; and the sacrifices which I bring by living in extreme loneliness, etc., I have been bringing in fact for a long time no longer for life, but only for writing. The value and the intensity of my life lies in the times when I am poetically productive, therefore precisely those times when I am giving expression to the inadequacy and despair of my life.[37]

The artist who "realizes himself" as an artist often does so with a bad conscience. To the question: where is Goldmund's bad conscience? the answer must be: it is in the whole novel. *Narziss and Goldmund* with its burning anguish over transience and its apprehensive wooing of death, its seesawing moods—"this oscillation between lust for life and sense of death" (V, 277)—is closer in feeling to "Klingsor's Last Summer" than to any other of Hesse's works; and "Klingsor" was written in Montagnola a few months after the total collapse of the author's family life. Despite contradictory evidence,[38] it appears that in the late twenties, before his third marriage, Hesse experienced another attack of disillusionment and loss of faith (later reflected in part in *The Journey to the East*); he ceased to believe in self-development. Just as, when he fled from Bern to Tessin, he felt that devotion to his literary work alone could give his life meaning, so also now in 1929 he holds to the same idea; except that this is no longer a notion but a *fait accompli*. Hesse says that it is no longer possible to reach his ideal aims in life—he means, of course, the goal of spiritual self-perfection; the conclusion of *Siddhartha* has revealed itself, with time, to be an utterly unattainable wish-dream. Even *The Steppenwolf*, that optimistic catharsis, ended with a touch of resignation; for Harry perceived that progress along the Way would be very gradual and would involve, maybe, many seasons spent in hell. Now we find Hesse confessing that his spiritual aspirations have been broken upon the wheel of reality: he has reached only a partial goal; only in his writing has he really achieved something; only in his art, now an end in itself, is there meaning; and in his art, therefore, even by the fact that he still creates it, he gives expression to the inadequacy and despair of his life.

*Narziss and Goldmund* is, then, superficially, a novel of self-realization, but in its essential tenor much more one of tragic resignation, its conclusion is still instinct with aggression against the world-view of the "idealists," of Plato and the theologians. It is all very well for Narziss to pour the balm of "thinking" upon Goldmund's accumulated "spite against us theologians" (V, 276); it remains true that Goldmund dies declaring he has and wants no peace with God: "Do you mean peace with God? No, that I have not found. I do not want peace with Him. He has made the world badly, we don't need to praise it, and it will not be of much concern to Him whether I extol Him or not" (V, 318–319). The conclusion of the novel, properly understood, presents precisely the attainment of that "partial goal" of which Hesse speaks in his letter. The two friends are of course not united in any harmonious entity, but remain utterly separate and different to the very end. Goldmund may have blended mind and matter in his art, but he has scarcely done so in his life. And as for Narziss, the message which his counterpart brings back from the world may incite his wonder but cannot help him to be saved.

On his return to Mariabronn, Goldmund sees his *vita* spread out before him in three great divisions: "the dependence upon Narziss and its resolution—the period of freedom and wandering—and the return, the homecoming, the beginning of maturity and the harvest" (V, 280). We recall "A Bit of Theology" and certain discrepancies between its rigid triadic structure and the actual course of Siddhartha's life. In Siddhartha's case the *via purgativa* was not taken to the point of the breaking of the will and the coming of grace; illumination came to Siddhartha only by way of total submersal in the life of the senses. For Goldmund the *via illuminativa* is replaced by art, which also comes to him through the senses; Narziss remains upon the *via purgativa*, upon which Goldmund had so erroneously set out, and follows it to its highly uncertain end. Thus it is evident that in this novel, as in *Siddhartha*, Hesse distorts the traditional mystical framework to accord with his own permanent dualistic dilemma. The aspiring saint is divided into two halves, which proceed in parallel upon what should be successive stages of the Way. The third step of Goldmund's life, described here as "the return, the homecoming, the beginning of maturity and the harvest," is full of ambiguities. It appears that Goldmund becomes, to use the *Siddhartha* term, "perfected." Working at his sculptures in the monastery, he even acquires a pupil—a sure sign of advancement on the Way—Erich, the smith's son. His retirement, in order to create, parallels exactly Narziss' retirement to commence the spiritual exercises which precede ordination: "For the monastery it was as though he had vanished" (V, 292) may be compared with the previous: "A few days later, already, it was as though Narziss had vanished" (V, 74). Goldmund's smile belongs only to those figures in Hesse's novels who are perfected; it is a smile "which looked so old and fragile and which seemed sometimes a little half-witted, sometimes had the appearance of pure kindness and wisdom" (V, 321). He is illuminated; he accepts that his dream one day of portraying Mother Eve will never be realized; she does not wish her mystery to be revealed; instead of him giving form to her, her fingers now mold him.

Some play is now made with Goldmund's aging. He is alarmed to be repulsed by a girl he approaches who finds him old; restless, after two years in the monastery, he sets off on his travels again, secretly in search of Agnes, who then in her turn rejects him. He comes back sick and exhausted, aged by many years; true to his pattern, this suddenly old middle-aged man studies his face in a mirror, finds therein, for the first time, a touch of equanimity. He is perhaps "no longer quite present" (V, 314)—beginning to be depersonalized. His depersonalization, however, is unlike that of Harry Haller's Immortals; for it is a sinking back—for this sensualist who believes in no afterlife—into a formless void. There was ambiguity, in *Demian*, between the will-to-be and the desire to dissolve into nonbeing (the ultimate sense of Frau Eva); in *Narziss and Goldmund* the will-to-be has been sublimated in works of art, while the life succumbs.

Goldmund's last journey is not recounted as his previous journeys are; this last breakout has about it the quality of legend: "A few fragments from Goldmund's accounts and confessions were transmitted by Narziss, others by the assistant" (V, 315). A switch of point of view occurs, such as was noted in the middle of *Beneath the Wheel* and at the end of *Siddhartha*; when Goldmund leaves the monastery this time, Narziss with his thoughts remains behind, pondering whether Goldmund's Way is not after all a better one than his own. The author has ceased to write from within Goldmund's mind; we read not "he was weary" but "he seemed to be terribly weary" (V, 311). For indeed Goldmund now takes on some of the qualities of the saint and his life those of legend; for a short moment before his hagiographical death he becomes the *imitabile* who Narziss would fain be like; he is Siddhartha, Narziss Govinda; Narziss kisses Goldmund on hair and brow. The canonization of Goldmund to some extent disguises the truth, that this novel uses the Way of the artist as a despairing *pis-aller* for the Religious Way, that its glorification of art and form is but the surrogate of the disappointed mystic, while the sinking into the arms of the mother, into the formless ground, is the love-death of the Romantic pessimists relived.[39] As art is supposed to substitute for life, so the polished, melodious language exorcises the burning and and all-too-poignant confession and transforms it largely into music. This sublimative process throws a good deal of light on the novel's style; it is the style of an author who always believed that content by itself was of no significance.[40]

Though the book lacks the stridency of *The Steppenwolf*, it is at bottom an equally painful and indeed a more pessimistic work. It is a veiled, elusive novel; false comparisons in regard to it may lead to gross misinterpretations. The conversations between Narziss and Goldmund should not be compared, for instance, with those between Naphta and Settembrini in *The Magic Mountain;* such analogies (which are inclined to be tendentious anyway) lead to the certainly unjustifiable derogation of Hesse as a thinker and moreover to a total misunderstanding of the book. In the formal world of this novel the conversations are not primarily profound philosophical analyses of specific and—as is often the case in Mann's novels—sometimes slightly extraneous issues; they should rather be seen as restatement in reflective form of the two life patterns, the twin themes, now wooing, now marrying, now divorcing. Both the reflective and the symbolic modes are equally important, both variations on the same motifs. While the book's so-called realism[41]—the description of the plague, Goldmund's killing of the rapist,—is constantly muted by the lyricism of words and structure, the most striking feature of the style is the predilection for direct or—as it may often appear—overdirect statement. There are the beginnings of *Altersstil* (style of old age) here. Time and again the symbol is not allowed to speak for itself, but is interpreted by commentary; but this technique, as has been shown, was always an integral feature of Hesse's work, for these lyrical novels are also all didactic novels, poem and tract are combined in them. Schiefer has observed (in connection with *The Glass Bead Game*) that it is unreasonable to reproach this particular writer for the fact that he constantly resolves the poetic image by interpretation and reflection; for in Hesse's mature work no figure, no image, no action is portrayed for its own sake, but everything subserves the exemplification of a convinced and uncompromising view of the world.[42] That is to say—Hesse can only be properly evaluated as a didactic writer. No doubt, this overstates the case. It is, however, true that works which spring simultaneously from the lyrical and the didactic impulses court certain risks, both subjective hazards of composition and objective hazards of critical judgment. Goldmund's terrible, dying question to Narziss: "But how will you die one day, Narziss, if you have no mother?" (V, 322) may be construed as a warning to the mind. As the reflective mind and the didactic will may damage the lyrical work of art, so the tyranny of the father threatens Narziss. A synthesis is needed, and it cannot be found, neither in the work nor in the life. Perhaps the real "sense" of *Narziss and Goldmund* lies in its confession: "I have become a writer, but I have not become a human being. I have reached a partial goal, but not the main one. I have failed."

# NOTES

1. Cf. a similar comment in "The Beggar" (IV, 844); "The Beggar" first appeared in 1948.

2. *Letters* (VII, 683).

3. "Interrupted School Lesson" (IV, 868).

4. "Aus einem Tagebuch des Jahres 1920," *op. cit.*, 198–199.

5. "Engadine Experiences" (VII, 864).

6. *Ibid.*, 866.

7. *Ibid.*

8. Karlheinz Deschner, *Kitsch, Konvention und Kunst: Eine literarische Streitschrift* (Munich, 1958).

9. *Ibid.*, p. 127. The term "Goldschnitt" alludes to the epigonal poetry of the middle and later nineteenth century; it is totally misapplied as a stricture upon *Narziss and Goldmund*.

10. "Konrad" should surely read "Adolf" (V, 87).

11. Max Schmid, *Hermann Hesse: Weg und Wandlung*, p. 112.

12. *Spa Visitor* (IV, 115).

13. In Ball, *Hermann Hesse*, p. 260.

14. *Op. cit.*, p. 100. He adds (and this one doubts, since it appears to contradict the premise) that between them they can be expected to support successfully the existence of a Steppenwolf.

15. By Weibel, but surely unjustifiably. There is in *Narziss and Goldmund* nothing like the objective sweep of *Witiko*.

16. 1907–1908; first edition, however, Zurich, 1945.

17. Cf. also "The Cyclone": love is "a closed garden" (I, 768).

18. "Good old Barbie!... Now she'll have to ordain this clod too" (I, 861). The popular profanity displays the characteristic Hesse nexus.

19. Otto Basler, writing in Ball, *op. cit.*, p. 296.

20. Perhaps meant in part as a symbol of extraversion. Cf. Max Schmid, *op. cit.*, p. 107.

21. "Narziss is to be taken just as seriously as Goldmund" (*Letters*, VII, 584). The formulation is rather curious.

22. VII, 305. An important passage in *Spa Visitor*, in its implications, supports Goldmund's priority of place: "There are two ways of redemption: the way of righteousness, for the righteous, and the way of grace, for the sinners. I, who am a sinner, have once again made the mistake of trying the way of righteousness. I shall never succeed in this" (IV, 104).

23. Cf. V, 48.

24. We recall the maternal farewells, at the opening of the Maulbronn term, in *Beneath the Wheel*.

25. Cf. here also Jung, *Symbols of Transformation*, pp. 63–64.

26. In the actual illustrations to *Pictor's Transformations* we have a flower with eyes and mouth, and a tree with human head and shoulders.

27. See especially "The Hiking Trip" (III, 394). Cf. also "Engadine Experiences" (VII, 852) and its reference to travel, in a passage which mentions Goldmund's "privileged moment."

28. Cf. the figure of Alois Beckeler in "Walter Kömpff."

29. Cf. Jung, *Symbols of Transformation*, p. 205: "The heroes are usually wanderers, and wandering is a symbol of longing, of the restless urge which never finds its object, of nostalgia for the lost mother." Cf. also Stekel's observation that Don Juan is perpetually unfaithful precisely because of his unchanging mother-fixation. However, Goldmund is not normally disappointed by his women; and his metaphysical attitude is not the cosmic hostility which, for instance, Hoffmann notes in his "Don Juan." And yet the revolt and the metaphysical despair are undeniably there.

30. This section caused Hesse some trouble. He rejected Nazi suggestions that he cut the passage out, and the novel thereupon vanished from the German book market.

31. Again we note the significance of the name "Johannes"—Narziss' name in religion and also that of Hesse's father.

32. *Letters* (VII, 508).

33. Cf. Gide, *Romans, Récits et Soties* (Paris, 1958), p. 478.

34. It is unclear just how many; no satisfying chronology of Goldmund's career can be established. There are contradictions: it is "a good ten years" (V, 219) since Goldmund last saw Narziss; yet soon thereafter he returns to the city which he first visited "so many years ago" (V, 235); though Julie, when he sees her again, has not yet lost her beauty, his first visit to her château now belongs to his "legendary youth" (V, 282). Chapter 13, in particular, involves much compression of time.

35. Cf. P. Schiefer, "Grundstrukturen des Erzählens bei Hermann Hesse," p. 89.

36. "The Hiking Trip" (III, 412).

37. *Letters* (VII, 487).

38. The assertion in the important letter to Rudolf Pannwitz (January 1955) that this period was one of "tolerable comfort after a serious crisis" is an example (*Briefe: Erweiterte Ausgabe* [Frankfort, 1964], p. 437). However, it is vital to see on what the relative tranquillity of Hesse's intellectual and emotional life during these years was apparently based: it was founded on

humor, that is to say, essentially on resignation and compromise, on the abandonment of lofty spiritual aspirations without denying the existence of a higher world. A poem written in 1929 may be adduced in further support of this argument: "Gedenken an den Sommer Klingsors" declares: "no longer to wish for the unthinkable/Is now my wisdom..." and affirms as present desire and purpose a purely artistic function:

> "nichts als Spiegel sein,
> Darin für Stunden, so wie Mond im Rhein,
> Der Sterne, Götter, Engel Bilder rasten" (V, 716).

> (to be nought but mirror
> In which for hours, like moonlight in the Rhine
> Rest images of stars, gods, angels.)

In a recovery of personal spiritual hope *The Journey to the East*, which stands at the end of this period, tries to show that this very resignation itself is a stage upon the Way.

39. Cf. Gerhard Mayer, "Hermann Hesse: Mystische Religiosität und dichterische Form," *Jahrbuch der deutschen Schillergesellschaft*, IV (1960), 545: Klingsor and Goldmund are seen both to be seduced, by their veneration of Mother Eva, to a point at which they abandon their efforts after spiritual "perfecting" and seek "unconscious extinction in the arms of Mother Nature." However, the phrase "to the heart of the mother" (*Spa Visitor*, IV, 105) is confessedly a figure for the state of grace. "The Steep Road" has "breast of the mother" (III, 327). This ambiguous identity of rebirth and oblivion is characteristic of all Hesse's work.

40. "And I thought...that my book, like every poetic work, does not just consist of content, that rather the content is relatively unimportant, just as unimportant as whatever the author's intentions may be, but that for us artists it is a question of whether, à propos of the intentions, views, and ideas of the author, a work has been formed, woven of the material, the yarn of language, whose immeasurable value is high above the measurable value of the content" "Notes While on a Cure in Baden"; IV, 925–926).

41. The evocation of the Middle Ages is tentative and poetic, and in no sense does it have the texture of the historical novel proper.

42. *Op. cit.*, p. 96.

HENRY HATFIELD

# Accepting the Universe:
# Hermann Hesse's Steppenwolf

"The value of illness: it gives a man time to acquire the insight that his position, his business, or the society he lives in has made him ill."

—Nietzsche, *Human, All Too Human*

Hesse's *Steppenwolf* (1927) is his most exciting and extreme book, at times deliberately sensational—and it is probably his best. Known as the most romantic of the important German writers of his time, as a continuer of the traditions of Eichendorff and Mörike, Hesse wrote here in a consciously crass, often shocking manner which recalls the cruder aspects of expressionism. The book is an account—among other things—of neurosis, depression, and schizophrenia, in which the hero, Harry Haller (an especially transparent mask for Hermann Hesse), narrowly avoids a complete breakdown. In that sense the story is a flower of evil, though far from evil in itself.

As Ralph Freedman has shown, Hesse tended to write "lyrical" novels, in which poetic expression is far more important than plot or characterization. The lyrical novel—apparently the term is Freedman's own—is especially prevalent in German literature. He mentions *Werther*, Hölderlin's *Hyperion*, and Novalis' *Heinrich von Ofterdingen*, among others.[1]

From *Crisis and Continuity in Modern German Fiction.* © 1969 by Cornell University.

Accepting Freedman's useful rubric, one can note that by definition lyrical novels tend to be highly autobiographical. This links the type with that characteristically German form of fiction, the *Bildungsroman*. Hesse's more distinguished narratives may be seen as parts of one enormous educational novel. Thus in *Demian*, his first really notable success, we read of the attempts of an adolescent to emancipate himself from a pietistic family, and recall that the *Bildungsroman* grew out of the pietistic tradition in the eighteenth century and often implied a critique of that heritage. In other novels of Hesse's, we read of the hero's struggles to establish himself as a writer or artist, of his loves and marital entanglements, his philosophical flights, his sense of isolation. As in *Wilhelm Meister's Apprenticeship* and its successors, we learn of the cultural experiences, especially the literary ones, which shape his mind.

By the twentieth century, the *Bildungsroman* seemed to be an exhausted form: too many of the most accomplished German novelists had used it; it was associated with romanticism, or the bourgeoisie, or both. Thomas Mann and Hesse were able to revive it only by introducing new approaches and devices—parody, myth, and in Hesse's case Jungian symbolism. Probably the success of his own *Demian* in 1919 and of *The Magic Mountain* five years later encouraged Hesse to employ the form again.

*Steppenwolf* is an educational novel with a difference. As Egon Schwarz has pointed out, the "Steppenwolf" Harry Haller must undergo a reverse development (Rück-Bildung).[2] He is a "man of fifty years"—the title of a novella by Goethe to which Hesse himself alludes[3]—embittered, far from well, with graying hair. Yet like Wilhelm Meister he encounters helpful guides and amiably seductive girls. In his case it is a question of rejuvenation, not of normal growth: he must "die and be born again" or he will be utterly lost; he is closer to Faust than to Wilhelm Meister.[4] Another departure from the usual pattern of the educational novel is that Hesse has provided three narrators. Most of the story consists of the recollections of Harry Haller himself, which he has naturally written down in the first person, but the first chapter is narrated by a former acquaintance who claims to have found these memoirs; he is intelligent and sympathetic to Haller but very bourgeois. The enlightening "Treatise about the Steppenwolf," which comes third, is written "from above," with sarcasm as well as irony, by an anonymous, highly sophisticated author. His diagnosis is so incisive and impersonal that the reader suspects he may be an astute physician or a psychoanalyst.

It soon appears that not only is Haller very sick indeed, but that his sickness is a stigma of insight. Novalis, one of the poets Hesse particularly cherished, has a great deal to say about the positive value of sickness, as does

Thomas Mann. In *The Magic Mountain* illness is the mark of European society in the seven years preceding the First World War; Mann's account of life on the mountain is a "time novel" as well as a story of education. *Steppenwolf*, which owes a good bit to Mann,[5] also has this dual aspect. Even the middle-class narrator realizes that Haller's story is a "document of the time":

> For Haller's psychic illness—I realize this now—is not the eccentricity of an individual but the illness of the time itself, the neurosis of his generation, which apparently does not attack only the weak and inferior individuals but precisely the strong, the most intellectual, most gifted [p. 37].

The age is ugly, vulgar, and hypocritical—though the course of the novel makes it clear that it has other, saving aspects which Haller, to his great peril, has scorned or ignored. The contemporary world seems a veritable wasteland. (Appropriately, Eliot quoted Hesse's essay "Looking into Chaos" in the notes to his most famous poem.) Haller is convinced that the respectable forces in society are busily preparing the next war, and is confirmed in this belief when he finds the professor to whom he pays an unfortunate visit sure of the subversive role played by all "Jews and Communists" (p. 92). Further, the Steppenwolf holds that his whole generation is living in an epoch of radical transformation, and that when two cultures intersect, life becomes intensely painful, in fact a hell (pp. 38–39). Kafka's stories "A Country Doctor" and "In the Penal Colony" make the same point.

If *Steppenwolf* is very much part of a tradition, it is at the same time intensely personal. The strong autobiographical element is hardly veiled: Haller's name is only the most obvious of many hints. The style is forthright to the point of ferocity; in this novel Hesse has abandoned the decorum of his earlier books. Yet he has transmuted his experiences into art. Comparison with another of Hesse's works, which records the same experiences in relatively raw form, makes this clear. The verses contained in the volume *Krisis* (1928) are full of images and themes familiar to the reader of *Steppenwolf*, but the difference is enormous. To quote:

> Ich aber saufe und fresse,
> Heisse nicht mehr Hesse,
> Liege bei den jungen Weibern
> Reibe meinen Leib an ihren Leibern,

Kriege sie satt und drücke ihnen die Gurgel zu,
Dann kommt der Henker—bringt auch mich zu Ruh.


Bleibe im Nichts und ungeboren....
Da kann man über alle diese Sachen,
Lachen, lachen, lachen, lachen.[6]


(But I guzzle and gorge,
Am no longer named Hesse,
Lie with the young females,
Rub my body against theirs,
Get enough of them and choke them to death,
Then comes the hangman and puts me to rest too....
I stay in nothingness, unborn....
Then, about all these things, one can
Laugh, laugh, laugh, laugh.)

These lines could almost be a synopsis of the novel, written by the crudest and most brutal of readers.

It is evidence of Hesse's great talent that he could transform impressions and reactions of this sort into the most challenging of his novels. Perhaps his most striking feat was to make his Harry Haller into a fascinating individual, when he could so easily have been a cliché: another misunderstood intellectual, a "deep," romantically miserable outsider. Largely he accomplished this by viewing Haller—and the whole concept of the "two-souled" rebel— critically, often ironically.

As the novel opens, Haller is obviously on the brink of psychological disaster. He believes that he is half man, half beast; the name Steppenwolf is no mere metaphor to him. Apparently he has lived for many years in a state of controlled schizophrenia; now the disease seems about to get out of control. A specific concern with schizophrenia often is evident in Hesse's work. Beyond that, he was obviously fascinated by duality in general, as the frequent pairs of antithetical characters in his narratives—Sinclair and Demian, Narcissus and Goldmund, and so on—attest. Often the two characters are basically only two aspects of the same person. From the point of view of *Der Steppenwolf*, the possession of two or more "souls" is a sign of complexity as well as a danger. With part of his being, Haller admires and longs for the life of the burgher, like another Tonio Kröger; and very possibly it is this desire for human warmth which enables him to survive.

According to the "Treatise," the Steppenwolf type plays a cardinal role in bourgeois life. It is the half-adjusted, the semioutsiders, who provide vitality and originality for contemporary society, which otherwise would be a mere herd. By an implicit bargain, such half-domesticated wolves are tolerated by the burghers. It is a thoroughly ambivalent relationship, with mixed feelings on both sides.

This compromise, however, does not satisfy Haller. A suicidal type, full of self-hatred, he has long felt the pull of death but has resolved to remain alive until his fiftieth birthday, some two years away at the time the book opens. An oversevere, moralistic education has given him a chronically bad conscience. He is, moreover, one of those who feel with Schopenhauer that individuation is in itself guilt; he longs for "dissolution, back to the Mother, back to God, back to the All" ("Treatise," separately paginated, p. 13). Haller's very heavy drinking seems a deliberate attempt to dull the pain of consciousness in a sort of partial and temporary suicide.

The "Treatise" is most interesting when it becomes a critique of the whole notion of the two-souled man. Real human beings have not two selves but a thousand. Haller comprises not only a wolf, but a "fox, dragon, tiger, ape, and bird of paradise" (T, p. 40). It is up to him to develop all the creative aspects of his being, not to try to "return to nature" or innocence. There is no way back, Hesse proclaims with Schiller, but only a seemingly endless road ahead. "Man" is not something already created but a postulate of the spirit.

Haller, we read, is "enough of a genius to venture the attempt to become a real human being." He is one of the very few who is so qualified, and thus he should no longer live in a world controlled by "common sense, democracy, and middle-class culture" (T, pp. 39–40). (At this point the "Treatise" is extremely Nietzschean; its point of view is more radically aristocratic than that of the novel as a whole.) Haller is called a genius, not because of his earlier writings, which are mentioned only casually, but because of two insights: he sees, however dimly, the goal of becoming human (*Menschwerdung*), and he senses an eternal world of pure form behind the veil of ordinary existence.

What then must the Steppenwolf do to be saved? For the purposes of this novel, it is not a matter of rising to the superhuman heights alluded to in the "Treatise." Rather, to survive at all, he must become human in an earthy, rather humble sense. His education is largely a matter of learning to accept the world, the flesh, and—himself.

Haller learns his lessons largely from "publicans and sinners": he has plunged into the demimonde of a European city of the 1920's, and his companions are the two courtesans Hermine and Maria, and Pablo, a saxophone player. He is also instructed by the figures of Goethe and Mozart, who appear to him in dreams and try to guide him away from morbid obsession with himself. In terms of practical behavior, he must learn not to sulk like a child, not to brood but to find joy in the moment, and above all to laugh. Despite his pietistic upbringing, he learns to enjoy the "garden" of sex without the anxious feeling that he is tasting forbidden fruit. Goethe tells him that the immortals prefer jest to heavy seriousness. Reproached by the Steppenwolf for his untragic view of life,[7] Goethe instances *The Magic Flute* as a serene work of art which is as profound as the tragic works of Kleist or Beethoven. It is a shrewd stroke, for Mozart is not only Haller's favorite artist, but in the novel, his name is a cipher for sheer beauty. Appropriately, it is Mozart who leads Haller to come to terms with the modern world. As a fervent intellectual—and intellectual snob—he has always scorned radio music; Mozart brings him to see that even a crude receiver of the twenties "cannot destroy the essential spirit of such music" (p. 304)—a concerto grosso of Händel's. Haller, in a way, is prepared for such an insight. Early in the book (p. 64), he admitted that the naïve sensuality of American jazz was "honest." Since anti-Americanism is and was so often the stock in trade of certain self-conscious European intellectuals, the admission is significant.

Haller's relations with Goethe and Mozart are very much in the tradition of the *Bildungsroman*. Thus Wilhelm Meister learns from Shakespeare, Keller's Green Henry from Goethe, Mann's Castorp from all and sundry. The basically optimistic point is the same: a man can learn from others not mere facts but insights which may reshape his life.

The climax of Haller's life is the account of his experiences in the section devoted to the Magic Theater; it is, like the "Treatise," one of the two high points of the book. The theme of the theater is announced very early, in the first section of Haller's autobiographical papers. Clearly, it is of major strategic importance. In its own advertising, it is described as "not for everyone. Only for the insane!" (pp. 55–56). Here extraordinary people, crazy or at least crazed, may see the acting out of events, perceive the semblance of reality. It is suggestive that the insane appear both superior and inferior to the average—a view which accords perfectly with the Steppenwolf's (and Hesse's?) feelings of mingled condescension and envy toward the solid citizens. Also, it must be significant that when Haller does enter the Magic Theater, mirrors are everywhere: he is always seeing himself.

When he ventures into the theater, Haller is in a most exalted state: he has reasons to believe that he will become the lover, and perhaps also the

slayer, of Hermine there. (The "love-death" theme is predictably sounded—
a regrettably banal touch.) Further, Pablo has just primed him with alcohol
and apparently with drugs. This is also a signal to the reader not to interpret
Haller's experiences literally. In the theater he is freed of all his inhibitions,
finds compensation for all his defeats, acts out all his aggressions. (The
psychiatric jargon seems appropriate.) He had to leave the fiction of his
"personality" in the checkroom before he entered. Then he takes part in a
variety of shows (pp. 251–290); he is in a sort of psychological Coney Island,
offering every possible experience. Hesse presents it with great verve. "All
the Girls are yours!" one sign proclaims, and the Steppenwolf relives all his
erotic experiences. This time each is rewarding.

Another sign runs: "Come to the Merry Hunt! Open Season on
Automobiles." In the sideshow Haller can act out his hatred of machines,
which as a good European *Kulturpessimist* he loathes, or affects to loathe. The
account of Harry and a friend ambushing cars while perched in a tree is
wildly comical, comparable to the films *Modern Times* and *A Nous la Liberté*,
but more drastic—in fact quite sadistic. Other attractions include a scene
devoted to instruction in the Indian art of love (not banal in 1927), another
to a presentation of suicide, and a third to one of homosexuality.[8] The most
immediately relevant signboard reads: "Guidance for Constructing One's
Personality Success Guaranteed." Another, clearly self-mocking, satirizes the
"wisdom of the Orient." (Hesse had published *Siddhartha* only a few years
before.) The style reaches a feverish height: thus when Mozart appears to
him in the theater, he recites a Joycean sort of "pome," beginning "He, mein
Junge, beisst dich die Zunge, zwickt dich die Lunge?" (Hey there, young
one, what's eating your tongue, or is it your lung?—p. 296). The episode of
the theater ends with Haller's symbolic murder of Hermine and the
"punishment" which ensues.

It has long been realized that *Steppenwolf* is an account of Hesse's own
psychological crisis. It would seem that the Magic Theater is a carefully
worked out allegory of psychoanalytic treatment: despite his resistance, the
subject is led to relive his past, dramatize his aggressions, and so forth. Here
one can destroy automobiles, commit murder, and so on, without sinister
consequences. The hoped-for outcome is the one to which the real theater
has normally aspired—catharsis; and Haller does seem purged, exhausted,
and a bit battered at the end of the "performance."

Haller, to be sure, has not changed so much that he will live the life of
an epicure, nor is *Steppenwolf* a eudemonistic book. Rather, the protagonist
needs to learn the value of pleasure in order to bring his personality into
some sort of balance; otherwise suicide or some other disaster seems certain.

Happiness is not his destiny, and he cannot linger indefinitely in the garden of sexuality. Doubtless, life with Maria and Pablo would eventually bore him, but his hedonistic period is one of the numerous metamorphoses he must undergo. Similarly, the end of the book brings no final resolution, any more than a successful psychoanalysis does; but Haller's sense of guilt and dread has been contained and made manageable. Presumably he will no longer find masochistic satisfaction in isolation. Above all, his courage to live has been restored, so that he welcomes being "sentenced" to eternal life: "I was resolved to begin the game once more, once more to taste its torments, to shudder once more at its senselessness, to explore once more and often the hell of my inner self" (p. 313). "I go to encounter for the millionth time the reality of experience," Hesse's fellow exile James Joyce had put it. An earlier Steppenwolf, Nietzsche, phrased it differently; undoubtedly Hesse knew his lines: "Was that life? Very well, then, once more!"[9]

One reason that Haller cannot base his life on the "pleasure principle" lies in his basic *Weltanschauung* (which presumably reflects Hesse's own). While his way of living has been radically changed, this philosophy has remained. Deriving from Schopenhauer (thus ultimately from Buddhism) and Nietzsche, it involves a radical dualism: reality is divided into the realms of time and eternity. Hesse also uses the symbol of the mother (nature) as opposed to the spirit (masculine) or intellect (*Geist*). "Time" contains the tangible world, "reality"; it is equivalent to Schopenhauer's will, and is related to Nietzsche's Dionysiac principle. In other words, its "reality" is ultimately an illusion, but it is nevertheless the very stuff of life. Beyond and above time lies the world of eternity, symbolized by the stars, by classical music, by the immortals, and above all by Goethe and Mozart. It is the realm of disinterested contemplation, aesthetic or intellectual. A few lines from the poem "The Immortals," which just precedes the episode of the Magic Theater, contrast the two realms succinctly:

> Immer wieder aus der Erde Tälern
> Dampft zu uns empor des Lebens Drang,
> Wilde Not, berauschter Ueberschwang,
> Blutiger Rauch von tausend Henkersmählern,
> Krampf der Lust, Begierde ohne Ende,...
>
> Wir dagegen haben uns gefunden
> In des Aethers sterndurchglänztem Eis,
> Kennen keine Tage, keine Stunden,
> Sind nicht Mann noch Weib, nicht jung noch Greis.

Eure Sünden sind und eure Aengste,
Euer Mord und eure geilen Wonnen
Schauspiel uns gleichwie die kreisenden Sonnen [p. 214].

(Ever again, from earth's valleys
The stress of life rises up to us like vapor—
Wild need, drunken excess,
Bloody smoke from a thousand last meals,
Convulsion of lust, desire without end,…

But we have found each other
In the icy space of the starry sky;
Know no days, no hours,
Are neither man nor woman, young nor old.
Your sins and your anxieties,
Your murders and your lecherous bliss
Are a spectacle in our eyes, as are the circling suns.)

The sphere of the immortals is as cold as interstellar space. While the "world" is submoral, eternity appears to be supermoral; one can understand that neither Christianity nor democracy would appeal to Haller's "heroic pessimism." Nor can even the most exquisite caresses, the most refined drugs long attract a man who has had glimpses of the eternal.

Since the eternal world is nonmoral, Haller is neither condemned nor forgiven for his offense, the "murder" of Hermine. There is no sort of ethical judgment: men act as they must. But as Haller has broken the rules of the game, confusing appearance with reality, he is "punished": the entire chorus of the immortals laughs at him. Instead of judging him, they announce a diagnosis, in a sardonic but benevolent way.

In arguing that man has not two but a thousand souls, the "Treatise" is very close to Jung's notion of archetypes. (Hesse had been treated, apparently with striking success, by the Jungian analyst Dr. Joseph B. Lang.) [10] Jung gave several different descriptions of the archetype, some of which partially contradict others.[11] The meaning most relevant here is that of a primordial image, found in most or all men: the "Great Mother," the "eternal boy," and the serpent are examples. Since, however, the archetypes are not mere images but shape the personality of a given individual, Hesse can legitimately refer to them as souls. Of course Jung's theories are enormously speculative; they are also often extremely ambiguous.[12] One can see, however, that the theory of archetypes might well appeal to a poet: it is based on the belief that symbols have incalculable psychic power. Jung was a far more appropriate guide for a romantic like Hesse than Freud would have been.

A second Jungian notion, that of the anima or animus, is exploited in *Steppenwolf*. Each man has within him his complementary soul, which appears in the image of woman—his anima; each woman has her complementary animus. The courtesan Hermine, intimately and mysteriously linked to Harry Haller, is indeed his other self, as her name (which of course suggests Hesse's own) implies. Since she is Haller's alter ego, she can also appear masculine and is called Hermann several times; like Goethe's Mignon, she has a hermaphroditic aspect.[13] Toward the end of Haller's symbolic "descent into hell" he kills Hermine (or rather her image) in a fit of sexual jealousy. Apparently the point is not so much that "each man kills the thing he loves," although it is relevant that killing Hermine is a form of partial suicide; it is rather that a man must "interiorize" his anima;[14] that is, he must come to understand its nature as an image, not an autonomous personality, and thus "overcome" it by dealing with it consciously and rationally. Differently put: we should smile at, not try to destroy, the relics of our "dead selves." Similarly, Pablo may represent a childlike, pleasure-oriented aspect or "soul" of Haller, and Maria is an archetype of the temptress, appealing to sheer sexuality. (Her role corresponds to that of Philine in *Wilhelm Meister*.) Perhaps it is best to see these three figures— Hermine, Pablo, and Maria—in two ways: both as individual characters in the story and as archetypes or "souls" of the Steppenwolf. Thus, in life, if John Smith projects his archetype of the Great Mother upon Betty Jones, she is from a Jungian point of view both herself and an element of his psyche. The technique seems particularly appropriate to the lyrical novel: one "I" speaks through a variety of masks.

The most striking aspect of the form of *Steppenwolf* derives from its use of three narrators;[15] all touch upon many of the same things. In the introduction, the hero's "wolfishness," his suicidal tendency, his illness, and the illness of the age are all presented. Haller's memoirs are naturally much concerned with the same major themes; he comments upon them at length and illustrates them, acts them out, in the course of his narration. Here there is a wealth of incident, episode, and "gallows humor" not found elsewhere in the novel. In his turn, the author of the "Treatise" makes many of the same points as the first narrator, but from a sardonic point of view anticipating that of the immortals. The poem "The Immortals" also restates a central theme of the book.

Thus Hesse relies largely on the technique of repetition and variation, in fact to a degree which suggests a debt to Thomas Mann. The Homeric laughter of the immortals at the end of the novel, for instance, is foreshadowed by the remarks of the "Treatise" on the saving role of humor and by Pablo's affectionately regretful words: "Poor, poor fellow. Look at his eyes! He can't laugh" (p. 165). Leitmotifs are also of great importance; thus the araucaria symbolizes bourgeois life and taste. As Freedman points out, mirror images form a strategic motif throughout the novel, most obviously in the Magic Theater.[16] The "Treatise" is itself a mirror,[17] as is the introduction. Perhaps the most effective and concentrated symbol is that of great music heard over a radio. As the inferior instrument distorts but cannot ruin the music, so time and matter cannot destroy the eternal, and Haller will never survive to view eternity unless he accepts the temporal world—"the radio music of life" (p. 309).

Like many of Gide's works, *Steppenwolf* seems to be intended as a book of liberation and joy. Not that one can imagine Haller as a truly joyful person, but that is the direction of the book. To restate its themes at length would be to trivialize them; taken out of the fabric of the novel, they seem banal. To recapitulate briefly: the Steppenwolf comes to realize that he must love himself as well as his neighbor; he is freed, at least partially, from the sense of guilt; he comes to cherish the surface as well as the depths. Yet we sense that it will be a very long time before he learns to laugh. Steppenwolf is a Nietzschean type, striving toward a health he will hardly attain, a martyr of heroic pessimism rather than a superman. Much of the appeal of the book lies in this paradoxical tension. The novel is a deliberately dissonant hymn to joy.

## NOTES

1. *The Lyrical Novel* (Princeton: Princeton University Press, 1963).

2. "Zur Erklärung von Hermann Hesses *Steppenwolf*," *Monatshefte*, LIII (1961), 198.

3. *Krisis* (Berlin: S. Fischer, 1928), p. 81.

4. Schwarz, "Zur Erklärung von Hermann Hesses *Steppenwolf*," pp. 192, 197.

5. Compare for instance Mann's phrase "problem child [*Sorgenkind*] of life" (my translation) and Hesse's use of the word *Sorgenkind* in *Der Steppenwolf* (Zurich: Manesse Verlag, n.d.), p. 37. Page numbers in the text refer to this edition; all translations are my own. The quotation from "The Immortals" is by permission of Suhrkamp Verlag.

6. *Krisis*, pp. 10–11; used by permission of Suhrkamp Verlag.

7. For a similar criticism of Goethe, see Erich Heller, "Goethe and the Avoidance of Tragedy," in his *The Disinherited Mind* (Philadelphia: Dufour and Saifer, 1952), pp. 27–49.

8. In "psychedelic" circles, it is claimed that Hesse took drugs; it has also been maintained that he was an "overt homosexual" (*New Republic*, July 13, 1968, p. 24). Doubtless these assertions will interest persons of certain persuasions; they have no literary relevance, and remind one of questions like "Was Shakespeare a sailor?" "Could Goethe swim?"

9. *Sämtliche Werke*, VI (Stuttgart: Kröner, 1965), 173.

10. See Malte Dahrendorf, "Hesses *Demian* und Jung," *Germanisch-Romanische Monatschrift*, XXXIX (1958), 89.

11. See Edward Glover, *Freud or Jung* (New York: Norton, 1950), esp. pp. 30–32, 61–62.

12. *Ibid.*, esp. pp. 187–195.

13. Schwarz, "Zur Erklärung von Hermann Hesses *Steppenwolf*," p. 193.

14. See Paul Roth, *Anima und Animus in der Psychologie C. G. Jungs* (Winterthur, Switz.: Keller, 1954), pp. 50–51.

15. See Theodore Ziolkowski, *The Novels of Hermann Hesse* (Princeton: Princeton University Press, 1965), pp. 178–228.

16. *The Lyrical Novel*, pp. 76–77.

17. *Ibid.*, pp. 78–79.

JOSEPH MILECK

# Narziss Und Goldmund: *Life's Double Melody*

## THE PAST, REVIEW, AND REVERIE

By the beginning of 1927, Hesse's storm had run its course, and in the relative tranquillity of the lull that followed, a frantic participant and acrid recorder became a composed observer and wishful dreamer, an embittered Haller was forgotten and an amiable Goldmund was enthusiastically espoused, and the dramatic tempo of *Der Steppenwolf* yielded to the more epic tread of *Narziss und Goldmund*. This marked the end of that turbulent decade during which Hesse was intent primarily upon coming to grips and to terms with himself. The many tales of this period reflect not only the anxieties, tensions, and general anguish of this undertaking, but also Hesse's dogged persistence, his unflagging hope, and his spells of elation. *Demian*'s proclamation of emancipation and self-realization begins these years with vigorous aspiration and high optimism. *Klein und Wagner* mirrors the initial agonies and despair of Hesse's actual emancipation. *Klingsors letzter Sommer* documents his almost manic surrender to life and art during the summer of 1919. *Siddhartha* is the resolving philosophical lull following this flurry of activity. *Kurgast* records one of the many desperate sieges of physical pain and mental distress that Hesse suffered in the twenties: crises illustrative of the artist-thinker's conflicting need for isolation from and for contact with life. *Der Steppenwolf* depicts the most critical of these periods of depression,

From *Hermann Hesse: Life and Art*. © 1978 by The Regents of the University of California.

aberration, and renewed hope; it was also the cathartic experience that brought the relentless phase of Hesse's self-quest to its end. Center of interest was soon to shift from the self to the community. In the interim, Hesse looked to his past, reviewed his thoughts, permitted himself to dream, and wrote his *Narziss und Goldmund*. According to an unpublished letter to Helene Welti, December 19, 1928,[53] the novel was begun in mid-1927 and completed in December 1928. The book appeared in the spring of 1930.

Both *Siddhartha* and *Narziss und Goldmund* were written during lulls following considerable turbulence, and each followed in the wake of a tale contrastingly autobiographical and gripping in its immediacy. Both were as much the consequence of equanimity as *Klingsors letzter Sommer* and *Der Steppenwolf* were the effects of agitation. Regarding thought, feeling, conflict, and aspiration, Siddhartha and Goldmund are no less self-projections than any other of Hesse's protagonists, but their worlds are basically novel and their actions are largely imagined. In *Siddhartha*, there is nothing in outer detail that is discernibly autobiographical, and in *Narziss und Goldmund*, very little. Hesse's Maulbronn obviously lent its name to Goldmund's Mariabronn. It also left its physical imprint on the monastery. Mariabronn's arched entrance, large courtyard, dormitories, refectories, its double early Gothic church, ornately carved choir pews, and small cloister garden and fountain are clearly recollections. Goldmund is brought to the monastery at the age of fifteen, with the expectation that he will in time become a cleric; Hesse had entered Maulbronn at fourteen and with similar parental hope. Goldmund's fisticuffs with a strong schoolmate are reminiscent of a similar tangle in which Hesse had conducted himself equally admirably and which had first received literary expression in *Unterm Rad*.[54] As had Hesse before him, Goldmund applies himself diligently in school, ruins his health, even thinks of taking French leave, becomes generally abrasive, finds solace with an intimate, and eventually loses all interest in school and studies. He leaves the sanctuary of the monastery at the age of eighteen, just as Hesse at the same age had left the shelter of home and parents. What follows on Goldmund's departure is story and not converted fact.

*Narziss und Goldmund* is an amalgam of pre-1914 narration and post–*Demian* thought. In his storytelling, Hesse returned to his Gaienhofen years in general, and specifically to *Berthold*, the three-chapter fragment put aside in 1908 for want of interest, inspiration, or ability. Fragment and novel are similar enough to suggest that one was the narrative springboard for the other. Both are located in South Germany and the Rhineland, and both begin as school tales. Like Goldmund, Berthold is reared by his father, has no memory of his mother or earliest childhood, and is sent to a church school at the age of fifteen to be educated for the priesthood for which he, too, is not at all suited. In both cases, studies once attractive soon become tedious, and initial spiritual concerns give way to worldly interests. Both youths are strong, handsome, and naïve, puberty proves trying for both, each has vivid sexual fantasies, and each gladly allows himself to be seduced by an older and practised young woman. Each also latches onto a slightly older and more sophisticated confidant and teacher, and both pair of intimates engage in long philosophical discussions. Though anything but a saintly Narziss, Berthold's friend Johannes is a similarly attractive young man, with the same long dark eyelashes, just as courteous in manner, shares Narziss's air of solicitous superiority, courts his high aspirations, and also awakens his ward to the realization that the church is not his calling. Both Berthold and Goldmund also fall in love with a blond-haired Agnes who precipitates a severe crisis for each, both murder in jealous rage, and both flee church and school for life at large, while still in their late teens. *Berthold* breaks off at this juncture. It seems as though Hesse had just not been up to the epic demands of his protagonist's subsequent adventures as a soldier in the Thirty Years' War. A discarded fragment of 1908 proved to be a suggestive narrative source in 1927, and an intended picaresque novel became a well-disguised *roman à thèse*.

But *Narziss und Goldmund* harked back to more than just *Berthold*. Its monastic situation returned to the more detailed depiction of Maulbronn in *Unterm Rad*, and much of Goldmund, of his family situation and school experiences, and even some of his relationship with Narziss, is prefigured in Giebenrath and his family situation, school experiences, and friendship with Heilner. In fact or in memory, Hesse must also have returned to Knulp, his favorite pre–*Demian* protagonist. Both are handsome vagabond-artists and childlike voluble charmers, and both sing and dance and are facile storytellers. Knulp writes poetry and plays a harmonica, and Goldmund recites verse and plays a lute. Neither has talent for work, both are footloose, and each treasures his freedom and lives his own life regardless of consequences. Both age prematurely, and both return home pale, haggard, and mortally ill. God appears to Knulp in the delirium of his illness, counters his lurking regrets, and consoles him. Mother-Eve (*Eva-Mutter*) confronts Goldmund in his hallucinations, alleviates his pain, and expunges all fear of death. As God's voice trails off, it suggests that of Knulp's mother, that of his first sweetheart Henriette, and then that of Lisabeth, the mother of his son. Analogously, Goldmund's Mother-Eve is a composite of all the women in his life. But for Goldmund's insatiable and freely exercised sexuality, he and Knulp are unmistakable birds of a feather. Indeed, Hesse's beloved protagonist of 1927 was largely a resurrected prewar ideal upon which he imposed a postwar favorite, his sensual and uninhibited Klingsor.

The origins of Narziss and of his relationship with Goldmund were no less diverse than Goldmund's derivation. His lineage began with Wilhelm Lang, Hesse's own bosom companion in Maulbronn, and his literary antecedents were legion. He and his role in Goldmund's life were prefigured in the earliest of Hesse's trail of double self-projections, and returned most immediately to *Demian*'s interplay of friendship. With *Demian*, erstwhile intimate friend and contrasting personality had become a veritable guru practised in psychoanalysis. Narziss was a return to and a slight humanizing of this Demian concept of friend, foil, and guide. Like his predecessor, Narziss is slightly older than the protagonist, is also a schoolmate, and is just as quick to take his newfound friend under his wing. Both Demian and Narziss are dark-haired and sad-faced, courteous and disciplined, deadly serious and hyperintelligent, and consciously aloof and supremely self-confident. Each is more man than boy, more scholar than student, more guide than friend, and more function than fact. Both wards are immediately fascinated by these haughty young princes among lesser commoners, and both quickly succumb to their slightly mocking solicitude. Like Demian, Narziss knows more and better than his troubled friend, is determined to awaken him to himself and to life, engages him in religious, philosophical, and moral discussions, and helps him break out of a restrictive shell, that he may find, live, and realize himself. Like Demian too, Narziss can read thoughts, is present or appears when needed, and in deep contemplation assumes an open-eyed, trance-like, rigid posture. In his being, his function, and in the mechanics of his relationship with Goldmund, he was clearly a harking back to Demian. He was to Demian very much what Goldmund was to Knulp.

Demian was borrowed from Sinclair's tale and accorded more reality, *Eva-Mutter* was simply lifted from it and rendered more clearly symbolic. Both Demian and his mother *Frau Eva* are basically concepts actualized. Their actuality is thin and pale and their symbolism is inordinately complex. Both are too many things too mysteriously veiled to be entirely satisfactory. Such is not the case in *Narziss und Goldmund*. In Narziss, Hesse resurrected only the person Demian, and in *Eva-Mutter* only the symbol *Frau Eva*. Unlike Demian, Narziss is not a disguise, not a person who is essentially but a projected *daimon* or externalized imago, but an independent reality, an actual friend and guide. *Eva Mutter* too, unlike *Frau Eva*, is not an implausibly disguised anima and Magna Mater, but pristine idea. Narziss was rendered more actual than Demian, *Eva-Mutter* became more symbol than

*Frau Eva*, and *Narziss und Goldmund* emerged a tale more plausible and less murky than *Demian*.

## DICHOTOMY AND ITS POLARITIES

From *Demian* to *Der Steppenwolf*, Hesse was bent on self-quest, obsessed by life's dichotomy, and absorbed by its complexity of polarities. Life and thought became a fluctuating and faltering upward progression, and began to revolve about the spirituality and animality of man, about art and life, the artist and the nonartist, about thought and feeling, erotic and social love, the transitory and the permanent, culture and the bourgeois world, appearance and the real, contact and isolation, multiplicity and oneness, and about time and timelessness. During these years, Hesse was only twice able to relax enough to review his rapidly evolving thoughts. *Siddhartha* was a meditative summation and culmination of his initial thinking, and *Narziss und Goldmund* was his calm concluding reconsideration of most of the period's major concerns.

Like most of Hesse's protagonist's, Goldmund is a man with a pressing quarrel. His dispute is with himself and with life, and his grievance is dichotomy and its many polarities. Man is male or female, becomes a voluptuary or ascetic, a dreamer or a thinker, a thinker or an artist, an artist or an ordinary citizen, a citizen or a vagabond, is caught between the sensual and the spiritual, between evil and good, and experiences joy or sorrow, and love or hatred. Thanks to this flaw in God's creation, life is a frustrating either-or and never a rich simultaneous experiencing of its diverse possibilities. This dichotomy is the critical fact of existence with which Goldmund, like his predecessors, has to come to terms. Like theirs, his whole life is governed by this challenge.

For Sinclair, dichotomy extends little beyond the duality of incompatibles inherent in Christian belief and morality, and a Nietzschean emancipation is enough to resolve his quandary. Able to cope neither with inner nor outer dichotomy, Klein elects to escape it all in suicide. Klingsor's response to life's dualities is desperate affirmation and wild revelry. Siddhartha's is a general affirmation, systematic exhaustion, and an ultimate transcending of dichotomy. In *Kurgast*, life's poles and man's swinging back and forth between them are enthusiastically acclaimed. And an embittered Haller, whose eyes are fixed on an ethereal realm beyond dichotomy, requires a touch of gallows humor to make the spirit and flesh polarity of life even tolerable. In his grappling with and resolution of dichotomy, Goldmund is something of a very human compromise between two intimidating possibilities: the magnificent ideal depicted in *Siddhartha* and Haller's heroic retreat into Platonism.

Like Siddhartha's, Goldmund's emphasis is upon life for all that it is and upon its living, and like Siddhartha, he experiences and realizes himself, and accepts death. Unlike Siddhartha, however, though Goldmund accepts life's dichotomy, he does not cease to quarrel with it. He makes his peace with himself, but not with life; God could have fashioned it better. Siddhartha traverses and transcends dichotomy, whereas Goldmund continues to be troubled by it to the end. He does not experience Siddhartha's revelatory timelessness, oneness, and meaningfulness of life, but he does achieve a very human insight into himself and life.

Like Haller, Goldmund is troubled by and quarrels with life's dichotomy, unlike him, he chooses, notwithstanding, to live life fully. For Haller, dichotomy is life's most regrettable flaw and he can only agonize in his oscillation between its poles. He turns his back upon the flawed phenomenal world to the extent he can and finds his sustenance in the perfect noumenal realm of his Immortals, endures his lesser physical self and pampers his spirituality, starves his appetites and fattens his dreams. His sporadic adventures of the flesh are but brief aberrations tolerated for their therapeutic value, minimal exposures necessary to immunize himself against life and to render secure his isolation and passionate dedication to things spiritual. In contrast, and despite his quarrel with dichotomy, Goldmund learns to revel in his to and fro between life and art, between animality and spirituality. Pendulation is life's curse, but it is also life's glory, a blissful agony to which man owes much of his achievement, and wherein alone self-realization is possible.

For Siddhartha, all is well with world and man, neither is ideal enough for Haller, and Goldmund has serious reservations about both. Siddhartha affirms reality for all it is, his life is living, and his reward is transcendence. Haller takes bitter issue with and rejects reality, his life is trying quest, and his goal is a world etherealized and man spiritualized, Goldmund questions but accepts reality, his life is to live fully and to create, and his goal is self-realization and death. Siddhartha knows no disparity between what is and what could or should be, Haller is tormented by it, and Goldmund is able to put up with it. Siddhartha feels no need to reconcile anything, for all is a reconciled oneness, Haller cannot reconcile his spirituality and animality or phenomena and noumena, and Goldmund manages to reconcile himself to life's frustrating dichotomy. In Hesse's recapitulation and synthesizing of the past, a new possibility emerged, an ideal more possible than Siddhartha's and an adjustment more attractive than Haller's: all in all, a more human coping with the self and with life.

## TWO POSSIBILITIES

Like most of Hesse's major tales, *Narziss und Goldmund* juxtaposes and scrutinizes two human possibilities: the ideal possible and the dubious actual. Goldmund is obviously the possible, and Narziss the actual. Protagonist and intime are yet another variation of Hesse's customary double self-projection: Goldmund is the ingratiating artist-voluptuary he would have liked to be, and Narziss is the retiring thinker-ascetic he knew himself to be. Contrary to the implications of the title, the novel is not a balanced recounting of the lives of two protagonists, nor was it ever intended to be. From its inception, the story was to be Goldmund's. Its initial array of titles makes this amply clear: *Goldmund oder Das Lob der Sünde; Goldmund und Narziss; Goldmunds Weg zur Mutter.*[55] The final bipartite title and its sequence was an appropriate afterthought for a tale featuring dichotomy in both its substance and form, and a sensitive response to metric flow. Nor does it do the novel justice merely to consider it allegory, to argue that protagonist and friend are but flesh (*Natur*) and spirit (*Geist*) personified and that their intimate friendship only demonstrates Hesse's belief in the necessary and desirable interplay and interdependence of these poles of life. Goldmund and Narziss are not just unidimensional personifications but complex personalities. They, like all of Hesse's very human protagonists, are caught up in life's polar tug of war, and each adjusts in a manner that most accords with his psychology. Neither adjustment is without its drawbacks and each has its virtues. Goldmund swings freely and with no compunctions between sensuality and spirituality, is both a disciplined artist and a roving voluptuary, and as much at home in the monastery as in the world. His rewards are life's intensities, and the price he pays is equanimity. Narziss chooses to deny his body, to turn his back upon the world, and to cultivate things spiritual in the seclusion of the monastery. His reward is peace and its price is human warmth. Each is envious of the benefits of the other's adjustment to the self and to life, but neither can nor will exchange roles with the other. For Goldmund to live like Narziss would be a violation of the self, and for Narziss to emulate Goldmund would be to violate himself even more than he does. Though Hesse gives obvious preference to Goldmund's resolution of the dichotomy, he clearly condones both approaches to life; both are psychological necessities and not mere caprice, and both can unveil life's mysteries.

It was not given to Hesse to live and to create as spontaneously and unconcerned as Goldmund—but he could dream. Narziss, like Haller before him, was Hesse's real predicament and lot. Narziss's kinship with his antecedent is manifest. Haller's suppression of his sensuality and his Platonic rejection of the world became Narziss's chastity and monastic withdrawal from the world, his realm of the spirit became Narziss's Kingdom of God, and both have their eyes fixed on eternity. Haller is likely to continue to swing between man and wolf for some time before he is able to join his serene Immortals. What still lies between mortality and eternity for Narziss remains conjecture. Goldmund's dying reference to the impossibility of death without life smolders ominously in Narziss's heart. He is a Haller more firmly in control of himself and of life, but he is also a potential *Steppenwolf.* Narziss and Haller sacrifice themselves for a purpose and a possibility. Goldmund surrenders to actuality, simply yields himself to himself and to the rhythm of life and death. A wistful dream died with Goldmund's death, and Hesse was left with Narziss and a way of life that was immediately far less attractive, but that was in accord with his being and that promised to be far more satifying.

## Art and Life

Art was a concern for Hesse as persistent and almost as insistent as life's dichotomy. He was as fascinated by one as he was troubled by the other. Most of his protagonists and many of his minor characters are artists by vocation or avocation, much of the argument of their stories is focused on art, and this serial exegesis clearly traces Hesse's own evolving attitude toward and notions about art. Art was for Hesse the substitute for life it is for Lauscher, it became as wretched a profession for him as it does for Camenzind, as great a consolation as it is for Kuhn, the all-absorbing fated profession it ends up being for Veraguth, the passion it became for Klingsor, the loneliness and self-exposure it is for Haller, and Goldmund's reconciliation of life and art became a culminating ideal that Hesse nurtured but himself never realized. Each of the tales in question paints an inner portrait of an artist, and under the aegis of psychoanalysis, these studies became progressively more penetrating in their psychology. In 1918, this psychological interest in the artist began to spill over into Hesse's essays. His tales, together with these essays from 1918 to 1930, afford a composite psychological portrait of the artist and a detailed supplemental psychological theory of art.[56]

At the outset of Hesse's career, art and life were virtually incompatible and mutually exclusive areas of human experience. Like the author-protagonist of *Eine Stunde hinter Mitternacht* and Lauscher, Hesse believed or wanted to believe that true art neither derived from nor dealt with drab life at large, but was inspired by and depicted a romantically ideal world behind appearances, a realm accessible primarily in dream or poetic imagination. This wondrous world behind the ordinary world became the subject of his art. Spirituality and sensuality, too, were as incompatible for Hesse as they are for the author-protagonist of *Eine Stunde hinter Mitternacht* and for Lauscher. For him, just as for his two self-projections, seductive sensual experiences—deviations actually imagined more than experienced, and frequently alluded to but never depicted—were cause for guilt and reason for fervent atonement. Sensuality sullied, spirituality edified. For young Hesse, the world was a wretched detraction, sexuality a questionable urge, and both were heroically renounced for art and spirituality.

From *Peter Camenzind* to *Rosshalde*, and particularly in the Swabian *Novellen*, art and life were interrelated, but the bland mixture became as unsatisfactory to Hesse as his futile attempt to reconcile his sensuality and his spirituality, and to be both an artist and a respectable citizen. Life as an artist-citizen proved to be as confining and frustrating as life dedicated to beauty. From *Demian* to *Der Steppenwolf* the old cleft between art and life reappeared and widened progressively. Depicted life narrowed down again to Hesse himself, and as earlier, with primary emphasis upon inner world and not outer circumstances. But this was no return to the past. Art had once been an ornate depiction of an innocent young aesthete's dreams and sorrows, now it became a raw exposure of a wayward middle-aged artist's psychology. Sexuality, once carefully shunned in life and art, was now indulged in both. Spirituality, however, continued as always to be Hesse's true love. Sensuality remained suspect, affirmed fully in theory, but less accepted than just tolerated in fact. Hesse was a Haller and Siddhartha was a dream.

It was to dream that Hesse returned in *Narziss und Goldmund*. What he had not been able to settle satisfactorily in life, he now resolved in yet another ideal. Goldmund's tale not only again accords life at large a real role in Hesse's art, but makes life an integral part of creativity, and thereby justifies and renders acceptable the spirit-flesh dichotomy. Instinctuality, previously a detraction for the artist, now became a necessity for his art. Goldmund concludes from his experience that true art derives from life itself. To create, the artist must live and allow life's experiences to imprint their images upon his soul. These images are the source of his inspiration and became art in disciplined application. Art is a product of both the flesh and the spirit, and exemplifies their necessary and desirable interaction and inter-dependence in life as a whole. This theory of art and life was Hesse's latest sentiment, and Goldmund personifies what temporarily became a new ideal following *Der Steppenwolf*. Hesse had been a troubled aesthete and a discontented artist-bourgeois, had become a wayward artist-seeker, had ended an artist-recluse with aspirations after immortality, and now he imagined himself a freewheeling, self-affirming and life-accepting artist-voluptuary.

## ART AND TIME

Life's transitoriness and death became the source of anguish and fear early in Hesse's life. His first response was flight into the world of his imagination, a Lauscherean retreat into the timeless and wondrous real realm behind the ever-changing ugly façade of life's appearance. Dream's solace lasted only as long as Hesse's short-lived aestheticism, and he was left again to lament and to endure the ravages of time. Siddhartha's theory of timelessness was Hesse's second attempt to eliminate the reality of time. This second effort to anesthetize himself was as futile as the first. He had been able to imagine a life without time, and could think timelessness, but he continued to live in time. Hesse had meanwhile begun to pursue a more conciliatory approach to time. If this painful fact of life could not be wished away, it could perhaps be rendered more palatable. And this it was, when like his Knulp and Kuhn respectively, he began again to recognize that life's very transitoriness heightens the appreciation of its beauties, and provides the thrust in man's creativity. These early notions evolved in greater detail following *Demian*, and received their culminating expression in *Narziss und Goldmund*. Klingsor hates and fears time and death, but he also loves them, for they are the driving impulse in both his life and his art; death kindles an appreciative passion for life, the frenzy of creativity blots time out, and his art, a veritable weapon against death, lends some degree of permanence to the evanescent. In *Kurgast*, Hesse insists that transitoriness and death are the *sine qua non* of beauty and its appreciation, and even argues that permanence could be a drab and lifeless tedium. His return to this theme in *Narziss und Goldmund* was essentially a repetition of old sentiment become more continent and modified in its emphasis. Fear of death is again the creative thrust, and Goldmund, like his predecessors, is anxious to rescue something of life from the dance of death, but he is no longer interested in making death more palatable, or in blotting out its reality, or in lauding it. Art is now simply man's attempted conquest of time and his partial victory over death and despair, and death itself ultimately becomes for Goldmund but a welcome culminating experience, an almost erotic reunion with the Primal Mother. Goldmund's life was Hesse's dream, his tranquil death had become his hope.

## THE BOURGEOIS WORLD

Though generally conciliatory in his review of the past, Hesse remained adamant in his deprecation of the bourgeois world. In *Demian*, this is the world of the herd, of the cowardly weak and of their self-protecting herd morality and religion. In *Klein und Wagner*, the bourgeoisie is the stifling society of socially conditioned, self-righteous hypocrites and philistines. In *Klingsors letzter Sommer*, it is the bland everyday world of the ordinary. In *Siddhartha*, it is the world of trivial material concerns and absurd anxieties, peopled by child-adults. In *Kurgast*, it is the world of dignified appearance, fat wallets, good stomachs, and also of vulgar normality, mental indolence, and tasteless superficiality. This swell of vituperation peaked in *Der Steppenwolf*. Middle-class society is enviable in its cleanliness, diligence, orderliness, in its emphasis upon duty, and its consciousness of law, but beyond all this, it is everything that is wrong with our age humanly, politically, and culturally: empty mechanical existence, nationalism and militarism, materialism and utilitarianism. Haller's touch of ambiguity, his basic animosity, and his bitter invective carried over into *Narziss und Goldmund*. His sentiment is essentially Goldmund's. The sedentary members of society (*die Sesshaften*) are less to be envied for their well-being and self-satisfaction than to be soundly berated for their emotional and mental stagnation, their vulgarity and avarice, vacuity, petty pursuits, and easy satiety. For Goldmund to join this staid and stark world of bickering merchants, fishmongers, and tradesmen, would have been to become another artistically crippled and embittered Master Niklaus, the malcontent artist-bourgeois Hesse had himself once been. Like most of his predecessors, Goldmund is irked by and never makes his peace with the bourgeois world. Hesse himself had not done so, nor was he about to. This world was tantamount to the establishment, and the establishment was almost by definition inimical to the individualist.

### Verbal Counterpoint

For Goldmund, successful art is an organized composite whose multiple parts are consonant with each other. Forehead must accord with knee, knee with shoulder, shoulder with hip, and all must be in keeping with nature and temperament. His Apostle John is a partial and his Virgin Mary a perfect realization of this artistic ideal. Goldmund's theory of art was also Hesse's, and *Narziss und Goldmund* was obviously another of his more deliberate responses to this conception. In *Siddhartha*, human possibility evolving through three areas of human experience found its conscious and accordant expression in a tripartite structure, and in action and language characterized by a three-beat rhythm. In *Narziss und Goldmund*, life's basic dichotomy with its constellation of polarities found its appropriate and just as conscious expression in a thoroughly contrapuntal manner: setting is bipartite, movement fluctuates, personae are paired, actions and attributes are coupled, attitudes are opposing, emotions are polar, and mode of expression affects a primary two-beat rhythm. Manner itself becomes matter! In *Kurgast*, Hesse had expressed the fervent desire to be able some day to give simultaneous expression to the two voices of life's melody in both the substance and form of his prose. He doubted that he would ever realize this aspiration, but would never cease trying.[57] *Narziss und Goldmund* approaches this envisaged verbal counterpoint as closely as prose ever can.

The antithetical setting of *Narziss und Goldmund* immediately focuses attention upon dichotomy and polarity. Monastery and world not only exemplify life's intrinsic dichotomy but, like Narziss and Goldmund, they are also a visible expression of the polar concepts of spirit (*Geist*) and flesh (*Natur*), about which all things human revolve. Ten of the tale's twenty chapters are properly given to the monastery, ten to the world, and Goldmund twice moves from one to the other. Each of these halves is in turn appropriately bisected. The monastic half begins in the Mariabronn of Goldmund's youth and awakening, and ends in the Mariabronn of his manhood and death. The secular half silhouettes two situations and possibilities: the bishop's city, domestication, and art; the world at large, the open road, and life. The splintered structure of *Klingsors letzter Sommer* accords with the fractured structure of its protagonist's life; the symmetrical tripartite structure of *Siddhartha* is consonant with its protagonist's systematic three-stage progression through life; Goldmund's confrontation with dichotomy found its correspondent expression in this balanced bipartite structural segmentation and fluctuating movement.

Life's dichotomy and the polar predicament of man are equally accentuated by the narrative itself. A father and son arrive with two horses at Mariabronn, a monastery with an entrance arch resting on double columns, with native walnut trees and a southern chestnut, and with two exceptional inmates: the old Abbot Daniel, simple and wise, and the young novice Narziss, learned and haughty. Handsome and delicate Goldmund, the student newcomer, immediately becomes attached to both abbot and novice, finds himself torn between two ideals, and soon becomes troubled and angry. It is with trepidation and expectations that Goldmund agrees to accompany Adolf and two other schoolmates to visit two young girls in a nearby village. He also declines two further invitations. As a student in Mariabronn, Goldmund becomes ill twice, is twice put into an infirmary, and twice enjoys the monastery's traditional medicinal wine. He and Narziss are opposites and complements: one is blue-eyed and has blond hair, a dreamer and a child, and the other is a dark-eyed brunet, a thinker and an analyst. Convinced by Narziss that he is neither monk nor scholar, and that he belongs to those with strong and delicate senses, to those who are at home in the garden of love and in the land of art, Goldmund's interest in learning and his enthusiasm for dispute wane and die. Goldmund resembles his once beautiful and wild mother in both figure and face. In his frequent dreams, the reawakened mother-world envelops Goldmund, suggesting not only kindness, love, happiness, and consolation, but also all that is dark and frightful, all greed and anxiety, sin and sorrow, birth and death. Twice Goldmund leaves the monastery stealthily via mill and stream, and he also has two sexual encounters with the gypsy Lise before he wanders forth into a receptive and waiting world. He wanders frantic and hungry for two days and nights through a forest alive with birds and animals, then chances upon a hovel with an old woman and a young child, a peasant and his wife, and two goats. A year or two of incessant wandering and frugal fare follow. Women and love become Goldmund's destiny, he learns rapidly and forgets little. Desire is sated as quickly as it is roused, and after each affair, Goldmund is left both happy and sad.

This mannered two-beat narrative rhythm continues to the very end of the tale. Before lapsing into unconsciousness, Goldmund leaves Narziss with a pair of statements alluding to the impossibility of death without life, and for two days and nights, Narziss watches over dying Goldmund and ponders his last words.

Matter affected mode of expression as thoroughly as it determined structure, narrative movement, choice and arrangement of cast, physical action, and emotional reaction. Dichotomy left its imprint even on the mechanics of Hesse's prose. The first paragraph emphatically establishes the two-beat rhythm that pervades the novel. The paragraph comprises two sentences, the first of these sentences consists of two major segments, and the second of these segments is introduced by a pair of parallel principal clauses and followed by two parallel clusters of five principal and subordinate clauses. This coupling of sentences and paired clustering of clauses is too patterned to be anything but design. A closer examination of syntax reflects this same design. The first segment of the first sentence consists of four syntactic couplets: two prepositional phrases that locate Mariabronn's lone chestnut tree, the tree-subject and an appositive, two more prepositional phrases that account for the southern origin of the exceptional tree, and a second appositive reference to the tree, together with a qualifying prepositional phrase. The second segment of the first sentence draws attention to the appearance of the tree in the spring and in the autumn, and is composed of at least twenty syntactic couplets. The second sentence again stresses the foreign origin of the tree, draws attention to the contrasting reaction to it of the Latins and the natives, and consists of at least another eight syntactic couplets.

Not only syntax but Hesse's choice of words and juxtaposition of concepts was influenced by his dichotomous concern. Compounds and bisyllabics are almost obtrusive in their abundance. The first paragraph includes no fewer than thirty-two of these bipartite nouns, adjectives and adverbs. This duality is broached by Hesse's immediate allusion to the double columns of Mariabronn's arched entrance, and then made explicit by his spaced antithetical references to the chestnut and the walnut trees, the north and the implied south, the spring and the autumn, the youngsters and the prior, and to the natives and the foreigners. Matter's way is well prepared, then constantly accentuated by manner.

The entire novel is not as thoroughly mannered as its opening paragraph, but this two-beat pulsation remains the prevailing rhythm of its style. Just as in *Siddhartha*, deviation from characteristic mode of expression occurs primarily when outer situation and inner state become exceptional. In particularly novel, threatening, or otherwise exciting situations, and at times of nervous expectancy, intense anxiety, or sheer elation, pattern yields as usual to asymmetry. Sentences normally more or less comparable in length, slow and steady in flow, and even in their two-beat rhythm become an animated intermixture of longer and shorter units with gripping successions of irregularly brief clauses and phrases, liberal parataxis emphatic repetitions, rousing word accumulations, lively exclamations and rhetorical questions, and with a resultantly rapid and fluctuating flow and decidedly varied rhythm. As usual, Hesse's language adjusts to and accentuates changing situation and state. Such is particularly evident where he recounts Goldmund's initial expectant wandering through a forest teeming with animal life, his frantic stumbling across a stark, wintry landscape following Viktor's death, his manic experiencing of the plague, his night of despair and desperation in the governor's castle, and his sieges of inspiration and creation.

Apart from its pervasive two-beat rhythm, the manner of *Narziss und Goldmund* shows the usual hallmarks of Hesse's prose. Although the tale may suggest a return to German Romanticism's best tradition of storytelling, it is anything but traditional narrative. But half of Goldmund's very short life is recounted. He arrives at Mariabronn at the age of fifteen and with no more than a skeletal past. Only the remaining sixteen or seventeen years of his life are brought into focus, and of these merely ten are actually accounted for, and then but spottily. Hesse's customary thin thread of narration is as usual repeatedly broken by time fissures, descriptions, commentary, and protracted interior monologue and expository dialogue. Goldmund's first three years in Mariabronn are skimpy narrative: he attends school, engages in a scuffle, takes part in an illicit outing, experiences two bouts of illness, gathers herbs, and is seduced by Lise. Only the first few days and the last few months of Goldmund's first year and a half in the outside world are focused upon: his night with Lise, two days and nights in a forest followed by a day with a peasant's family, and his second sexual experience; autumn months on a homestead with an old knight and his two daughters, two days in a village, birth of a child, another sexual encounter, Viktor's death, and wintry struggle for survival. The year preceding Goldmund's months on the homestead, and the year and a half following Viktor's murder are disposed of with but brief references to the passing seasons, the tribulations of the road, and to Goldmund's continued adventures of the flesh. Allusions to more affairs and to a great deal of brawling suggest that much transpires during Goldmund's next three years in the bishop's city with Master Niklaus but little is narrated. Only the first two and the last few days of this period are accounted for; all else is rumination about and dialogue involving art and life. Goldmund's subsequent four years of hunger and adventure are accorded but a brief paean to the knights of the road. Only Hesse's description of the plague and its summer of mayhem and mania, and his recounting of Goldmund's encounter with Robert, Lene, and Rebekka enjoy a touch of epic breadth and detail. But for his affair with Agnes, his apprehension, and his rescue, and but for his briefly recalled second and last sortie into the world, and his death, Goldmund's brief return that autumn to the bishop's city and his last three years in Mariabronn are again primarily interior monologue and expository dialogue. As usual, Hesse's tale is more an airing of views than a depiction of life, more an exposing of minds than a telling of deeds, less a narrative that unravels than a portrait that emerges. And this inner portrait of Goldmund evolves more fully through a succession of expository monologues and dialogues revolving about nodal situations and episodes, just as the image of Goldmund's Primal Mother assumes detail as he proceeds along his road of self-experiencing, and emerges full flown when he has exhausted himself and life.

Goldmund's story is clearly not a traditional romantic narrative, nor is it a realistic historical novel, and it does not pretend to be either. Like *Siddhartha*, it is a simple romance, which is located in time and place removed, in which Hesse features his usual protagonist and foil who for him exemplify two human possibilities, and in which he again peruses life's polarity and again airs his evolving views. And like most of Hesse's tales, Goldmund's is anchored firmly in neither time nor space. The setting is not *the* Middle Ages, but *a* medieval world of monasteries, castles, churches, and remote villages, of monks, and priors, peasants, townsmen and knights, artisans and vagabonds, guilds, masters, and apprentices, and of vast forests, mountains, and a large river, presumably the Rhine, and the bishop's city which may be Cologne. All this is again but incidental, albeit interestingly exotic staging for life's polar drama. As such, stage property and supernumeraries are only contoured in Hesse's usual sparsely enumerative manner: evocative concepts more than visible reality. Even Goldmund and Narziss are accorded minimal necessary physical attributes; theirs, like that of all Hesse's heroes, is primarily a reality of words, thoughts, feelings, and acts.

*Narziss und Goldmund*'s characteristic concomitant evolving of portrait and argument lends inner coherence to its twenty rather straggly segments. Outer coherence is achieved by Hesse's customary concatenative linkage of chapters. As usual, each chapter broaches the major action or theme, or both, of the following chapter and, as is customary in Hesse's novels, the last chapter ends on a suspensive upbeat: Goldmund has lived and died and his story has been told, Narziss has known only service and sacrifice, may not be able to die, and his story has yet to be told. Narziss was an anticipation of things to come in *Das Glasperlenspiel*. In 1927 to 1928 Hesse was obviously not yet prepared either to give him his merited attention or to accord him the self-justification that he so willingly grants his Goldmund.

NOTES

53. In the Welti-Nachlass, Schweizerische Landesbibliothek, Bern, Switzerland.

54. See *Kindheit und Jugend vor Neunzehnhundert* (1966), p. 148.

55. See manuscript of the novel in the Bodmer-Hesse-Collection, Schiller-Nationalmuseum, Marbach a.N.

56. See Chapter 5 above, "Art and Disease."

57. See *Gesammelte Schriften* (1957), Vol. 4, pp. 113–115.

MARTIN SWALES

# *Hesse:* The Glass Bead Game
# *(1943)*

Hermann Hesse's *The Glass Bead Game* closes with a number of short poems and stories which apparently constitute Josef Knecht's posthumous writings. The three stories, or *Lebensläufe* (biographies), derive directly from the educative process which Knecht has undergone (all Castalian students are required, as part of their training, to compose such fictional lives). Knecht's stories all concern a protagonist who ultimately finds insight into the right way of life, thereby attaining that integrity of purpose and being which he seeks. The final story tells of a young prince who comes to realize that all experience is vanity, that the path to truth and peace proceeds through contemplation, through acquiring the skills of the Yogi. When Prince Dasa begins this life of spiritual service, "There is no more to be told about Dasa's life, for all the rest took place in a realm beyond pictures and stories. He never again left the forest" (612).[1] Dasa has reached the point where his life leaves behind that mode of being which can be chronicled narratively. The lived peace, the certainty beyond friction and change, the wholeness of wisdom—these cannot be conveyed in plot or palpable image. This perception, with which Hesse's novel closes, focuses for us the central thematic concerns within *The Glass Bead Game*: the nature of the story and of the hero, and above all, the relationship of that life, of that selfhood, to notions of human and cultural wholeness.

From *The German Bildungsroman from Wieland to Hesse.* © 1978 by Princeton University Press.

The story is told by a narrator who belongs to the elite province of Castalia and who writes this account some time after the death of the great Magister Ludi. The opening few pages of the novel are devoted to the problem of Knecht's significance within Castalia. We learn that "obliteration of individuality, the maximum integration of the individual into the hierarchy of the educators and scholars, has ever been one of the guiding principles of our spiritual life" (8). The narrator is at pains to distinguish his biographical enterprise from that of earlier writers:

> Certainly, what nowadays we understand by personality is something significantly different from what the biographers and historians of earlier times meant by it. For them and especially for the writers of those days who had a distinct taste for biography, the essence of a personality seems to have been deviance, abnormality, uniqueness, in fact all too often the patho-logical. We moderns, on the other hand, do not even speak of major personalities until we encounter men who have gone beyond all original and idiosyncratic qualities to achieve the greatest possible integration into the generality, the greatest possible service to the suprapersonal. (9)

This is, I would suggest, a passage that reminds us very much of the passionate onslaught on individuation that informs Stifter's *Indian Summer*. Hesse's narrator, while he at times pays lip service to the notion of person-ality, essentially writes from a position in which the manifestations of individuality are to be regretted as some kind of pre-Castalian aberration. It follows from this (and from comments he makes on bourgeois degeneration in the "newspaper supplement age") that our narrator is bitterly critical of the bourgeois convention of storytelling because it implies a cult of *individual* selfhood. The narrator asserts that he is interested in Knecht insofar as he is the paradigm of the suprapersonal life of Castalia. And yet, of course, Knecht's life is the story not only of "impersonal" service to Castalia, but of defection precisely in the name of *personal* commitment and responsibility. The narrator's account enacts a largely unacknowledged paradox: Knecht's life is, in spite of, or, more accurately, because of Castalia, a "life" in the old bourgeois sense. Which is another way of saying that *The Glass Bead Game* opens as a work written against the demands of traditional novel expectation, but progresses to the point of validating the novel genre as personal biography.

This tension takes us very much to the heart of the theme and narrative technique of Hesse's novel. It has been suggested, most notably by Theodore Ziolkowski in what is by far the liveliest and most suggestive account of Hesse's art,[2] that the discrepancy between avowed narrative intention and actual narrative realization is to be explained in terms of the prolonged gestation and growth process of the book. This is, of course, a possible explanation; but I find it deeply unsatisfying. Writers are, after all, capable of rewriting earlier sections of a work if this is demanded by a later change in overall conception. In my view, the narrative tension of *The Glass Bead Game* was not obliterated for significant artistic reasons (which are, incidentally, particularly suggestive for any understanding of the Bildungsroman tradition). The closing stages of Knecht's life, unlike those of Prince Dasa's, take place within the realm of stories and pictures. However much the conclusion may be symbolic of Knecht's "service" in its truest and finest sense, yet it also reports an *event* that is both irrevocable and concrete.[3]

*The Glass Bead Game* opens with a leisurely statement of Castalian beliefs. The narrator proudly proclaims himself a Castalian, a "modern," that is, someone who inhabits a world that has gone beyond the bourgeois fetish of individuality. (Thereby, of course, he implicitly recognizes the historical *donnée* of his own intellectual position, and, as we shall see, history emerges as one of the major themes of the novel.) The highest expression of Castalia is to be found in the Glass Bead Game which is so much its intellectual and spiritual center. We are told that the game had its precursors wherever and whenever scholars and intellectuals looked beyond the confines of their specific, specialist disciplines in order to find some integral principle that binds together human culture into a total, synchronic phenomenon. We learn that "the symbols and formulas of the Glass Bead Game combined structurally, musically, and philosophically within the framework of a universal language, were nourished by all the sciences and arts, and sought in play to achieve perfection, pure being, the fullness of reality" (40-41). The game is the expression of the Castalian "tendency toward universality" (88): people of intellectual potential are encouraged to devote themselves to free study of even the most abstruse topics because their work, however esoteric, does feed into the generality of the scholarly community. (We are reminded here in some ways of the Society of the Tower in *Wilhelm Meister*: the context of the community provides the wholeness by being the intersection of many discrete lives and interests.)

To this Glass Bead Game Josef Knecht offers devoted and strenuous service, although he is not unmindful of the dangers in the Castalian way of life. These dangers are manifold, and they become the psychological substance of Knecht's unease, which will finally produce the break with Castalia. Knecht comes to see that any attempt at realizing a totality within the life of man must, by definition, operate with abstractions from discrete, individual experience. Abstraction, bloodlessness, and ahistoricity are therefore the besetting sins of Castalia. (One thinks of the present-day battles of Structuralists and Marxists, in which the role of history likewise becomes more often than not the essential bone of contention.) Many of Knecht's reservations are stated in discursive form in his open letter to the authorities of Castalia. But these vital thematic concerns are also underpinned in a variety of ways. History itself becomes a source of constant pedagogic debate in the novel. From Pater Jacobus, Knecht "learned to see the present and his own life as historical realities" (178). The process of this specific learning is not an easy one for Knecht. Jacobus at one point sternly reproaches him: "You treat world history as a mathematician does mathematics, in which nothing but laws and formulas exist, no reality, no good and evil, no time, no yesterday, no tomorrow, nothing but an eternal flat, mathematical present" (179). Knecht comes to realize that Castalia is part of history, that it is *of necessity* a historical phenomenon: "we forget that we ourselves are a part of history, that we are the product of growth and we are condemned to perish if we lose the capacity for growth and change" (386). He will live out that principle of growth and change by his act of defection.

The deepest import of the theme of history, however, takes us into the very heart of the narrative tension which informs *The Glass Bead Game*. When Knecht discovers history as an ontological dimension, he discovers something that not only modifies the intellectual teaching of Castalia but also radically transforms his own understanding of himself. Knecht's perception of history as a general principle entails the vital notion of personal historicity. Knecht acknowledges that he himself has a "history," a story, a linear chronology of experiences for which he is responsible. His defection from Castalia not only expresses his intellectual disagreement with the province but also enacts the personal, existential concomitant of his convictions: he asserts that he has an individuality, a story which cannot be obliterated in the pictureless and storyless world of Castalian ideals.

Early in the novel, the narrator declares that "the writing of history—however soberly it is done and however sincere the desire for objectivity—remains literature. History's third dimension is always fiction" (45-46). One is here reminded of Kant's "cosmopolitan history" which threatens to become a novel! Moreover, we could turn the narrator's statement around to say that all literature, and for our purposes this applies particularly to narrative literature, must partake of history, must in other words be concerned with the historicity of a life, with its chronology, with its lived sequence. Knecht, despite the narrator's opening polemics, is the hero of a novel. However much his life may be directed toward the service of suprapersonal goals and ideas, he has a personal story which the narrator chronicles, thereby giving thematic enactment to the values inherent in Knecht's life: the protagonist becomes the supreme Magister Ludi, but only to repudiate his eminence and the principles which he has hitherto served.

Knecht is helped to overcome an early crisis in his life by talking with the Music Master. The latter reveals something of his past and of his personal difficulties and uncertainties. What comforts Knecht is the realization "that even a demigod, even a Master, had once been young, and capable of erring" (109). That personal history which antedates the Music Master's translation into Castalian greatness is made up of conflict and uncertainty and groping for insight. The story has the friction of struggle and conflict, of erring, and it therefore antedates the attained goal in which the self is submerged in the universal principle that is Castalia. Knecht's story is interesting precisely for those aspects which do not easily fit in with the Castalian ideology which the narrator so stridently affirmed at the beginning of the novel.

We sense the full measure of Knecht's difficulty with Castalia in his various dealings with the authorities shortly before his resignation. Master Alexander attacks Knecht: "You have an excessive sense of your own person, a dependence on it" (438). The conflict between Alexander and Knecht is irreparable because it is one of fundamental principle. The President also reproaches Knecht: "Here you are speaking about your own life, and you mention scarcely anything but private, subjective experiences, personal wishes, personal developments and decisions. I really had no idea that a Castalian of your rank could see himself and his life in such a light" (440). Knecht answers by invoking precisely those principles which are anathema to the President: "I am trying to show you the path I have trodden as an individual, which has led me out of Waldzell and will lead me out of Castalia tomorrow" (440). Knecht asserts both the reality and the value of the individual path in answer to the uncomprehending Castalian ideology. Some of this ideology remains with our narrator, particularly in his somewhat defensive opening statements. It is, of course, one of the deepest ironies of the book that the narrator, in spite of himself, chronicles the life of a man whose intractable individuality and historical self-assertion transcends Castalian ideology and is potentially the source of the province's regeneration. Yet one wonders whether Castalia would be able to absorb the import of Knecht's life. The narrator's empathy with his protagonist may on occasion take him beyond the confines of that somewhat defensive Castalian position which he espoused at the opening. But on the other hand, the ending to Knecht's life can somehow be deprived of its sting by being incorporated into a manageable legend. The title of the book gives continued primacy to the cultural institution—the Glass Bead Game—while relegating Knecht's life to the subtitle, "Attempt at a Biography of the Magister Ludi Josef Knecht together with Knecht's posthumous papers, edited by Hermann Hesse." Certainly, the opening pages give no hint that the significance of Knecht's experience has been seized. Thereby a narrative tension is established which heightens the significance of those moments when the narrator glimpses the complexity and resonance of Knecht's life.[4] At one point, for example, he praises Knecht:

> Knecht was a great, an exemplary administrator, an honor to his high office, an irreproachable Glass Bead Game Master. But he saw and felt the glory of Castalia, even as he devoted himself to it, as an imperiled greatness that was on the wane. He did not participate in its life thoughtlessly and unknowingly, as did the great majority of his fellow Castalians, for he knew about its origins and history, was conscious of it as a historical entity, subject to time, washed and eroded by time's remorseless power. This sensitivity to the living experience of historical processes and this feeling for his own self and activity as a cell carried along and working with the stream of growth and transformation had ripened within him and become conscious in the course of his historical studies and under the influence of the great Pater Jacobus. The predisposition to such consciousness, its germs had been present within him long before. Whoever genuinely tries to explore the meaning of that life, its idiosyncrasy, will easily discover these germs. (288-89)

Such observations on the part of the narrator are, as it were, generated by the story he has to tell; they remain glimpses which are not allowed to ripen into a fully articulated attitude. They are moments which bring into focus the narrative tension of the book, and that tension is thematic enrichment rather than artistic inconsistency on Hesse's part. Over and over again we sense that the narrator is impelled to recognize qualities which conflict with the Castalian ideal. One example is the narrator's remark about Plinio Designori at the beginning of Chapter 10: "nevertheless, he was not simply a failure. In defeat and renunciation he had, in spite of everything, acquired a specific profile, a particular destiny" (350). For the narrator of the opening pages, "a specific profile, a particular destiny" could hardly have constituted any kind of achievement. Or again, toward the end of the novel, the narrator comments on the void left in Castalia by Knecht's withdrawal:

> The laconic, sensible remarks [of Knecht's final testament to the province] stood there in neat, small letters, the words and handwriting just as uniquely and unmistakably typical of Joseph Knecht as his face, his voice, his gait. The Board would scarcely find a man of his stature for his successor; real masters and real personalities were all too rare, and each one was a matter of good luck and a pure gift, even here in Castalia, the province of the elite. (448)

The remarks sound valedictory: the emphasis falls on precisely those details that are unique to Knecht, and the closing sentence implicitly links "real masters" and "real personalities." The narrator, while only rarely acknowledging as much, has moved a long way from his opening remarks on the questionableness of personality. The story told in this novel is of growth, movement, change. And the narrative voice becomes an accompaniment to those processes; it grows and changes with the life it is obliged to chronicle.

Once a year each student in Castalia has to write a fictional "life" in which the explores certain potentialities he feels to be inherent in himself. Our narrator notes that "while writing these lives many an author took his first steps into the land of self-knowledge" (120). We are allowed direct access to three such lives, all of them by Knecht. It is tempting to assume that these lives are an unequivocal celebration of a certain goal, of the decisive attainment of self-knowledge on the part of the protagonist. In this way the stories can be invested with a straightforwardly didactic import. Yet one might view their significance differently and stress that the essential interest in the lives is the way rather than the goal, for the simple reason that the attained goal implies an integrity of being and purpose, an absence of friction and wandering that is foreign to the specifically *narrative* act. Certainly, the story of Josef Knecht is important precisely because it is a *story*. The pattern in this life is, I would suggest, one familiar to us: Wilhelm Meister emerges from the Society of the Tower feeling as intractably unenlightened and baffled as ever; Hans Castorp gradually forgets the snow vision; Josef Knecht, with full moral and intellectual knowledge of what he is doing, repudiates that special province which is devoted to spiritual wholeness and harmony. The friction between story and totality, between *Nacheinander* and *Nebeneinander*, between, in the terms of Hesse's novel, historicity and the Castalian ideal, has profound implications for both plot and characterization in the novel. And these implications are, as I have tried to suggest, structurally central to the German Bildungsroman.

Virtually all of Hesse's novels are concerned with human striving for integrity and wholeness. In this sense his fictional world can be profitably viewed within the context of the Bildungsroman tradition. A novel such as *The Steppenwolf* would, I think, interlock suggestively with a number of the issues I have been raising. (It would, for example, be interesting to compare the function of the theater in this novel and in *Wilhelm Meister's Apprenticeship*: in both, I suspect, the theater has special thematic significance within the hero's quest for perspective on his own selfhood. One wonders also about the role of the "Immortals" as emissaries from a world that knows of the complex coexistence of specific talents and proclivities. In this sense they are akin to the Society of the Tower. Indeed, both have in common a certain sententiousness, in the maxims to which Wilhelm is referred, and in the "Treatise" which Harry Haller acquires.) But I have chosen to restrict my discussion of Hesse to *The Glass Bead Game* for one very simple reason. To me, it is the one novel of Hesse's in which the Bildungsroman tradition occupies a specific and overtly indicated place in the novel fiction. The name of its hero, Knecht (servant) is a quizzical echo of that of Goethe's hero, Meister (master), and Knecht becomes Master of the Bead Game. Moreover, the Castalian province clearly recalls the "Pedagogic Province" of *Wilhelm Meister's Travels*. The stress throughout *The Glass Bead Game* on learning and growth clearly announces an indebtedness to the Bildungsroman. When Josef Knecht becomes involved with Plinio Designori, we read that he has "come to feel that this other boy would mean something important to him, perhaps something fine, an enlargement of his horizon, insight or illumination, perhaps also temptation and danger" (98). Here we sense the characteristic principle that informs so much of the hero's experience in the Bildungsroman: the other figure is important for the protagonist's growth and self-understanding, he matters insofar as he catalyzes a certain inner potential slumbering within the hero. Even the eccentric Tegularius is important in this way for Knecht: he is "a small open window that looked out upon new vistas" (295). One wonders also whether there are not specific echoes in Hesse's text. When Knecht reflects on the primitive world outside the confines of Castalia we read: "this primitive world was innate in every man; everyone felt something of it in his own heart, had some curiosity about it, some nostalgia for it, some sympathy with it. The true task was to be fair to it, to keep a place for it in one's heart, but still not relapse into it" (104). Both the ideas here, and their formulation, call to mind Hans Castorp's insights in the "Snow" chapter of *The Magic Mountain*. (Moreover, Thomas Mann himself figures as a distinguished Castalian under the thinly veiled pseudonym of Thomas Van der Trave.) Finally, when Plinio asks Knecht, "which of us is really the authentic and valid human being, you or me? Every so often I doubt that either of us is" (340), he raises one of the paramount intellectual issues of the Bildungsroman tradition.

Moreover, one should note that the concern in Hesse's novel for *Geist* marks it as a work unmistakably embedded in the generality of the German intellectual tradition. *Geist* is a realm which allows the limiting dimension of the real to be transcended by the abundant potentiality of human consciousness. Even Plinio expresses his lasting indebtedness to Castalia "for not letting anything coerce me into a course of studies designed to prepare the student as thoroughly as possible in the shortest possible time for a speciality in which he could earn his livelihood, and to stamp out whatever sense of freedom and universality he may have had" (325). Castalia is, then, a realm which allows for "freedom and universality" in answer to the constrictions of everyday social practicalities. But at the same time, it is a world dangerously determined to insulate itself from actualities; it is an ivory tower, an elite province which will not acknowledge its own embeddedness in history as the given dimension of human being and activity. In this novel Hesse offers an affectionate, yet deeply critical, examination of a familiar pattern in German thinking. The all-pervasive presence of the Bildungsroman is the measure of the specificity of Hesse's engagement with the German tradition. The tensions that inform the novel suggest precisely his uncertainties and misgivings. And these are also the tensions present in the major Bildungsromane. In its finest examples, this novel tradition is never an unproblematic odyssey toward human wholeness. None of the major novels ever unquestioningly endorses that strident equation, made by Fritz Tegularius, of "real history" with the "timeless history of the mind" (303). Knecht has *his* "history"—as do Agathon, Wilhelm Meister, and the other protagonists. The *Nacheinander* of plot, of personal history, is simply not an eradicable quantity.

One final comment about the theme of history in *The Glass Bead Game*: the novel is, of course, set at some future date when the dilemmas of bourgeois individualism (as outlined in the narrator's denunciation of the decline into the "newspaper supplement age") have been transcended in the creation of Castalia, the ideal province.[5] Hesse takes as the prehistory of Castalia precisely those bourgeois-individualist values which produced in the

Bildungsroman the attempt to mediate between individual and totality, between the increasing specialization and restriction of practical life and the need for human wholeness and community. By projecting that future world of Castalia, Hesse postulates, as it were, the actual attainment of the so frequently intimated (but hardly ever realized) teleology of the great Bildungsromane. Yet, precisely because of its provenance, Castalia remains a problematic utopia, one whose ideals are but the wish-dream of that bourgeois culture from which it has sprung. In every sense, then, Castalia has a history: paradoxically, its very aversion to history serves to reveal its roots in history. In this context, Knecht's life takes on a truly exemplary function. He is offered the opportunity of lasting escape from the world of practical reality by being absorbed into an elite enclave dedicated to spiritual harmony and totality. But he comes to repudiate that opportunity as a falsity. In *The Glass Bead Game* the aspirations of the Bildungsroman, and their inherent questionableness, find intense, thoroughgoing exploration. And once again, the result is a work shot through with an unremitting narrative argument with, against, and ultimately for the novel form with its bedrock credo of the story told in chronological, that is, historical, sequence. The theme of history in *The Glass Bead Game* is, then, intimately bound up with its own historicity as a literary text. For like Thomas Mann's *Doktor Faustus* (1947), this novel, first published in 1943, is Hesse's urgently critical examination of his own intellectual roots. It was an examination necessitated by the course of European, and particularly German, history. In both novels (and the same can be said of Mann's specific exploration of the Bildungsroman tradition in *The Magic Mountain*), present understanding involved activation of and debate with the German tradition.

Hesse's *The Glass Bead Game* is in this way very much a part of the heart-searching and self-examination that followed the collapse of the Third Reich. One urgent feature of this debate was the question of whether there were, so to speak, two Germanies, a "good" and a "bad," or whether there was but one Germany, the evil self being inextricably intertwined with the good. In this context one can appreciate the special force and cogency of Hesse's taking issue with the Bildungsroman tradition. This novel genre was surely one paradigm for an exploration of the "German problem": in one sense it was the repository of the great humanistic tradition of Germany, providing a link with the eighteenth-century *Humanitätsideal*; but in another sense it was the embodiment of that questionable inwardness, of that lack of thoroughgoing concern with practical affairs and political facts which had so bedeviled the German nation.

The resonance of Hesse's undertaking can be measured by recalling the closing pages of Friedrich Meinecke's *The Great Catastrophe* (1946), in which Meinecke looks for a way forward and out of the devastation that has befallen Germany. The emphasis of his solution is characteristic: "Everything, yes everything, depends upon an intensified development of our inner existence."[6] He suggests the need for Germany to draw new strength from its Golden Age of Weimar:

> The heights of the Goethe period and of the highly gifted generation living in it were reached by many individual men, bound together merely in small circles by ties of friendship. They strove for and to a large degree realized the ideal of a personal and wholly individual culture. This culture was thought of as having at the same time a universal human meaning and content.[7]

Meinecke goes on to speak of the need for organizations to promote this renewal of German spiritual identity. But the relationship to "organization" is characteristically grudging. What is essentially involved is German *Bildung* in all its inwardness: "does organization alone promote spiritual culture? Does not spiritual culture demand a sphere for individual inclination, for solitude, and for the deepening of one's self?"[8] Insofar as Meinecke explores the practical question of how to restore the integrity of the nation, he suggests the setting up of "Goethe communities," which could meet "at a late Sunday afternoon hour, and if at all possible in a church,"[9] in order to listen to German music and poetry being performed and read. Beyond this he does not go: "I shall not sketch this further here, in order not to anticipate the free creative activity of individuals. The whole idea must start with individuals, personalities, the special few who first build among themselves only one such Goethe community, and then let it develop here in one form, there in another."[10] Meinecke offers here an unreflective reinstatement of the ideal of *Bildung*: social and political life is to find its center of gravity in an elite group of spiritual leaders bound together by a special distinction and wholeness.

Where Meinecke can take up a tradition which, for him, is still left intact, Hesse finds himself obliged to mount a critique of that very tradition from within. As I hope my inquiry has suggested, the authors of the major Bildungsromane were often more differentiated and questioning in their espousal of *Bildung* than were the theoreticians, the philosophers, or, as in Meinecke's case, the historians.

## Notes

1. References throughout are to Hesse, *Das Glasperlenspiel* (Frankfurt: Suhrkamp Taschenbuch, 1973). My translations are heavily indebted to the version by Richard and Clara Winston, *The Glass Bead Game* (Harmondsworth, 1972).

2. Ziolkowski, *The Novels of Hermann Hesse: A Study in Theme and Structure* (Princeton, 1965), 294. Ziolkowski's argument has been challenged (see G. W. Field, "On the Genesis of *Das Glasperlenspiel*," *German Quarterly*, 41 [1968], 673–88). Whether Ziolkowski is right or wrong about the genesis of the novel, he is, in my view, *interpretatively* right to stress the tension at work in the book; other critics have some-how dissolved that tension into serene thematic progression.

3. See Mark Boulby's contention that the ending of the novel involves "service...of the self" (*Hermann Hesse: His Mind and Art* [Ithaca and London, 1967], 320). Many critics have commented on Knecht's break with Castalia. It has been variously suggested that the ending is to be seen as a higher and truer fulfillment of Knecht's mission of pedagogic service, that it represents a commitment to life and practical activity, or that it negates the spiritual significance of Castalia, thereby relativizing the whole import of the novel. All these arguments have pertinence, but to me they are slightly off center. The real force of Knecht's decision can, I think, only be sensed in terms of the kind of cultural debate with novel tradition which I have stressed in my analysis. Within this framework, the narrator's Castalian ideology brings into focus the whole spectrum of issues suggested by Knecht's act of defection.

4. See Hans Mayer, "Hesse's *Glasperlenspiel* oder die Wiederbegegnung," in *Ansichten: Zur Literatur der Zeit* (Reinbek bei Hamburg, 1962), esp. 52. Throughout my analysis I am indebted to Mayer's essay, which suggests the full range of immanent contradictions in the novel.

5. Field, "On the Genesis of *Das Glasperlenspiel*," has shown how Hesse, in the gradual reworking of his material, removed the specific references to the 1930s, to nationalism, political brutality, and Nazism. In place of historical specificity we are given a cultural-typological analysis which, in my view, suggests the generality of cultural values from which the Bildungsroman derives. The reworking process is a further illustration of that urgent debate with novel tradition which is so central to *Das Glasperlenspiel*.

    6. Meinecke, *The Great Catastrophe*, trans. Sidney Fay (Boston, 1963),
115.
    7. Ibid., 115.
    8. Ibid., 116.
    9. Ibid., 120.
    10. Ibid., 121.

EUGENE L. STELZIG

# *The Aesthetics of Confession: Hermann Hesse's* Crisis Poems *in the Context of the* Steppenwolf *Period*

> For at least a year now I have been in the worst crisis of my life,
> and I still hope even now that it will not pass, but break my neck
> instead, because I am sick of life to the point of throwing up.
>
> Hesse in a letter of 1926

I

What is possible, for poetry, today? The question is so formidable that it seems forever to defer a palpable answer, one that would be in any sense definitively or philosophically considered. Shrinking back from such an overwhelming vista, I turn to Hermann Hesse's radically self-confronting poetry of the twenties, which raises fundamental aesthetic issues that have only found a tortured resonance in the American poetic scene of the sixties and seventies, in the work of some of the leading confessional poets, such as the later Lowell, Plath, Berryman, and a host of others of whose work it is yet too early to say whether it is merely trendy and epigonal, or whether it carries a genuine poetic charge that can ground a future poetry. Hesse's hardwon ideal, during his forties, of an unflinching autobiographical art— *Kunst als Bekenntnis*—can fructify in a concrete and perhaps exemplary

From *Criticism* 21, no. 1 (Winter 1979): 49-70. © 1979 by Wayne State University Press.

fashion our meditation on the possibilities of poetry today, a stark poetry of the here and now that doesn't cower in the face of chaos in the borrowed robes of a timid formalism, but gives chaos itself a veritable voice and shape.

## II

In the poem-cycle, *Crisis: Pages from a Diary (Krisis: Ein Stück Tagebuch)* published by Fischer in a limited edition of 1150 copies in April 1928, Hesse's confessional aesthetic of the twenties finds its most acute, forthright realization in a lyrical mode that is as courageous (as Heinrich Wiegand praised it in his review in *Kulturwille*[1]) as it seems to be unmediated by an artistic persona. This lack of a recognizable mask is the difference between *Crisis* and *Steppenwolf*, so that the critic is tempted to label the former *life* and the latter *art*, as Ralph Freedman does when he notes that *Crisis* is not, like *Steppenwolf*, "filtered through a transforming process of the literary imagination."[2] But the apparent absence of an aesthetically distancing filter is not necessarily a defect once we are willing to grant Hesse the freedom of his own premises in the poem-journal. What Freedman sees in the balance as a minus I credit as a plus of authenticity in the abrasive self-encounter of *Crisis*, which is an unvarnished life-study—although there is a good deal of mediation by way of form and style, as I will try to show—so that the stark verse-diary is to be valued in its own right, to quote its author, as "the frankest poet's confession since Heine."[3] I do not want to take the perverse tack of arguing that *Crisis* is better than the novel, but rather to examine it on its own ground in relationship to the *Steppenwolf* years as a whole, instead of reducing it to the status of raw material for the fictional frame of *Steppenwolf*, a line of reasoning by which the poems are swallowed up by the novel.

Hesse did not wish the lyrics to be thus liquidated, but to guarantee their independent existence as a cycle. In a letter of 1928 he explains the fact of a limited edition as a strategic move to preserve the poems' integrity: "I found no other way to assure the existence of this poem-cycle so that it cannot be lost any more, and to protect it at the same time from the popular craving for fashion and sensation."[4] He was almost embarrassed by the sensational success of *Steppenwolf*, and he wanted *Crisis* to be available only to the happy few who could appreciate its genuine meaning and intention beneath the shocking surface. He didn't want this intimate little tome to fall into *too* many wrong hands, because to state the paradox as succinctly as possible, his turn to a confessional aesthetics contained within it a strong reservation about the ultimate value of confession as art: to be published in a large edition, "these poems are not objective enough...are too much confession and momentary notice."[5] And at the same time, he felt that the only thing that mattered to him as an artist was confession, in a variety of forms, and whatever its ultimate worth. Contrasting himself with the "aesthetically irreproachable poets," Hesse announces the ironic credo of the *Steppenwolf* period, confession at any cost: "As far as I am concerned, I don't count in that regard any more; I have already abandoned the aesthetic ambition years ago and write not poetry (Dichtung) but confession (Bekenntnis), in the same way that someone who is drowning or who has been poisoned does not concern himself with the cut of his hair or the modulation of his voice, but simply screams out."[6] And *Crisis* is the purest expression of Hesse's aesthetics of the scream, decades before that ungodly sound began to make itself heard in American poetry, and at first in the Beat poets, especially Allen Ginsberg.

With the publication in 1975 of Ralph Manheim's spirited, free-wheeling translation into English of *Crisis*, the English-speaking reader has now for the first time available to him (with the exception of the letters, and some fragments and journal entries) all the texts of Hesse's troubled but protean *Steppenwolf* phase—or to use his favorite word here, *incarnation*—which opens with the 1922 fragment, "From the Journal of One Who Has Been Derailed" ("Aus dem Tagebuch Eines Entgleisten"), a pre-study, as Hesse describes it, to the novel,[7] and which closes in 1928 with the Kafka-influenced short-story, "Concerning the Steppenwolf." The major works that lie between these boundaries—*A Guest at the Spa* (1924), *Steppenwolf* (1927), *The Journey to Nuremberg* (1927), and, of course, *Crisis*—reflect the complex psychography of Hesse as Steppenwolf and outsider (he repeatedly uses the English word in his letters) suffering from a severely divided self or "schizomania" as Harry Haller has it, from suicidal despair concerning the fate of the poet in the modern world, and finally, from an uncontrollable oscillation or "pendulation" (to use Ziolkowski's term[8]) between the worlds of *Geist* (mind/spirit) and *Natur* (senses/instincts), which is also a conflict between the masculine and feminine sides of Hesse's psyche. The multifarious self-division which afflicted Hesse was such that no degree of magical thinking could help him to a synthesis, not even "that airy bridge," humor, "the old mediator between the ideal and the real," the "crystal that grows only in deep and enduring pain."[9] For even humor, of which he asked so much in the twenties, and which he tried to cultivate in works that are essentially unfunny, save for some sublimely grotesque moments in *Steppenwolf*, is a compromising mediation, and thus a bridge back to the bourgeois structure of values that he struggled to reject and that he recognized as a mode founded on the lukewarm middle, safe from all extremes where *Geist* and *Natur* act out their pure destinies. The striving for humor in *Journey to Nuremburg* and *Guest at the Spa* is indeed so heavy-handed, mawkish and hypochondriacally self-indulgent that only Hesse's desperate wish for some kind of bridge away from the abyss can even begin to account for the genesis of these strange works. But in *Crisis* and *Steppenwolf*, so different in form and content, yet so intimately bound up in a symbiotic relationship, his ambivalence is bodied forth in a laughter that in the former is at times purely nihilistic, and that in the latter points altogether beyond the bourgeois dilemma to the crystallized indifference of the Immortals, a goal which the novel can only adumbrate, and that is provisionally reached in *Journey to the East* and *The Glass Bead Game* with a resolution of the masculine/feminine split by way of mortifying *Natur* or the Eternal Mother. I say provisional, because the *magna mater* refuses to let herself be killed off, as we can see when Josef Knecht, the Magister Ludi, obeying the self-willed call of awakening or "Stufen," leaves the Castalian realm of a senescent *Geist* to plunge into the mountain lake at dawn, the amniotic fluid at the beginning of things, the maternal *Urquelle* that is at one and the same time the death-dealer and the baptismal font of life of the spirit grown weary of itself.

## III

The sexual leap into the lap of the eternal feminine, the return to the maternal matrix also constitutes the primary psychological gesture and *Bildungs*-program of the confession that is *Crisis*. The poem-cycle mirrors the psychomachia in Hesse's life cycle between eros and intellect, with eros— for this is what the forty-eight year-old writer has come to—as the appointed, necessary good. Extreme simplicity of style and content in *Crisis* masks the authentic complexity of a self that is absurdly yet courageously seeking to achieve some measure of reintegration through mortification and self-surrender of the intellect. The first surrender, however, is that of the purgation or voiding of confession itself, the will to truth concerning who one is, no matter how repulsive or unflattering that truth may be. Confession as exhibition: in Rousseau the act is literal, as the exhibition of confession is partly a confession of self-exhibition; in *Crisis* it is a venture to expose those areas of the self that have been most repressed because they are most un-palatable and infamous to a bourgeois sense of what life and art ought to be.

How far does Hesse carry this self-exposure in *Crisis?* Not quite far enough to suit his punctilious standards for frankness, because he feels constantly constrained by conventions of prurience that a middle-class reading public imposes on its authors. His postscript to the collection is a curiously hedging document, being both offensive and defensive, affronting and apologetic. Hesse wants to keep his audience's sympathy in the very act of cutting away the ground of sympathy on which a middle-class audience can stand, and the poet ends up in a a sense shadow-boxing with the philistine censor in himself. His psychic need is to explain so as to mollify: the poems reflect the fear of ageing and death of a man close to fifty, and not merely by way of a violent reassertion of too-long stifled instincts, but as a crisis-stage of middle age when the spirit grows weary of itself and yearns to abdicate to nature and chaos. The task is literally a life-saving counter-swerve from Hesse as Saint Siddhartha, and a turn to unsuccessfully sublimated impulses that have been either silenced altogether or prettified in his earlier works, and that are now allowed to come to voice under the moral aegis of *Aufrichtigkeit*: *Crisis* as therapy, and hopefully a more effective one than the expensive thermal cures in Baden. Although Hesse is more than willing to engage in vigorous sessions of self-hatred, he is still dependent on the love of his audience, which itself is a synecdoche or psychic trope for the first audience of man-as-actor:

> Once a man takes honesty as his ideal, he cannot confine himself to showing the pleasant and reasonable side of his nature. The other side is there. I must even admit that my honesty in this respect is flawed, for I have omitted from this book a number of poems publication of which would have been too damaging to my self-esteem.
>
> Dear friends, I attach no importance to your judgment. But I set great store by your love. Continue to love me, even if you do not approve of my poems.[10]

The hidden addressee is Hesse's mother now long-dead, and the plea re-enacts the plea of Hermann Hesse's self-willed child, adolescent, and fledgling author, whose disturbing acts and words were in a sense always a repeated, extreme testing of that infinite lode of mother-love—the prayer of the child in all of us, forever poignant: love me even if you do not approve of me.

The opening lyric of *Crisis* offers both a dedication and a program as the poet surrenders himself, turns or returns to the "Urmutter" to find in her embrace both salvation and the ecstatic release of eros ful-filled, an ultimate letting-go. Here, as later at the conclusion of *Narcissus and Goldmund*, the man re-enters the Eden of childhood in a sexual embrace with the eternal mother, to be consummated in and consumed by her kiss—Hesse's own myth of the Romantic *Liebestod*, via the family romance. The sensuous recovery of the original ground of being is an ambiguous rite of passage—life-giving and suicidal—because adult intellect and selfhood are surrendered, but a primal unity is regained through the incestuous death-swoon. The double-dealing character of this embrace which kills and renews is further enhanced by the fact that inherent in the reunion is not a return pure and simple, since it contains also a wish to violate the mother. There can be no innocent entry into the shadow realm of origins by the adult poet, and even though the explicit recognition of the sexual union as a violation of the mother as well as of the self is only implicit in "Dedication" (*Hingabe*, which also means a giving-of-oneself), a number of other lyrics make quite explicit the ferocity of the erotic urge in terms of violence against the self as well as the other.

Thus self-murder and the crime of passion are two leading, linked wish-images of *Crisis*. The poet's craving for death finds various expressions, from naked assertions of the wish itself, to grotesque fantasies of killing the enemy in his own breast ("In Vain," p. 55), being crucified ("Intimations," p. 95), or run over, fate of fates, by the car of a Catholic baker ("The Drunken Poet," p. 105). Correspondingly, the sadistic urge to murder the beloved, which figures also as the high or low point of *Steppenwolf*'s Magic Theatre sequence with the stabbing of the sleeping Hermine, is given a prominent place in the poetry, as the speaker thinks of strangling his nubile young partners after intercourse ("Poet's Death Song," p. 5) or even in the moment of passion ("The Debauchee," p. 87), and as he confesses to having stabbed to death his beloved, Erika Maria Ruth ("With These Hands," p. 115)—in fact, Hesse's second, much-younger wife, whose marriage to him was short-lived and ill-sorted, and ended, not in murder, but in the divorce courts.

Lest this catalogue of passionate misdeeds should prove too revolting, let me quickly add that it is presented for the most part through a high-gloss veneer of grotesque and sardonic humor, as a sort of farcical confessional fantasia. The intended effect of the humor is to stylize and distance such shocking imaginings; yet the humor, because of its biting, sardonic edge, is not exactly comforting or reassuring as the author holds the mirror up to the psychopathology of his everyday life. Like Baudelaire, Hesse is still (perversely) as much of a moralist as a nihilist or sensualist here, because in some measure he is working to get the reader—*mon semblable, mon frère*—to face up to the hidden monsters in his own breast. *Crisis* as a comic catharsis moves from fantastic confession to a purgation of the sick soul of the modern European insofar as Hesse feels that the psychic derangement of the artist holds a larger meaning for the society in which he lives: "the neurosis of a man of spirit is simulataneously a symptom of the soul of the time."[11]

Hesse in his *Steppenwolf* incarnation was acutely aware that one of the chief afflictions of middle-class culture is its denial or sentimental euphemizing of the instinctual basis of human life, to which the artist in pursuit of *Geist* is also particularly susceptible. The insight, of course, is almost a commonplace in the advanced circles of the twenties, when coming in the wake of Freud, such major artists as D. H. Lawrence made it over into the substance of their best-known works, and Hesse himself only came to it belatedly after undergoing psycho-analysis. But he felt it with a peculiar force, not merely because it helped him to cast off once and for all the last vestiges of the Protestant-Pietist mentality on which his childhood and youth were fed, and against which he struggled from early adolescence on, but especially because it helped him to redefine the aesthetic principle, or the relationship between life and art, experience and poetry. In an essay on Hölderlin written near the beginning of the *Steppenwolf* period, he posits that the poet's mental collapse was rooted in an unsuccessful sublimation of ordinary instincts: "He cultivated in himself a spirituality that did violence to his nature."[12] Behind Hesse's self-conscious dedication to the realm of the mother and of the senses we may discern his insight about Hölderlin as a representative cautionary figure impelling him, by way of negative example, to hazard in poetry the journey (as he puts it in the *Crisis* Epilogue) into "nature, chaos, and animal instinct" and to come to voice "this darker, perhaps deeper half of life" (p. 119) that he knows now had either been silenced or dressed up in borrowed finery in his earlier works. As Wiegand wrote in his 1928 review, here "nothing is beautified or silenced which governs most unspiritually below the navel." Wiegand praises this as a courageous act, and observes further how rare it is for an older writer to make such a disconcerting departure from his earlier works: "Radical youth doesn't signify much, as every sort of history will show. Revolutionary age is dangerous. Rebellious youth: normal. Revolutionizing age: deranged (verrückt)."[13] Although the reviewer's remark is apt because in the course of ageing most artists seem to pursue a path of retrenchment into and a further refinement of their most representative modes, there are always major exceptions, in art as well as life, as the famous example of the older Tolstoy, who raged in old age like a Russian Lear of the steppes, will show. But a glance at the decades supervening since Wiegand's comments may intimate to us that Hesse's way here may not be merely a brave divagation, but may prove to have been exemplary as far as the development of at least some major modern writers is concerned. Did not Yeats, roughly half a decade after *Crisis*, turn his back on the mosaic-like ideal of perfection of Byzantium, the artifice of eternity, to return full-force to "the fury and the mire of of human veins," and proceed to amaze his public in the thirties with the erotic wisdom of the incorrigible Crazy Jane, that "Fair and foul are near of kin,/And fair needs foul." And what of Lowell's breakthrough, in middle age, to a personal idiom and a vigorous poetic confession after the studied, opaque formalism and the mannered impersonality of his much-praised verse in the modernist vein?

IV

What enables a major writer to take a radical departure in mid-career? I have already touched upon Hesse's psychoanalysis as an important element, one that I would like to consider now in a little more detail in relation to his artistic development from the end of World War I to the *Steppenwolf* years. In Hesse's case, the turn in later middle age to a piquant confessional aesthetic can be seen in a sense as a delayed reaction to his earlier reading of the works of Freud, Jung and Stekel, and to the extended sessions with the Jungian analyst, Josef B. Lang, during the distressing situation of the war years when his literary and personal life fell into ruins because of his outspoken opposition to the war, the mental breakdown of his wife and the subsequent dissolution of his family. In a 1918 essay on "Artists and Psychoanalysis" (for which he received a polite acknowledgement from Freud), he lists as one of the major benefits of analysis for the artist that it demands a "truthfulness toward oneself to which we are not accustomed," and adds, revealingly, that such honesty "at the very outset of analysis is a powerful, indeed a monstrous experience, a shock that reaches to the root of one's being."[14] The initial result of this extensive shock is that it made it possible for Hesse to emerge at the end of the war as a new writer—literally so, pseudonymized as Emil Sinclair—with *Demian*, the novel that came, under great pressure and rather pell-mell, out of his experience of analysis, and that curiously enough caught the mood of a new post-war generation with a heady welter of Jungian symbolism. The hypnotic appeal of *Demian*, attested to by Thomas Mann, among other German intellectuals, is that the young men returned from the front were no longer enamored of public rhetoric and collective solutions, but willing to hearken to the inner voice, especially in the prophetic mystification and *clair-obscur* of a novel that was sufficiently compelling yet confusing to accommodate the private fantasies of a large number of readers. However, *Demian*, despite all of its psychic storms and stress, did not reach far enough for Hesse, at least from the perspective of a decade later: its author was unable to deal forthrightly with the strong erotic drives that stirred darkly in his imagination, especially in relation to mother figures, and which he rendered harmless through idealizing (Beatrice) and mythic (Frau Eva) character archetypes. When in 1919 Hesse settled down in Montagnola to the life of an ascetic recluse, the prolonged contemplation of his own psyche resulted in fictions whose "incarnations" begin to approximate more closely the erotic and anarchic currents that ran beneath the surface. *Siddhartha* (1919-1922), his semi-autobiographical saint's life by way of Indian romance is strongly idealizing and idyllic, but at least the romantic asceticism of Siddhartha as Samana is counterbalanced by his entry into the world of the senses and passion in the liaison with the courtesan Kamala. But the delectable love-goddess is largely a poeticized Indian paradise-dream; ultimately remote from Hesse's inner experience. Only in the contemporaneous *Klingsor's Last Summer* and *Klein and Wagner* (1920) does Hesse begin to focus more frankly–and shockingly—on the true character of his passionate drives with the portraits under a Southern sun of the painter Klingsor during his last summer of erotic, Dionysian intoxication, and Klein, the petty bureaucrat who takes the daring step (thus the name symbolism) of breaking with his marriage and career to plunge into the demi-monde of crime and sensuality. And in the remarkable (and neglected) short-story, *A Child's Soul,* Hesse for the first time faces explicitly the Oedipal stresses of his childhood without cloaking or distorting them with romantic Jungian archetypes. Hesse's frank version of the Freudian family romance here takes us to the threshold of—and makes possible—the new, exacting, and largely unromantic confessional aesthetic that he elaborates during the twenties, and that for my purposes here can be typified by his statement in 1928 on the artist's vocation: "[he] doesn't have the job of forging an idiom for any generally accepted world-view, but to express as forcefully…as possible his own, unique fashion of living and experiencing."[15] This is Hesse's personalist creed, to be contrasted with the modernist accent on impersonality prevailing in European and especially Anglo-American poetry. The monstrous shock attendant upon undergoing psychoanalysis had tranformed Hesse as a writer by way of a belated but fundamental insight in his forties into the basis of his instinctual life; thus toward the end of the *Steppenwolf* phase it is so grounded in his artistic outlook that he is now able to redefine the aesthetic principle itself in generic terms that reach far beyond the modernist impersonality theories that were to dominate English and American poetics for several decades more.

In addition to Hesse's earlier encounter with psychoanalysis, there is at work as well in his changed aesthetic outlook the nihilism and spiritual media that afflicted him enormously during the *Steppenwolf* years. The mood of suicidal despair, nausea, and disgust at oneself and one's world is of course a normative characteristic of the literature that emerged after World War II, and many leading modernists gave compelling expression to it during the twenties and thirties—indeed, the literature of despair has been with us so insistently since that for a major contemporary writer the virtues of a genuinely-founded cheerfulness might be something of a new discovery. Harry Haller's consoling resolve (which was Hesse's own, as the letters show) to have an accident with his razor at the age of fifty if he can't get out from under the burden of life-in-death has been acted out in actual life by many poets since. Hesse was particularly burdened by a sense of the worthlessness of modern literature, and the futility of artistic creation and of any higher spiritual or intellectual striving in a world where the commercial values of the market place, having pre-empted other faiths, brand all such pursuits as pitiable delusions. In such a world the artist is a wolf of the steppes, an outsider come to it from another plane of being who can only watch in stunned despair as he realizes that all he holds dear has no legitimate currency in this hard, material realm. Perhaps at such a time the serious writer too is a fallen creature; his work at worst pointless, at best problematic. "I don't think anything of the whole of today's German literature, my own, naturally, included" is the refrain that echoes through the correspondence of the *Steppenwolf* decade, and that reaches its low point in an epistle of 1926 with the querulous plaint:

> It doesn't go well ... I can't escape this filthy mess any more. The inner resistance is lacking, the will to health and to keeping on. I'm fed up, and feel the increasing paralysis of my powers bitterly. It started during the war, with the collapse, with fatherland, public morality, etc., then came the collapse of the family, the increasing loneliness (my second wife hasn't been to Montagnola in two years), then slowly came the most difficult: the insight into the worthlessness of my intellectual and literary labors. That is to say, I believe I don't underestimate the relative worth of my talent and my mental world as measured against the contemporary average—but the time is pursuing other goals, and the collapse of the spirit in favor of other life-values renders the work and

striving of someone like us a pure illusion—We might just as well be blowing soap-bubbles.[16]

The feelings here voiced privately and informally are part of the spiritual malaise that tortured the best minds between the two great wars, and Hesse's sense of the collapse of the norms of the spirit is the troubled chorus of modern European-man-thinking, running the gamut from Kafka's poignantly absurd hunger-artist to Valery's magisterially prophetic assertion in a 1935 essay that

> a disorder to which no end could be imagined was observable on every hand. We find it around us and within us, in our daily habits, in our manners, in the newspapers, in our pleasures, and even in our knowledge. Interruption, incoherence, surprise are the ordinary conditions of our life.[17]

Nihilism and despair, however, are double-edged emotions, for they can be as creative and fructifying as destructive and sterile. The task of the true artist, as Keats knew in the "Ode on Melancholy," is to make his despair a source of productive energy, and to wrest creation from the destructive element in which he has perforce to immerse himself. Thus, paradoxically, it is Hesse's very despair that enables him to make a fundamental break with the epigonal Romantic vein in which he had been mostly content to work as a poet up to the end of World War I. It has been noted how formally innovative his sonata in prose, *Steppenwolf*, is, and how it can stand beside such experimental modernist masterpieces as *The Wasteland*, *Ulysses*, and *The Counterfeiters*. But it has not been acknowledged that *Crisis* in its own way parallels the novel in its departure from the poetic molds that had hitherto been adequate to Hesse. In the case of the poem-cycle as well as that of the prose-fiction, the reader is faced, not with a complete break with the heritage of German Romanticism of which Hesse was probably the major literary exponent, but with a substantive transposition of basically Romantic themes and modes into a modern idiom, setting and mood where Romantic nostalgia gives way to surreal and grotesque evocations of present and future. In *Steppenwolf* and *Crisis*, twentieth-century Romanticism (if there is even a hybrid), rather than imitating the moribund and decadent later nineteenth-century versions that were popular in Hesse's youth and that frequently passed for the original article, affronts the chaotic modern world with a vision that for the first time creates a genuinely contemporary Romantic perspective on that world. Hesse does not merely translate the sensibility of the preceding century with the refurbished props of an updated setting, nor, conversely, does he reject that great tradition from Goethe to Hölderlin with which he feels most at home as a writer, in the way Pound and Eliot tried to turn their backs on the English Romantics. Hesse knew that what you reject too overtly will come back to haunt you in its cruder forms which you will not be able to recognize or control. His procedure is to assimilate and subsequently transform and restructure a literary inheritance to come to terms with the unprecedented demands of an age of accelerating change and confounding discontinuity. How could a serious writer, after the double-shock of psycho-analysis and World War I, do anything else? Drawing upon the past (and not merely by way of cleverly fragmented, parodistic allusions, like the author of *The Wasteland*) to meet the creative demands of the present, Hesse's novel and poem-collection perhaps also funnel into the future, whereas—and by now this is a question to be asked—some of the master-pieces of Anglo-American modernism that try to reject the nineteenth century out of hand may end up as the half-forgotten period pieces in some hypothetical museum of literature.

The exacting truth-standards arising out of Hesse's psychoanalytic sounding of the self, then, juggled aside both his self-love and the timidity or artistic inhibition imposed by conventional canons of respectability, and he was able to etch a new kind of self-portrait in *Crisis*, one that by a principle of psychic symmetry or aesthetic complementarity counters the ideal of Hesse as Saint Siddhartha. The artist as saint or sinner: the polarity isn't particularly novel, but Hesse's nihilistic basking in his new-found profligacy in the name of *Aufrichtigkeit* allows him to win for his art a new range of material and expression, thus revitalizing it sufficiently for him to be able to propel himself at the end of the *Steppenwolf* period to the threshold of the *Spätwerk*, the assured mastery of *The Glass Bead Game* with which his career culminates, where confession is dissolved back into a type of cosmic allegory of the evolution of consciousness throughout the different phases of history. But could the fictional biographies of that wondrous meditation, from the Rainmaker to the Magister Ludi, have been possible without the autobiographical experimentation in prose and verse of the twenties? And conversely, isn't the serene spirituality of the final phase in a sense earned and legitimated by Hesse's earlier *Crisis* incarnation? We might go further: whatever forms of spirituality are yet to be developed in the art of our late Western culture, they must surely have come to terms in a substantial way with the grotesque realities engaged in *Crisis*; if not, then they will ring as hollow as the chants of young Hare Krishna followers on a Brooklyn sidewalk.

# V

Integrity of spirit won through nihilism and despair—that is the essential achievement of *Crisis*, one forced by the alembic of both laughter and tears. The poem-cycle seeks to front the terrible chaos lurking behind the glittering facades of modern European urban life between the wars; to inoculate the self against its elegant corruption in the process of partaking of its anarchic pleasures and pains with anacreontic gusto. To get some sort of genuine purchase on these sub-merged patterns of chaos, Hesse makes a bold break with the Romantic convention of the lyric poem as euphonious song, to let jangling dissonances come to the fore. He had adhered rather automatically and unswervingly to the *Lied* tradition from his first volume of poems on, *Romantische Lieder* (1899), but in *Crisis* he largely breaks with his favorite mode to project the disordered perception of a contemporary *poète maudit* who has run amok in a labyrinth of automobiles, callgirls, and jazz bars. This world has a rhythm of its own, one whose fevered, Dionysian pulsations cannot be formally rendered in the *Lied* tradition of latter-day Romanticism, with its languid, liquid and melancholy vocables more suited to a faint-hearted pathetic fallacy than to the frenzied swirl of the street and night-life of a modern city. So Hesse turns to a different set of stylistic strategies to convey the contemporary hurly-burly that he sees in and around him at certain demonic moments in Zürich. Perhaps the most challenging question about the ultimate poetic worth of *Crisis* is, to what extent do Hesse's formal resources adequately engage and capture in language the burden of disordered experience that he bears witness to in these poems? A larger but related issue here is, how far can poetry open its doors to chaos without being blown to smithereens? Can form figure forth the formless, or does chaos in fact possess a form of its own, an inner demon that can be vowelled in the poet's voice, and ordered, Prospero-like? Perhaps the question is false and chimerical, like asking if unicorns can dance on water. But it needs to be asked, nevertheless, at a time when poetry and science are remerging in the half-glimpsed idea that both the inner and the outer world, the psyche and the cosmos, are possibly the crystallized disjecta of a primal and unbounded chaos.

The answer to the question concerning the value of the *Crisis* poems as art is that they are finally only a qualified success, because—to jump the gun on a conclusion which must be supported by further discussion-although Hesse makes a considerable departure from his previous poetic practice, he does not make enough of a clean break because he still cannot relinquish the trappings of a formal stylistic armor in hazarding the forces of chaos. This

armor reveals him in a sensational new guise as a modern knight errant
willing to break a lance or two against the refractory surfaces of urban life,
but the armor is nevertheless too self-protective to provide a genuine
opening or clearing for an unprejudiced jousting with chaos. As Faust needs
the protection of Mephisto to be able to partake of the infernal festivities on
the Brocken on Walpurgisnight, so Hesse turns to a set of traditional
rhetorical devices that will serve as a passport to guarantee his safe passage
through the quotidian inferno of modern life that is *Crisis*. The poems
succeed because of the risks they take, and they fail as well because these risks
are always too limited and calculated: Hesse's illuminations are guided so as
not to end in a premature terminal silence, like Rimbaud's. Further, Hesse
can elude our criticism as well as his own by the nihilistic disclaimer, the
poetic vanishing point that literary success and failure, and the question of
value, are simply meaningless in the cultural situation out of which he is
writing.

It is something of a truism that poets don't so much create forms as they
inherit them, and the degree of formal originality they possess manifests
itself in their ability to bond or adapt the inherited forms to the exigencies
and demands of the context in which they find themselves, which will always
be both relatively unique and relatively timeless. Hesse too, in *Crisis*, rejects
one aspect of his Romantic legacy, the *Lied* tradition, to explore another and
a "lower" mode of the lyric, that of *Galgenhumor* and *Knüttelvers* (gallows
humor and doggerel), with which he was familiar from his study of Villon
and Goethe, among others, and which he adapts with wit and bravado to deal
with contemporary material. The bawdy persona of these satiric poems
represents them as impromptu, improvised trifles, to be taken in not so much
as art but as a kind of documentation of momentary moods, impulses, and
experiences. At times both mood and mode are not that far removed from
Byron's improvisational high-jinks in *Don Juan* ("I write this reeling,/Having
got drunk exceedingly today,/So that I seem to stand upon the ceiling"),
including the fact that some of Hesse's stanzas too are presented under the
guise of having been composed under the influence ("To John the Baptist
from Hermann the Schnappsist"). The alcoholic apologetics help the poet to
disarm impending critical strictures, to treat material not normally admitted
into the temple of serious poetry because of the rules of decorum, and to
present a seemingly disordered, tippler's perspective that is in fact as carefully
organized and controlled as the doggerel rhyme and meter chosen to convey
it.

Thus in *Crisis* Hesse breaks for once with the elevated Romantic lyrical
vein in which he had worked as a prolific but largely second-rate poet, to turn

with verve and vigor to a satiric mode, that albeit in its constituent formal elements just as traditional as his epigonal Romantic songs, nevertheless represents an abrasive encounter with modernity that makes these poems in truth more serious than his intentionally "serious" poems. Both in style and content they force an opening for disorder and confusion to enter the stage, and to be engaged by Hermann-the-Schnappsist, the satiric self for whom the unfunny issue is that of the survival of self and poetry. Tempered in the crucible of his (heroic) despair, these crisis lyrics are, in the form of gallows humor and doggerel, articulate screams, cacophonous litanies that take to their logical extreme the confessional aesthetics of the *Steppenwolf* period. The sardonic collection may be seen as the *avant garde* of a highly creative, deranged, and suicidal decade in Hesse's life, for it is a calculated slap at the bourgeois friends, readers and critics who wanted to embalm Hesse as a venerable Great Writer, and who characterized his new works as "irresponsible derailments," insisting that the author of *Siddhartha* owed it to himself to maintain a more dignified public posture. As if Hesse could care less. Like the wolf in the short story that closes the *Steppenwolf* phase, Hesse wanted to bite the childish hand that was trying to feed him chocolate through the bars of his cage. He wasn't so much interested in the sweets to be had from his audience as in the survival of his troubled *daimon*, no matter what the cost.

## VI

Hesse's self-willed rebellion against respectability and convention in *Crisis* proceeds simultaneously on the sexual, social and literary planes. The revolt of the forty-eight year old poet as *enfant terrible* is enacted under the auspices of Dionysian intoxication, fueled by wine, whisky and cognac, which serve also as the necessary sensual dissolvents of decades of inhibition or repression of libidinous impulses. The active surrender to the realm of the eternal feminine, the career of the flaming senses, is moreover a flight from the idyllic self-isolation of the mountain-retreat at Montagnola—the contemplative seat of the cool *Geist* which with its perpetually regulated rhythms holds the fear of death in abeyance—to the flickering and irregular contortions of urban night life, where Hesse hopes to have one last romp before capitulating to the onset of old age. The erotic crossing from the realm of spirit to that of instinct is ironically a movement from country to town in the concerted effort to recapture there the lost *Natur* of childhood, to recover its wholeness in the fractured angularities of revelling. From the midst of this self-renewal Hesse could write in a lighter moment that one does everything in life, or most of it, on account of women. If I struggled the greater part of my life, and thought up systems to defend myself against them, I now do just the opposite. If I strove for wisdom in my younger years, I now take pains to be childish for once. And it succeeds, not always, but often enough, and gives me pleasure.[18]

The Goethe tradition is never far from Hesse's art, for his excursion in organizing a latter-day innocence is in a sense akin to Faust's rejuvenation in the Witch's Kitchen scene, where he is privileged with a burning vision of female pulchritude and drinks off a flaming potion that will make him a lady killer. So too Hesse's entry into the world of the senses in *Crisis* is replete with animal icons and beast images (dog, wolf, pig), as well as the associated Faustian violation of innocence, as Hesse (in a blasphemous poem ultimately not included in the volume, "The Man of Fifty Years") imagines himself stripping down a young girl "instead of reading a tome by Goethe" at least one time before—"in God's name"—the arrival of death.[19] Faust's Walpurgisnight adventure is also replicated in the shorthand of fragmentary references to the revels of a masked ball (one which Hesse actually attended, and which is expanded in *Steppenwolf* into the surreal, hallucinatory Magic Theater sequence). But in *Crisis* there is no epiphanic uplift by way of Pablo-Mozart and the golden track of the Immortals; what remains is the galling frustration of the fallow dawn, when the hung-over partier can only curse Lola, the flirtatious wife who fanned his lust all night long only to disappear at party's end into her husband's marriage-hearse, a "Fiat car," with the parting shot, "go to the devil" ("Morning After the Masked Ball," p. 99).

And so Hesse's pocket Brocken-bestiary in the style of the roaring twenties—jazz, booze, the foxtrot and the onestep—ends in a failure reflected back to him in the sordid mirror of self-hatred the morning after. The repeated, linked invocations of the myths of the Prodigal Son and of Don Juan, noted by Mark Boulby,[20] finally fail to fulfill the poet in a childhood paradise dream of sensual gratification, an achieved epithalamion of the innocent senses fully consummated. The attempted *Bildungs*-program of a self-abandon in eros culminates in nausea and a feeling of the ridiculous, grotesque nature of the attempt. The result is a type of catharsis not envisioned at the outset, for the lust to cram the empty self and to incorporate the female ends in a purgatorial voiding of that self. The dedicatory surrender or *Hingabe* to the "dark one, primal mother of all desire" undergoes an ironic inversion in the closing poem's sarcastic farewell to female arms, and the numb dread of the unavoidable end betokens the

return of *Geist*, whose resources will have to make that stark thought
supportable:

### The End

The flame that lured me through the pain
Of frantic pleasure has flickered and gone out.
My rigid fingers scream with gout,
And suddenly I'm in the wilderness again.
Recoiling from the shards of luckless revels,
Glutted, exhausted, disappointed, I,
Steppenwolf, have packed my bag. I'm going
Back to my native steppe to die.
Goodbye to sparkling, smiling masquerades,
Ladies too lovely, too ingratiating.
Behind the suddenly fallen curtain,
I know the old familiar dread is waiting.
Slowly I go to greet the enemy.
Harried by anguish, with laborious breath
And pounding, apprehensive heart,
I wait, wait, wait for death.

### Am Ende

Plötzlich ist verzuckt das Flackerlicht,
Das mich lockte durch so viele Lüste,
In den starren Fingern schreit die Gicht,
Plözlich steh ich wieder in der Wüste,
Steppenwolf, und speie auf die Scherben
Der verglühten Feste ohne Glück,
Packe meinen Koffer, fahr zurück
In die Steppe, denn es gilt zu sterben.
Lebe wohl, vergnügte Bilderwelt,
Maskenballe, allzu süsse Frauen;
Hinterm Vorhang, der nun klirrend fällt,
Weiss ich warten das gewohnte Grauen.
Langsam geh dem Feinde ich entgegen,
Eng und enger schnürt mich ein die Not.
Das erschrockne Herz mit harten Schlägen
Wartet, wartet, wartet auf den Tod.

The foundering at the finish of the erotic dream is, however, not an
unwelcome result, but a necessary defeat that Hesse pursued with clear-eyed

passion. From start to finish, the poem's "desperate and vain effort to drown the corrosive, cauterizing intellect in sensuous experience"[21] was a willed, ironically belated but coherent struggle to live out his long-pent-up sexual impulses in an all-encompassing symbolic incarnation of Hermann Hesse the Profligate. What we have in *Crisis* is not so much wish-fulfillment as a type of creative self-healing, a restoration of psychic equilibrium brought about by the purging of a hypertrophied intellect through modern Don-Juanism, the necessary context of which is the *Aufhebung* of that incarnation once its task is done and the spirit can re-emerge sublimed and freed for new tasks. The failure is thus fated, one which can no longer be put off or elided. Hesse's *amor fati* makes it the occasion of a strenuous self-creation, which allows him to go on and complete the novel, *Steppenwolf*, and to proceed to a different self-fictionalizing altogether in the serene *Spätwerk*, beginning in *Journey to the East* (1932). To rekindle his creative energies at the conflagration of a short-term failure in willful dissipation is the most intriguing strategy of *Crisis* that should be viewed as one more facet of Hesse's lynx-like and roguish personality. Thus it should not surprise us that in a prose fragment written four years before *Crisis*, he already foresaw in foreshortened form the whole Don Juan cycle to come, only to dismiss contemptuously this "current incarnation": "Put an end to yourself, mannikin, you belong to the old iron."[22] Nor should it amaze us, finally, that at the beginning of the next decade, Hesse turns his back on the acute confessional aesthetics that had served as the seedbed of his creative drives during the problematic *Steppenwolf* years, and begins to speak with Castalian calm of the poetic ideal of impersonality, of "the disparition of all that is personal and accidental in the secret of form"[23]—a fitting epitaph to the powerful, troubling self-imago which by the 1930's was no longer current, but already moribund in Hesse's imagination.

## VII

If there is a genuine failure in *Crisis*, it is to be found, as signalled earlier, in Hesse's inability or refusal to go far enough in engaging the disintegrative forces governing our mass culture. Although his poetry comes closer here than anywhere else to the real language of men—an early reviewer stressed how he "forges from everyday speech, the monologue and the letter a flexible, life-like idiom of much grace"[24]—his entry into the destructive element is too calculated, stylized and formally defensive, what with its easy and witty elegance; its ready reliance on rhyme, meter, formulaic colloquial blasphemy and cursing. The quasi Mephistophelean cleverness and bawdy negations ultimately mately prevent *Crisis* from being the major poetry it might have become, given a less programmed, more open-ended confrontation with chaos.

Even *Hesse's* chosen goal of erotic dissipation is rendered with rather conventional shock-tactics; lust is still too traditionally poetic, and there is little actual body language or erotic imagery beyond the obligatory breast, belly, hair and eyes. Hesse's *rendezvous* with sex is too willed and intellectual, and he stops where a contemporary of his like D. H. Lawrence will really get started. So also his stance *pour épater les bourgeois* is limited because his revolt against the middle-class assumes a middle-class framework to validate it, and reveals Hesse's dilemma to be that of the hypochondriac guest at the spa, who fulminates against bourgeois complacency safely ensconced in a luxury hotel, or of Harry Haller, who launches his attacks on Philistinism under the araucaria, the ruling icon of the bourgeois temple in which he dwells while living off his stocks and bonds. Similarly, the dramatic persona of *Crisis*, Hesse's alter ego, is no social outcast challenging the corrupt prerogatives of a privileged class; he is on the contrary a man of means, entering the playground of eros with the aid of smart clothes, liquor, and dance steps, and even the gay doings of the masked ball are only a *Fasching*-equivalent of genuine Bacchic ecstacy. In a sense the profligate here is only the other side of middle-class conformity, so that Hesse finds himself caught up in an unfruitful dialectic of respectability/debauchery that in the frame posited by the poems permits no synthesis or higher resolution. One of the deeper ironies of *Crisis* is that the demonic embodiment of worldly complacency, the Catholic baker with his expensive automobile that the poet would like to be run over by, could by a *volte-face* become the double or twin of the poet, or of the Harry Haller who engages in an absurd hunt after automobiles in the Magic Theater.

Consequently the sardonic humor—the laughter of despair—betokens the irresolvable bind the author finds himself in, which he is able to rise above only when he turns to the writing of the second half of *Steppenwolf*, where the warfare of the two selves (Faust's "zwer Seelen") opens into a vision of the infinite plurality of selves in a cosmic expansion of individuality that fans out to include the Immortals. There Hesse achieves a larger synthesis that assimilates but transcends the saint/sinner, blessing/cursing split in the surreal transformations of the Magic Theater. Whereas the laughter in *Crisis* is destructive of both the self and the other, in the last third of *Steppenwolf* it is corrosive only to move toward a greater construction. If in the poems Hesse doesn't get far beyond the problematics of the child (the

Prodigal Son, Don Juan), in the novel the child is reborn and integrated with old-age wisdom, which is joyful and gay, culminating in the laughter of the Immortals—indifferent in the best sense, but not nihilistic.

So Hesse, in *Crisis*, fails to go far enough in terms of either content or form. He does not hazard enough; he opens the door to chaos only a crack, to play, armed to the teeth, with a few disconcerting embodiments of the living dark, before the door is forced shut again with a verse-*Knüttel*. How easy it is to pass such a judgment in the secure warmth of one's study; how convenient to ponder chaos, keeping it at arm's length with pen, paper, typewriter, whatnot. Does any poet ever go far enough? Harry Haller's resolve was to have an accident with his razor on his fiftieth birthday: perhaps that is going too far, and not disorderly enough. Maybe too the failure the reader sees in the author is really his own as his critical specter is reflected back to him in a reductive ratio. But perhaps it is more important to raise questions than to find answers, those paltry birds that drop stillborn from the branches of one's best thoughts. And on that note I round back to my question at the outset: what is possible for poetry today? Or to recast it somewhat, is it possible for a poetry of crisis to find an authentic voice for chaos, a language that syllables the cosmic dark, that sounds into the black holes of space without being sucked in, that renders the configurations of disharmony? And does chaos possess an inner form that may be captured in a language that will not be mere gibberish, a mad cipher or inane howl? Is such a poetry possible, or is the very idea of it a terminal delusion? The reader can only raise the question; it is for the true poets to conjure the devil of chaos in utterance, bind him in speech, deliver his form, whatever that might turn out to be.

In the closing decades of our millenial century, it may be the only thing worth trying in poetry, even if only failure attends the poet's speaking-out-of the critical disarray of our multiverse. In this venture, the Hesse of *Crisis* may serve as a kind of Elder Brother, who in the twenties clearly heard the crack of doom, and tried to record some of its sound waves in an astonishing verse diary.

## NOTES

1. 1928 n.d., reprinted in *Materialen zu Hermann Hesses 'Der Steppenwolf,'* ed. Volker Michels (Frankfurt: Suhrkamp Verlag, 1972), pp. 306-309. Throughout this paper all translations of material quoted from *Materialen* are mine.

2. "*Person* and *Persona*: The Magic Mirrors of *Steppenwolf*," in *Hesse*: *A Collection of Critical Essays*, ed. Theodore Ziolkowski (Englewood Cliffs: Prentice Hall, 1973), p. 165.

3. Letter of October 1928, *Materialen*, p. 134.

4. *Materialen*, p. 134.

5. Letter of June 1928, *Materialen*, pp. 131-132.

6. Letter of October 1926 to Heinrich Wiegand, *Materialen*, p. 97.

7. Quoted by Volker Michels in *Materialen*, p. 39.

8. In his discussion of the light and dark worlds of *Demian* in *Hermann Hesse*: *A Study in Theme and Structure* (Princeton: Princeton Univ. Press, 1965), p. 96.

9. *Journey to Nuremberg*, in *Autobiographical Writings*, ed. T. Ziolkowski, trans. Denver Lidley (New York: Farrar, Straus & Giroux, 1971), pp. 206, 178.

10. *Crisis: Pages from a Diary*, trans. Ralph Manheim (New York: Farrar, Straus & Giroux, 1975), "Postscript to My Friends," pp. 119-121.

11. Letter of October 1926 to Hugo Ball, *Materialen*, p. 97.

12. "On Hölderlin" (1924), in *My Belief: Essays on Life and Art*, ed. T. Ziolkowski, trans. D. Lidley (New York: Farrar, Straus & Giroux, 1974), p. 128.

13. *Materialen*, p. 306.

14. *My Belief*, p. 49.

15. Letter of February 1928 to Cuno Amiet, *Materialen*, p. 126.

16. Letters of March and August 1926 to Ludwig Finckh and Georg Reinhart, *Materialen*, pp. 70, 95.

17. "The Outlook for Intelligence," *The Collected Works of Paul Valery*, Vol. 10, trans. Denise Folliot and Jackson Mathews (New York: Bollingen, 1962), 130.

18. "Verbummelter Tag," in *Materialen*, p. 71.

19. *Materialen*, pp. 197-198.

20. *Hermann Hesse: His Mind and Art* (Ithaca: Cornell Univ. Press, 1967), p. 169.

21. Boulby, *Hermann Hesse*, p. 167.

21. Boulby, *Hermann Hesse*, p. 167.

22. "From the Journal of One Who Has Been Derailed" (1922), *Materialen*, pp. 199-203.

23. "Mozart's Operas" (1932), *Materialen*, pp. 136-137.

24. Hans Böhm, *Der Kunstwart*, 44 (1930-31), 803-805, my translation.

SIEGFRIED UNSELD

# Hermann Hesse's Influence: Ethics or Esthetics?

O n the twentieth anniversary of Hermann Hesse's death on August 11, 1982, the *Frankfurter Allgemeine Zeitung* published an item under the sardonic heading "The Hesse Drug" in it, we find the following remarks: "World-wide sales of sixty million copies: twice as many as during the author's lifetime ... In other words, a global success it is safe to say. No wonder Hesse's publisher Siegfried Unseld beats the drum and tries to call the public's attention to this author; not to his *books*, to be sure, but— probably for good reason—only to their phenomenal *sales* ... After all, he has been raking in profits for years from the Hesse drug; he has no fewer than eighty-three Hesse titles on his list and large portions of the author's unpublished material still in his desk drawers." And then *this* concluding comment: "True, no German author is *more* successful than Hermann Hesse. Unfortunately[1]." (A letter to the editor a few days later pointed out that *seventy* million copies of Karl May's books have been sold, ten million more than of Hesse's.)

In *Acta Germanica*, the Yearbook of the South African Association of Germanists, Wolfgang Freese of the University of Natal in Pietermaritzburg criticizes *me* and my publishing house in these words: "Siegfried Unseld calmly dismisses all qualifications and reservations when he writes: 'However Hermann Hesse's works may be judged in the future, even an ideological

From *Hermann Hesse: Politische und wirkungsgeschichtliche Aspekte.* © 1986 by A. Franke.

opponent will not fail to respect Hesse's moral stature as it is documented in his political and religious pronouncements.'"

Was this statement of mine—as insinuated here—meant to point to the "true" Hesse? Did I thus intend to come to the rescue of Hesse the writer on political and ethical subjects at the expense of Hesse the literary artist?

Freese also attacks Suhrkamp's announcement of its publication of the *Politische Schriften* (Political Works). He quotes from our dust jacket: "Hesse's *Politische Schriften* are an exact mirror of his literary works, no matter how unpolitical the latter may appear at first glance[2]." Freese is of a completely different opinion: for him, scholarship that is concerned with literary evaluation is not interested in such mirroring; political matters are important but a judicious literary evaluation is *more* important. Another scholar, Rudolf Koester, comes to the following conclusion: "In order to disprove the cliché—one with especially wide currency in Germany—of the unworldly poet who is an introverted dreamer, Hesse's publishers have recently emphasized the practical and politically keen-eyed critic of his times by issuing some of Hesse's correspondence. This we assume is intended to demonstrate Hesse's relevance for our day. But a rehabilitation of his work on this basis would be too one-sided; for literature does not live from— social—relevance alone."[3]

Are we at Suhrkamp really interested merely in making the world aware of Hesse's opinions on contemporary topics? Are we trying in this fashion to divert attention from the literary weaknesses of his work? Are we attempting to say that the political message to be found in Hesse's writings is *one* thing, literary quality another? Does political content stand opposed to literary form, or does the correct political position also imply the correct literary quality? Moreover, by emphasizing Hesse's affinities with the counterculture, are we at Suhrkamp trying to encourage possible extreme leftist or even rightist tendencies on the part of young or no longer young nonconformists or conformists—tendencies which can have incalculable—perhaps even reactionary!—effects?

Walter Benjamin expressed his views on the question of correct literary quality in his famous address, "The Author as Producer," delivered in Paris on April 27, 1934. In it he quoted Lichtenberg: "It's not a matter of what kind of opinions a person has, but of what kind of man he is made out to be." And Benjamin adds: "Tendency is not enough" he must find forms of expression "that can provide the literary energies of his contemporaries with an incentive" for a new beginning. An author has a truly revolutionary function if he experiences "his solidarity with the proletariat, *not* as a producer but solely through his opinions".

I cannot deal here with the details of this important address by Benjamin, in many respects a contradictory document. But it is undoubtedly of great significance for its time, and we must definitely keep in mind the time and place at which he delivered his address. To Benjamin's mind, the struggle against Fascism could be carried out only by the proletariat, and at that point in history it was important to take a political stance. Benjamin was at that time strongly influenced by Brecht's theory of a didactic theater, by Brecht's idea that it isn't "private" or individualistic thinking that matters but the art of thinking inside other people's heads; it was probably this Brechtian influence that caused Benjamin to state that "an author who doesn't teach other *writers* anything doesn't teach *anyone* anything"[4]. Today few authors would be willing to fulfill such a requirement, but as I have already mentioned, we must keep the times in mind in which such demands were expressed.

But let us focus more clearly on our theme. Let us ask ourselves whether Suhrkamp is acting correctly in bringing out Hesse's "Political Writings" and considering them important, whether we are correct in publishing those works that contain Hesse's advice on the conduct of life. Must we ask ourselves, in other words, as Wolfgang Freese puts it in his essay, "whether a basic distinction ought to be made between the historical production of the author and the present-day production of the publisher (i.e., the Hesse industry)"?

Are we in fact trying to market Hesse's ethics to the detriment of his esthetic accomplishments? Are we overemphasizing Hesse's heroes as *models* for his readers to identify with and thereby neglecting, even denying, the *literary* artist for whom the instrument of his language is essential? Ethics versus esthetics, life's problems and uncertainties versus art and the theory of production? Various responses to these questions come to mind:

1. I could refer here, for example, to an intelligent, prophetic essay such as Egon Schwarz's "Hermann Hesse and the Future," in which the author predicts that "the demand [for Hesse's works] will be limited chiefly to the novels"—in other words, to the historical production. Although Hesse's essays, his moral and political observations, will enjoy temporary popularity, according to Schwarz, Schwarz believes that, "in spite of excellent translations, they will merely be carried along as insignificant appendages on the periphery of the great Hesse waves"[5].

2. Just what is the situation of the so-called Hesse industry today? Eighty-two Hesse titles are currently in print: of these, approximately one-third represent volumes in the same form in which they were issued by their author; one-third represent these same works in different combinations; and

only one-third are products of the Hesse industry. Of course, it is possible to object to collections dealing with topics such as butterflies or trees or the seasons, or to level criticism against Hesse calendars. In the case of *Lektüre für Minuten* (a volume of brief excerpts from Hesse's works), on the other hand, the fact that the little book has found a half million readers is surely of some importance. But who would want to voice objections to the publication of Hesse's *letters*, to collections with titles such as "What I Believe" or "A Mind of One's Own," to the publication of the author's observations on music, of his collections of older literature, collections that he, after all, had published himself: the *Gesta Romanorum*, *Morgenländische Erzählungen* (Oriental Tales), *Das Meisterbuch* (The Book of the Masters), *Der Zauberbrunnen* (The Magic Well)? Who would protest the publication of Hesse's impressions of Ticino, the Lake Constance, northern Italy, India? And certainly no one doubts the necessity of bringing out the two-volume edition of the political writings entitled *Politik des Gewissens* (The Politics of Conscience), which appeared in 1977. I might add that we have published *twenty-five* volumes of documents and secondary literature relating to Bertolt Brecht, whereas we have brought out only *ten* such volumes connected with Hesse.

But to return to our topic of ethics versus esthetics. Let us listen here to the words of Hesse himself, who wrote the following lines to Peter Suhrkamp on January 15, 1942: "... I have just reread [my novel] *Roßhalde* for the first time in almost twenty-six years. An external circumstance forced me to do it, and for a long time I hesitated to approach the task; I expected to feel ashamed. I thought I would find a form of 'Edelkitsch' [noble kitsch]. But it wasn't so. I liked the book, and it turned out to have withstood the test of time. There are only very few sentences in it I would omit or change today, and, on the other hand, there are a number of things in it I would now no longer be capable of. In those days, in this book, I reached the highest level of craft and technique possible for me, and I have never gone beyond it. Still, there was a positive side to the fact that the war came along and interrupted my development and instead of allowing me to become a master of 'gute Formen' (beautiful forms) led me into a problematic area where the purely esthetic could no longer survive[6]."

Two days later Hesse wrote to his cousin Fritz Gundert: "What has a lasting impact is not what is willed and contrived and constructed, but the gesture, the sudden inspiration, the little touch of fleeting magic—just as in an opera by Mozart it is not the plot or moral of the work that counts but the gesture and melody, the freshness and grace with which a number of themes are stated and varied[7]." On another occasion Hesse speaks of this topic in connection with Ödön von Horváth. In a letter to Alfred Kubin in early 1938 he writes: "I recommend a short book to you, a tale called *Jugend ohne Gott* (Youth without God), by Horváth. Perhaps you'll come across it somewhere or other; *it has flaws*, but it's marvelous all the same and cuts right through the moral squalor of today's world." Over and over again, we find this emphasis on morality: "The world needs morality more than cleverness and an ordering of values more than psychology[8]."

What, then, are Hesse's criteria for that which "has lasting impact"? Where do his priorities lie among the various criteria of ethics and esthetics, of political and literary relevance? This problem embraces more than the question of content and form, message and structure; it goes right to the heart of the author's self-image. We know that although Hesse was always firmly convinced of the importance of his life task, he never considered himself a great literary artist. Those familiar with his biography know that during every stage of his life his self-appraisal was low or, at the most, very modest. It became almost entirely negative at that time of existential crisis when he experienced the "hell of one's own self" and, with bitter irony, saw himself at best as a "purveyor of popular entertainment". In his diary entitled "Crisis," we read these lines of verse from the year 1925:

> Bald geh ich heim
> Bald geh ich aus dem Leim,
> und meine Knochen fallen
> zu den andern allen.
> Der berühmte Hesse ist verschwunden,
> Blob der Verleger lebt noch von seinen Kunden.

> Soon I'll go home
> Soon I'll fall to pieces
> and my bones will join those
> of all the others.
> The renowned Hesse is dead and gone
> But his publisher still lives off his readers.

Even when he was later awarded the Nobel Prize for Literature, he pointed out that there were other writers more deserving of this distinction than he. He repeatedly spoke of his "greater colleagues" as the "virtuosos" or the "classic virtuosos". But he also knew how to look at things relatively, as when he wrote to his friend, the painter Ernst Morgenthaler: "Perhaps the shortcoming lies merely in the fact that we are occasionally somewhat envious of the virtuosos instead of being content with our own gifts. And perhaps this discontent with ourselves and our tendency sometimes to overrate others is just what is good about us[9]."

When his son Bruno expressed doubts about his calling, about his abilities as a painter, Hesse wrote to him: "Each one of us artists, even if he has many self-doubts and thinks his talents and abilities are terribly minor, still has a purpose and a calling and, if he remains true to himself, accomplishes something in his station that only he is capable of... My dear son, both of us, you and I, are participating in a task that is as old as the world[10]."

I believe this phrase, "participating in a task that is as old as the world" is the most apt description that can be found for Hesse's appraisal of his own function. At approximately the same time he gave this advice to his son Bruno, the author returned to the question of ethics and esthetics in a letter addressed to Heinrich Wiegand: "When I read Eichendorff, who says the most incredible things through the vehicle of a naive folksong, I find your esthetically irreproachable poets, the [Stefan] Georges etc., with their beautiful, new, unwonted rhymes and exactly measured syllables, downright pretentious, even though at *other* moments I *too* am capable of enjoying and appreciating them. As far as I myself am concerned, I do not attribute importance to those things; I renounced my esthetic ambitions years ago and don't write literature but rather confessions, the way a man who is drowning or who has been poisoned is not concerned with how his hair looks or with the modulations of his voice but simply cries for help. You are right, dear friend, for finding fault with me for this, but you can't forbid a man from crying out as he perishes[11]."

Thus, we meet once again the familiar dichotomy between literature and confession, or, as someone else has put it, between "Dichtung" and "Wahrheit". There is without question a dichotomy here, but certainly it is not necessarily a matter of mutually exclusive antitheses. "In your writing," Hesse counseled a young author in 1951, "strive above all for truth, not for beauty. The latter will then come of itself[12]."

What kind of esthetic quality is this in Hesse that comes of itself? Or what are those problematic issues, in the face of which esthetic values cannot survive? It is noteworthy that these comments by Hesse occur with particular frequency during the period when he has to defend *Steppenwolf* to his own readers. (It is, by the way, quite remarkable how many of Hesse's critics have used his own self-doubts as their criteria for judging his work.)

In considering *Steppenwolf* I shall disregard the numerous polemics, damning reviews, and misunderstandings and simply call attention to the name Hans Mayer and the words with which he opens and concludes his memorable essay on this novel: "A book of personal crisis, of artistic crisis, of social crisis." It is easy to agree with this assessment, but then Mayer goes on to state that not everything in the book has successfully met the test of time and that Hesse would be the last one to dispute this. According to Mayer, under the stern gaze of Mozart in the Magic Theater the writer Hermann Hesse would be assigned the same fate as the composers Brahms and Wagner, whose punishment in the Hereafter was to lead "an enormous procession of several tens of thousands of men dressed in black". These were "the black thousands, all the players of those parts and notes that, according to Divine Judgment, were superfluous in the scores of these two composers". The author of *Steppenwolf*, Hans Mayer adds, would have accepted a similar judgment in his own case. And thus Mayer comes to the following conclusion: "Each of these three areas, therefore—the expression of personal crisis, the artistic dilemma, the cultural criticism—suffers from glaring weaknesses of composition and execution. Yet the unique combination [of these areas] produced what is still an extremely remarkable book[13]."

I beg to differ with Hans Mayer. How can "a book of personal crisis, of artistic crisis, of social crisis" suffer in each of these three areas from "weaknesses of composition and execution" and still, thanks to the "unique combination" of these weak, sickly, unsuccessful parts, turn out to be a compelling and influential book? In this connection, however, I should like to take issue with Hermann Hesse as well, when he says that his development, instead of allowing him "to become a master of beautiful forms, led [him] into a problematic area where the purely esthetic could not longer survive".

What does "master of beautiful forms" mean in this context? What *are* beautiful forms anyway? We know how difficult it is to find objective criteria for judging the formal aspects of a work of art; every great work is *sui generis* and must be examined according to its own rules, not with a view toward determining whether it possesses "beautiful forms" but rather whether the formal linguistic shape it takes is an appropriate expression of its inner intellectual and emotional character. Can a book that deals with a personal, artistic, and social crisis be given a "beautiful form"? Is the esthetic aspect of a book *merely*—"beautiful form"—can there not also be a critical form, a problematic form, an open form? Everything external in a work of art must be an externalization (or expression) of the internal. A work of art is truly a work of art when the form is the cognitive substratum of the content.

If we attempt to analyse the esthetics of *Steppenwolf* with this in mind, we shall make discoveries differing radically from those of Hans Mayer. True, we are not meting out a "Divine Judgment," yet it *is* one that is firmly based on esthetic principles. I ask for your indulgence if I go back to a brief passage from my dissertation on Hesse, submitted in 1951. At that time, I asserted, with the exaggeration typical of a student writing a dissertation, that *Steppenwolf* met precisely those specifications for the novel of the time established by Koskimies in his famous *Theory of the Novel* and that Hesse had also practised those "three methods of compositional procedure" that Koskimies had considered relevant for the modern novel[14].

Naturally, important as this discovery was for the young dissertation writer—that the principles of composition underlying *Steppenwolf* were in accord with Herr Koskimies' esthetic theories—this can scarcely be considered of any use in establishing the criteria we are searching for today. But at the time I also examined the *language* of Hesse's novel. Critics have often charged "The Treatise on the *Steppenwolf*," for example, with a lack of intellectual weight, but in so doing they overlook the narrative tone of this section of the novel: the Treatise begins with the fairy-tale formula "Once upon a time" and concludes with a smile. Likewise, the way the Treatise is printed in the first edition, as if it were a penny tract, demonstrates that Hesse wished to emphasize, as far as its form is concerned, that this part of the book is to be seen as lying somewhere between a pious, edifying homily and the *Tractatus logico—philosophicus*.

Major esthetic significance is also inherent in the novel's images and metaphors. What a strikingly successful invention is the name "Steppenwolf" itself, that mythological beast, as Hugo Ball called it, a name including "steppe," which evokes the Russian steppes—in other words, a wasteland—and "wolf," the animal as opposed to the human being. "Steppe" also denotes, however, a different place—a place for dropping out and of alternative lifestyles—while "wolf," as in Wolfgang von Goethe and Wolfgang Amadeus Mozart, evokes the world of the Immortals. "The stature of an artist," Hesse wrote in an unpublished review, "is determined by nothing other than the degree of density and power attained by his images, his visions[15]." It is just this that Hesse himself has attained in the example just cited.

Let me also call attention here to a passage of the novel—consisting in the German of a single sentence—that I believe can be seen to fulfill in exemplary fashion the requirement that form must be the cognitive substratum of content. Harry Haller is describing the room he rents in a bourgeois household:

Ich habe das gern, auf der Treppe diesen Geruch von Stille, Ordnung, Sauberkeit, Anstand und Zahmheit zu atmen, der trotz meinem Bürgerhab immer etwas Rührendes für mich hat, und habe es gern, dann über die Schwelle meines Zimmers zu treten, wo das alles aufhört, wo zwischen den Bücherhaufen die Zigarrenreste liegen und die Weinflaschen stehen, wo alles unordentlich, unheimisch und verwahrlost ist und wo alles, Bücher, Manuskripte, Gedanken, gezeichnet und durchtränkt ist von der Not der Einsamen, von der Problematik des Menschseins, von der Sehnsucht nach neuer Sinngebung für das sinnlos gewordene Menschenleben.

(On the stairs I like to breathe in this odor of quiet and order, of cleanliness and respectable domesticity. There is something in it that touches me in spite of my hatred for all it stands for. I like to step across the threshold of my room where all this suddenly stops; where, instead, cigar ash and wine bottles lie among the heaped-up books and there is nothing but disorder and neglect; and where everything—books, manuscripts, thoughts—is marked and saturated with the plight of lonely men, with the problem of existence and with the yearning after a new orientation for an age that has lost its bearings.[16]

The world of the burgher or ordinary citizen as opposed to that of the Steppenwolf; an area where norms are observed as opposed to one characterized by neglect; a sense of order versus disarray; the world of conformity versus that of the dropout—these polar opposites are contained and expressed in one extended sentence. The seemingly orderly world of the burgher is presented in clear syntax, whereas that of the Steppenwolf appears in a series of subordinate clauses loosely interconnected by the rather indefinite and abstract phrase "where everything..., etc." Calm, order, respectability, and domesticity are thus contrasted with the sufferings of the lonely, with the problematical nature of being human, with the longing for new meaning. Here again form is the cognitive substratum of content!

As a student, I came to the conclusion that Steppenwolf is one of the most profound and most carefully constructed of Hesse's works. "In every section of this work of art, in every sentence, the reader can pause; curiosity about the plot does not urge him forward, since the concluding pages are already anticipated in the Treatise. Yet the fact that the sections are self-contained does not mean that they are without function in terms of the whole. Each section stands by and for itself but at the same time is related to every other one by the musical technique of the fugue, for the Treatise contains all the motifs that are subsequently developed in the work, in its pictorial language, in its 'garment of visible events.' Thus, Hesse succeeded in transforming his 'attempt to express psychological experiences' into a genuine literary work of art[17]."

I have little to add today to my earlier conclusions. I am very glad that Theodore Ziolkowski has emphasized the musical nature of *Steppenwolf's* composition by using the analogy of the sonata form in his extremely enlightening essay entitled "A Sonata in Prose"[18]. I was also pleased when Ralph Freedman pointed out that the novel's pictorial language—for instance, the mirror images, the mirrorings, the metaphors of normal and distorting mirrors—is an important structural element in the book[19].

None of Hesse's novels has had more influence, has found more echo among generations of readers. Nor has any novel of his been subjected to more violent critical treatment, to more misinterpretation and misunderstanding. But after over half a century we can be certain of the book's enduring influence, and it is safe to say that this influence stems from the "problematic areas" Hesse treats in the novel. If these problems have been transferred from the author's head, however, into the heads of others, to use Brecht's language, then only the literary power of expression could have brought this about—in other words, esthetics!

Hesse was aware of this; he stressed esthetic values not only in his essays but also in his poetry and fiction. As an early example I shall quote here the fourth stanza of the poem "Morgen" ("Morning"), written in the summer of 1910:

> Aus dumpfem Leid und Freudenschwall
> Klärt sich mein Wille rein und kalt.
> Was gestern Spiel und Ungestalt,
> Ist heute Form, Gesetz, Kristall.

> From deep woe and surges of joy
> My will emerges pure and cold.
> What yesterday was playfulness and chaos
> Today is form, is law, is crystal-clear.

"Form [...] law [...] crystal [...]" strikes me as a beautiful poetic definition of esthetic quality. In 1915 in answer to the question "By what standards may one novel, one novella be judged to be better than another?" Hesse stressed formal esthetic criteria, and he later wrote that the tended more and more to put the quality of craftmanship higher than ideas and emotional content.

It would be easy to find many similar statements by the author, but I shall quote only one more in this regard, from a privately printed essay of 1947 with the Goethean title, "Geheimnisse" ("Secrets"). In it, Hesse advises us to approach a literary work in terms of "that question which is usually the most important one for its creator: the question of the esthetic value of his work, its degree of objective beauty[20]."

Are we faced with a contradiction here? On the one hand, the writer is forced into a "problematic area ... where the purely esthetic can no longer survive," and then, on the other, he recognizes once again that the most important thing is "the question of esthetic value". I do not necessarily see this as contradictory. I believe that Hesse judges literary creations in terms of esthetic value, of their degree of objective beauty, and he advises us, his readers, to do likewise where his own works are concerned. But he himself, in viewing his writing, adopted a freer, more independent point of view. He often spoke disparagingly of the way content could be measured yet esthetic form could not. "I should like," he wrote in *Kurgast* ("A Guest at the Spa"), "to find an expression for duality, I should like to write chapters and sentences where melody and counter-melody are constantly visible simultaneously, where multiplicity is constantly accompanied by unity, jesting by seriousness. For life consists solely in this for me, in the fluctuation between two poles, in the movements to and fro between the two basic pillars of the world[21]." Now, this is not exactly an esthetics that lends itself to being measured easily. It is no wonder that "the old competition between esthetics and ethics"[22] in *The Glass Bead Game* is carried on repeatedly, that it even functions as the "dynamic phenomenon" of the glass bead game itself. Joseph Knecht, experiencing a crisis in relation to the game and searching for its "meaning," writes to the Music Master; and the latter, evidently troubled, responds in detail: "Whatever you become, teacher, scholar, or musician, have respect for the meaning', but do not imagine that it can be taught ... If I were introducing pupils to Homer or Greek tragedy, say, I would also not try to tell them that the poetry is one of the manifestations of the divine, but would endeavor to make the poetry accessible to them by imparting a precise knowledge of its linguistic and metrical strategies. The task of the teacher and scholar is to study means, cultivate tradition, and preserve the purity of methods, not to deal in incommunicable experiences which are reserved to the elect—who often enough pay a high price for this privilege[23]." And a final example: when the mature Joseph Knecht is asked by Designori what he now intends to do, he replies he would like to write although, he adds, the subject matter would be of little importance to him: "The tone would be what mattered to me, a proper mean between the solemn and the intimate, earnestness and jest, a tone not of instruction, but of friendly communication and discourse on various things I think I have learned[24]." Again, this is not particulary easy to measure.

I should like to take the liberty of introducing here—in view of this contradiction or even dilemma—a consideration that may seem a bit bold given my insufficient knowledge of German studies. I ask myself the question: Can an esthetics consist of the attempt to avoid esthetics? Can an esthetics be an art of portrayal that is intended to give the impression of an absence of art, simply a portrayal of problems and uncertaintenties, of moral dilemmas? Hesse regarded his works as psychological biographies, as attempts to express psychological experiences in the garment of visible events. Could it then be that Hesse himself believed his esthetic achievement lay in portraying his problems and uncertaintenties, his reality, his truth, with an absence of art and esthetics? If this was indeed the case, it would represent a supreme triumph of the poetic art. T.S. Eliot's thoroughly ironic statement in his *Four Quartets* that "The poetry does not matter" occurs to us in this connection.

I hope I have now answered the question I raised at the outset of my remarks. The moral attitude of an author is *one* thing—it is the personal and subjective affair of every human being—but it takes on objective, social, and suprapersonal significance as a result of a kind of transformation, thanks to an esthetic achievement, even if this should consist in banishing esthetics in favor of ethics. In such a case, a "confession"—something that only one particular individual is capable of, and, if he is fortunate enough to have far-reaching influence, something that then concerns everyone. The subjective and objective aspects of the work of art I have just described here are actually two inseparable sides of *one* phenomenon.

I have often spoken of the fortunate case of Hesse's wide influence and have given four reasons for it: 1) Hesse's origins, which from the very outset assured him of a broad international horizon encompassing both Western and far-Eastern elements; 2) his language—simple, definitely traditional, not innovative, and comprehensible to the common reader; 3) his revolt against every type of repression, a revolt against out-dated, empty authority, against automatism, against norms and mediocrity, against mindless consumption, greed, and profits, against middle-class values and the middle-class state, against church and school and above all and repeatedly, a son's revolt against the father and his pedagogical methods. 4) I have pointed out that Hesse never restricted himself merely to analysis, to protest, or to refusal. In all his books, from the very beginning to the very end of his career—from *Peter Camenzind* up to the last prose he wrote—he depicts the process of individuation with an intensity and consistency displayed in no other literary body of work in this century. He searches for the answer to the question, "How do I become myself?"

All of this refutes, in my opinion, contemporary critics who attempt to dismiss Hesse's work as lovely fictional illusion, as literature dealing with private problems, who see him as the author of a "science fiction of inwardness" and regard his path to the interior as escape and evasion, as a flight to an ersatz world. Hesse's journey to the interior is vision *and* knowledge, it is comprehending *and* dreaming, it is reason *and* magic. In one of his last letters, written in February 1961, he said, "Where reason and magic become one ... there, perhaps, lies the secret of art[25]." By having a dream that goes beyond the world of present consciousness, as he has in *The Glass Bead Game*, Hesse is not creating ersatz worlds; rather he is perfecting reality in a utopia, and we know today from the study of Marxist theoreticians such as Ernst Bloch that reality without utopia is deformed reality.

From its inception in 1930, the writing of *The Glass Bead Game* was—and this we know only since we have been able to examine the author's posthumous papers—inseparably linked with the course of political developments in the Germany of those times. Perhaps one day we shall learn to see the great counter-vision to the barbarism and crimes of the Third Reich reflected in this book, containing as it does a keen analysis of its times, along with such classical utopian elements as the return to nature, and the concepts of eternal peace and a classless society. Hesse's Latin epigraph to the work, with its description of "non-existent things" and the "possibility of their being born," embodies the Ernst Bloch-like idea of "not yet".

Hesse does not flee from reality. He goes beyond it—thinking, dreaming, creating. He transcends reality. Transcending, a significant term used by Brecht in his later works, was likewise one of the aging Joseph Knecht's favorite words. Transcending also means going beyond boundaries, going beyond to open, indeterminate horizons. Such boundaries are crossed by Herman Lauscher, Peter Camenzind, Knulp, Emil Sinclair, Siddhartha, Klingsor, Klein, Harry Haller, and Joseph Knecht—all of them outsiders, saints, martyrs, heretics, and rebels. They criticize what exists. They offer no solutions but provide biographical models, designs for living, imaginative projections of the possible. This may have been what attracted Franz Kafka to Hesse, for Max Brod reports that Kafka read Hesse "with enthusiasm".

For the very reason that there are no solutions and no prescriptions in Hesse's work but merely descriptions of processes, the problems he depicts are relevant for our day and give his books their lasting impact. We may even ask ourselves whether it is not the unresolved nature of his problems and the open attitude he brings to them, the inevitable relevance for the individual of the questions he raises, that are responsible for the stature of his work. It is because he admits of no fixed values, recognizes no binding dogmas, because his characters are prepared for play, for Steppenwolf's "Magic Theater," for fantasy, for departures to ever new areas of existence, for ever new searching, for ever new goals, that portions of his work remain so vital and relevant for us today. Joseph Knecht's lines "Wir sollen heiter Raum um Raum durchschreiten, / An keinem wie an einer Heimat hängen ..." ("Serenely let us move to distant places / And let no sentiments of home detain us") could serve as a motto for our present-day society, which also finds itself in the position of making a new start, of searching for new paths. No one knows what the proper prescription is, but we see the symptoms and realize that the ailment must not continue. In the last two decades, popular belief in the power of collectivity has suffered a serious setback. This power preached the joyful gospel of the sovereignty of external forces; according to this view, the individual is to be understood merely as an extreme expression of a highly complex society. The individual became a passive object, an innocent victim of society, which is regarded as the sole active agent. The tendency toward determinism inherent in every form of social science has definitely gained the upper hand in our day, with the result that the individual has been forced to interpret all of his difficulties as caused by external forces. What was abolished here was the individual's will. The old maxim of Propertius, "In magnis et voluisse sat est" ("In great matters it is enough to have willed"), lost its validity, for collective enterprise abolished freedom in the name of emancipation.

Or look at the current communication glut produced by the media. Information that is supposed to orient us creates disorientation through its overabundance. To be sure, as the Chinese proverb points out, knowledge that doesn't increase must decrease. But in our case—according to the American social scientist Derek J. de Solla Price—when eighty to ninety percent of all scientists who have ever lived are alive today and when literature on the subject of the proliferation of literature has itself become a crucial problem, we find ourselves faced with the situation feared by Goethe. "Knowledge is no longer of any service in the rapid revolution of the world: by the time one has taken note of everything, one has lost oneself[26]."

It is this *Self* that we must not lose. And for this reason we need the power of the individual today more than ever, of the individual who makes his Self strong and then makes this Self responsive to the needs of others. In performing this task, so central for our times, the individual will find strength and support by reading the works of Hermann Hesse, all the more so because Hesse refuses to offer solutions and prescriptions. The characters Hesse describes invite the reader to identify with them; as a result, the inner world of this author can be seen as our outer world, insofar as his inner problems are also our common concerns.

Let us return once again to Walter Benjamin. In the Suhrkamp edition of his writings, Benjamin's encyclopedia article on Goethe follows directly upon his address, "The Author as Producer," which I quoted at the beginning. Writing to Gershom Scholem, he describes the "curious assignment" he received in 1926: "The great Russian encyclopedia would like to hear something from me about Goethe from the standpoint of Marxist doctrine. I couldn't resist the divine presumption of accepting such an assignment, and I plan to concoct the pertinent facts." What did Benjamin "concoct" in connection with *The Sorrows of Young Werther?* He came to this remarkable conclusion: "The book was perhaps the greatest literary success of all time. Here Goethe gave the perfect example of authorship of genius. For if the great author is one who, from the outset, makes his inner world into a matter of common concern, makes the questions of his time all into questions of his *personal* experience and thought, then Goethe in his early works represents this type of great author in unmatched perfection[27]." I am not trying to compare the influence of *Werther* with that of *Steppenwolf* nor to judge the comparative literary stature of the two works, yet it seems quite clear to me that Hesse too makes "the questions of his time all into questions of personal experience and thought".

In the quotation by Walter Benjamin as well as in my application of it to Hesse, I would stress that the word "make" ought to be understood as a poetic act. For Werther's fate would have remained merely that of one "unfortunate" human being had it not been Goethe who described it, producing with his novel a flood of suicides, yet at the same time transforming, through his art, his hero's death into a source of abundant new life. To be sure, the "questions of the time" referred to by Benjamin have changed, and we may not find the contemporary ones at all pleasing, but authors cannot be held responsible for this. Here again, however, I wish to emphasize the centrality of the act of creation, for this is what authors are ultimately responsible for. (We recall that the word "poet" is derived from the Greek verb "poiein"—to "make" or "create"). In this connection, consider a brief exchange in Beckett's *Endgame* where a customer asks a tailor to make him a pair of trousers. When after three months they are still not finished, he lodges a complaint:

"Customer's voice: God damn you to hell, Sir, no—it's indecent, there are limits! In six days, do you hear me, six days, God made the world. Yes Sir, no less Sir, the *world*! And you are not bloody well capable of making me a pair of trousers in three months!—Tailor's voice, scandalized: But my dear Sir, my dear Sir, look—disdainful gesture, disgustedly—at the world— Pause—and look—loving gesture, proudly—at *my trousers!*[28]"

## NOTES

1. "Hessen-Droge," *Frankfurter Allgemeine Zeitung für Deutschland* (August 11, 1982).

2. Wolfgang Freese, "Hermann Hesses Wiederkehr—Rezeption, Wertung und politische Dimensionen," *Acta Germanica: Jahrbuch des südafrikanischen Germanistenverbandes*, vol. 14 (1981), p. 111 ff.

3. Rudolf Koester, *Hermann Hesse* (Stuttgart: Metzler, 1975, Sammlung Metzler, vol. 136), p. 75.

4. Walter Benjamin, "Der Autor als Produzent: Ansprache im Institut zum Studium des Faschismus in Paris am 27. April 1934," *Gesammelte Schriften* unter Mitwirkung von Theodor W. Adorno und Gershom Scholem, 3 vols., ed. Rolf Thiedemann and Hermann Schweppenhäuser, vol. II, 2 (Frankfurt/M:Suhrkamp, 1977), p. 689, 696.

5. Egon Schwarz, "Hermann Hesse und die Zukunft," *Text und Kritik: Zeitschrift für Literatur*, ed. Heinz Ludwig Arnold, Heft 10/11 "Hermann Hesse" (May, 1977), p. 25.

6. Hermann Hesse, *Gesammelte Briefe*, 3 vols., ed. Ursula and Volker Michels, vol. 3 "1936–1948" (Frankfurt/M.: Suhrkamp, 1982), p. 201.

7. Hesse, *Briefe* 3, p. 203.

8. Hesse, *Briefe* 3, p. 453.

9. Hesse, *Briefe* 3, p. 199.

10. Hermann Hesse, *Gesammelte Briefe*, 3 vols., ed. Ursula und Volker Michels, vol. 2 "1922–1935" (Frankfurt/M.: Suhrkamp, 1979), p. 189.

11. Hesse, *Briefe* 2, p. 154f.

12. Unpublished letter to unknown addressee, dated 1951, Suhrkamp Verlag edition archives.

13. Hans Mayer, "Hermann Hesses 'Steppenwolf'," in *Materialien zu Hermann Hesses 'Der Steppenwolf'*, ed. Volker Michels (Frankfurt/M.: Suhrkamp, 1972), p. 330f.

14. R. Koskimies, "Theorie des Romans," *Annales Academiae Scientiarium Fennicae* (Helsinki, 1936).

15. Hermann Hesse, Review (unpublished), *in Hermann Hesse: Lektüre für Minuten: Gedanken aus seinen Büchern und Briefen*, selected and with afterword by Volker Michels (Frankfurt/M.: Suhrkamp, 1971), p. 220.

16. Hermann Hesse, *Steppenwolf*, tr. Basil Creighton and updated by Joseph Mileck (New York: Bantam Books, 1971), p. 33f.

17. Siegfried Unseld, *Hermann Hesses Anschauung vom Beruf des Dichters*, Inaugural Doctoral Dissertation, typed manuscript (Universität Ulm, 1951), p. 126.

18. Theodore Ziolkowski, "Hermann Hesses 'Steppenwolf': Eine Sonate in Prosa," tr. Ursula Michels-Wenz, *Materialien*, p. 353 ff.

19. Ralph Freedman, *Hermann Hesse: Autor der Krisis*, tr. Ursula Michels-Wenz (Frankfurt/M.: Suhrkamp, 1982). *Cf.*, the chapter "Die symbolische Stadt: Hölle des eigenen Selbst," p. 358 ff.

20. Hermann Hesse, "Geheimnisse," *Gesammelte Werke*, 12 vols. (Frankfurt/M.: Suhrkamp, 1970), vol. 10, p. 276.

21. Hermann Hesse, *Kurgast, Werke*, vol. 7, p. 111 f.

22. Hermann Hesse, *The Glass Bead Game*, tr. Richard and Clara Winston (New York: Holt, Rinchart and Winston, 1969), p. 136.

23. Hesse, *The Glass Bead Game*, p. 122.

24. Hesse, *The Glass Bead Game*, p. 415.

25. Hermann Hesse, *Ausgewählte Briefe* (Frankfurt/M.: Suhrkamp, 1964), p.531. Letter to Dr Joachim von Hecker, dated February 14, 1961.

26. Goethe, *Wilhelm Meisters Wanderjahre, Hamburger Ausgabe*, 10th ed. (München: Deutscher Taschenbuch Verlag, 1981), p. 438.

27. Walter Benjamin, "Goethe" (encyclopedia article), *Gesammelte Schriften* II, 2, p. 709.

28. Samuel Beckett, *Endgame, Dramatische Dichtungen in drei Sprachen*, tr. Elmar Tophoven and Samuel Beckett (Frankfurt/M.: Suhrkamp, 1963), English p. 467.

EUGENE L. STELZIG

# Ticino Legends of Saints and Sinners

I too must constantly struggle, now with the murderer, now with
the animal within me, but equally with the moralist and the wish
to attain harmony all too soon, with easy resignation, with the
escape into sheer kindness, noble-mindedness and purity. Both
have to be; without the animal and murderer in us we are
castrated angels without a proper life; and without the forever
new and supplicatory urge for purification, cleansing, and the
worship of the spiritual and the selfless we don't amount to much
either.

—Hesse letter of ca. autumn 1919

W hen in April 1919 Hesse put Bern and his marriage behind him to
settle in the southernmost, Italian-speaking canton of Switzerland, the
Ticino, he was belatedly acting out Veraguth's resolve at the end of *Rosshalde*
to begin a new life. It had taken the double impact of personal and cultural
crisis for Hesse to make a break with his past and to set out for new regions,
psychic and geographic. The movement south, as he describes it in the
opening piece of *Wandering* (1920, a collection of lyrical prose, poetry, and
drawings that reflects his eager embrace of his new surroundings), is the
crossing of a boundary that entails a harsh judgment of his past:

From *Hermann Hesse's Fictions of the Self: Autobiography and the Confessional Imagination.* © 1988
by Princeton University Press.

> I wanted to be something that I was not. I even wanted to be a
> poet and a middle-class person at the same time. I wanted to be
> an artist and a man of fantasy, but I also wanted to be a good man,
> a man at home. It all went on for a long time, till I knew that a
> man cannot be both and have both ... I increased the world's guilt
> and anguish, by doing violence to myself, by not daring to walk
> toward my own salvation.[1]

In the very productive decade that followed, Hesse's fiction was to be a
daring experiment in modern autobiography, a further sounding of "the way
within" initiated in *Demian* two years earlier. Like Klein's, Hesse's flight to
the south was exhilarating yet guilty, a definitive yet painful liberation from
his middle-class existence as a man and a writer. Freedom also brought
uncertainties: choosing where to live—the village of Montagnola, near
Lugano, Hesse's safe harbor for the remainder of his life—was easier than the
problem of how to make a living. His financial position was to remain
precarious for years, as most of his disposable income went toward the
support of his family, and as the earnings from his writings dwindled next to
nothing due to the rising German inflation.

Though Hesse's new-found poverty sorted well with the monastic and
reclusive self-image he cultivated during the early Montagnola years, it also
forced him onto the reading and lecture circuit, and even to the expedient of
selling handwritten and illustrated copies of selected stories and poems. And
even so, without the generous support of friends and patrons, he might not
have been able to keep afloat financially. These external constraints were
troubling, yet about the central issue of his new life Hesse felt no hesitancy.
His unwavering objective henceforth was the ideal of self-realization, even if
for the remainder of his career his particular pursuit of "salvation" was
marked by the conflict between his religious and his literary impulses.
Hesse's inward journey in the wake of *Demian* still carries the imprint of
psychoanalysis, but his style of thinking and writing moves progressively
away from the portentous chiaroscuro of that prophetic book. In his Ticino
legends he cultivated the image of the wanderer yet learned to be at home
with himself. As he wrote to his sister Adele a few months after settling there,
"in any event I have managed despite all worries ... to live intensively again
in my own way."[2] Intensive living translated into intensive writing, in a burst
of confession that had indeed begun well before his move from Bern, but that
peaked during the summer to make "the year 1919," as he noted in "Journal
1920–1921," the fullest, busiest, most prolific and blazing of [his] life."[3] The
mid-career break with his past released a flood of pent-up energies, and

initiated a new commitment to self-writing as the necessary center of his life. The amazing resurgence of Hesse's vitality during that memorable summer took other forms as well, however, as any reader of *Klein and Wagner* and *Klingsor's Last Summer* can readily guess: "I had hardly arrived in the Ticino when I began 'Klein and Wagner,' and hardly had I finished that when I wrote Klingsor, and besides that I covered day after day hundreds of sketch sheets; painted, and had active contact with many people; had two love affairs, sat for many nights in a grotto with wine—my candle burned at the same time at all ends."[4] One of his new creative activities, landscape painting, was both play and therapy. Freed from the pressures of "art" and of having to live up to a reputation, Hesse found through his charming post-impressionist aquarelles a means of expressing the light and childish side of his personality. A self-proclaimed amateur, he was able to jest about his avocation: "painting is marvelous; it makes one happier and more patient. Afterward one does not have black fingers as with writing, but red and blue ones."[5]

During his first year in Montagnola he was buoyed up by the knowledge that both his life and his work had undergone a "new beginning and upheaval." As he wrote in January 1920, the experience of psychoanalysis and the events of the time had completely altered his outlook and idiom. One consequence of this revolution—which he fears "will not delight his friends"—is that he "has worked ferociously this entire year nearly without a break."[6] Such is the literary consequence of an altered self-perception and an identity that, as he described it in "Self-Communion," was being "crystallized" anew. This brief but revealing essay (written in 1918 or 1919) evaluates the traumas of his recent past as conducive to renewal and rejuvenation, and concludes with the significant psychoanalytic comparison of his self to a lake, "whose deepest layers lay closed off, which led to suffering and the approach of death. But now what is above and below is busily intermingling, perhaps still imperfectly, perhaps still not actively enough—but in any event, it is flowing."[7] Water, which here on the threshold of his move to the Ticino is the image of psychic wholeness and the integration of conscious and unconscious, becomes in *Klein and Wagner* and *Siddhartha* the signifier of ontological plenitude and cosmic unity.

Psychoanalysis had broken up the stagnation by restoring the flow between the surface and the depths of Hesse's self; it had also made him take note of the myriad layers, currents, and shadings of light and dark of his inner world. To be sure, self-realization was more the goal than the product of his first Montagnola years,[8] and after the creative high of 1919 Hesse was to suffer repeated impasses, beginning with the prolonged depression of

1920, from which he sought relief through further psychoanalysis as well as
an immersion in Eastern philosophy and religion. The release of energy
Hesse experienced with his move to Montagnola, however, is that of a writer
busily confronting his inner self who is continually amazed at what he
discovers, and who now consciously owns up to the fact that his writing
(*Dichtung*) is confession (*Bekenntnis*).[9] As we saw in the last chapter, with
*Demian* Hesse tried to come to terms with the over-whelming impact of new
materials that had become available to him through psychoanalysis, and did
so through an attempted synthesis of the "light" and "dark" elements of his
psyche under the magical umbrella of the Abraxas symbol. In his subsequent
fictional self-probings during the following decade, the obscure symbolism
of *Demian* yields to a more immediate and tangible psychography that seeks
to document the plenitude of the self through confessional personas in whose
consciousness the polarities adumbrated in the personal myth of *Demian* are
more convincingly and cogently projected. Despite startling differences of
style, character, and setting, the leading self-reflectors of Hesse's early
post–World War I fictions reveal more of his inner life and problems than
anything he had written hitherto. In his powerful yet highly stylized Ticino
legends of saints and sinners, the extremes of grace and guilt, enlightenment
and despair, purity and corruption, *Angst* and bliss, dwell side-by-side in the
same character.

## The Psychomachia of *Klein and Wagner*

Hesse critics tend to agree that this novella that he wrote rapidly in the early
part of his first Ticino summer is a brutally frank confession.[10] A *tour de force*
of Hesse's new style, *Klein and Wagner*-resists "neat" interpretation because
of its juggling of heterogeneous elements—psychoanalytic, religious,
philosophical—that coexisted uneasily in its author's imagination.[11] The
surface parallels between Hesse and Klein are transparent, especially the
guilty flight from family and middle-class respectability into the freedom of
an unsettled and precarious existence. Even the differences between author
and protagonist only serve to underscore the transposition of life into art: the
crime of Klein (the bank employee who absconds with funds entrusted to
him) correlates with Hesse's sense of guilt at breaking with bourgeois
conventions in order to follow his inner urges—and the same is true of his
sexual relationship with the demimondaine Teresina who, like Hermine in
*Steppenwolf*, lives off middle-class society, yet has not lost the gift of
passionate living and giving. The deeper convergence between Hesse and his

character (in a tale that is, appropriately enough, full of mirror images) reveals that Hesse's new commitment to art as confession (*Kunst als Bekenntnis*) did indeed entail an unflinching examination of the psychopathology of his unpedestrian life.

From Klein's first glimpse of his "distorted face" ("a stranger's, a sad crazy mask")[12] in the train window, the story is a devastating résumé of Klein-Hesse's stifled individuality in marriage, and of a deep-seated resentment against his wife. Hesse's striking use of dreams here is almost too patly psychoanalytic as a revelation of suppressed impulses—for example, Klein's dream of taking charge of a car in which he is being driven, by wresting the steering wheel from the driver: "it was better to drive yourself even if it meant peril than always to be driven and directed by others" (50). The clue that the unknown driver was actually his wife is followed by Klein's admitting to himself his festering animus against her, which is in fact what led to his sudden flight. Klein's marital retrospect is Hesse's bitter recollection of his years in Gaienhofen and Bern: "He looked back ...upon his whole marriage, and the distance traversed seemed to him a weary, dreary road on which a man toils alone through the dust bearing heavy burdens on his back" (51). His "long-forgotten yearning for the south" (52) may have its sources in German literature from Goethe to Thomas Mann, but it is also the married Hesse's nostalgia for the happy foot-journeys of his bachelor days through northern Italy and of his "never clearly formulated craving for escape and liberty from the serfdom and dust of his marriage" (52). Conversely, the mirror image of "the sad and anxious face of Klein the criminal" is a reflection of Hesse's guilt at having taken this "leap into space," as is the telling exclamation, "if his father had lived to see this!" (57).

Klein's flight is a more desperate and less successful version of Hesse's attempt at self-realization and a progressive purging of the bourgeois assumptions that had governed his married life. In order to understand himself, Klein has to face up to his repressed self and "evil shadow" (65) represented by the double reference of the name *Wagner*, who is both the schoolteacher Klein had read about in the papers "who had butchered his entire family in a horribly bloody way and then taken his own life" (and whose act Klein had self-righteously condemned just when "the obsessional idea of killing his family had first gripped him," 59) *and* the famous composer whose music he had loved in his youth but condemned as a husband and father "because youth and artistic enthusiasm and Wagner reminded him painfully of things he had lost, because he had let himself be married by a woman he did not love" (64). It is only when, in a revealing nightmare that anticipates *Steppenwolf*'s Magic Theater in its projection of unconscious impulses as dramatis personae, Klein enters "the theater called 'Wagner'" and recognizes it as "his own interior being," that he fathoms the full relevance of the name: "Wagner was himself—Wagner was the murderer and the hunted man within him, but Wagner was also the composer, the artist, the genius, the seducer, lover of life and of the senses, luxury—Wagner was the collective name for everything repressed, buried, scanted in the life of Friedrich Klein, the civil servant" (116).

This traumatic yet therapeutic dream is the psychoanalytic centerpiece of a psychomachia in which the divided self of Klein ("one visible, and one secret," 56) achieves a larger self-awareness. The wordplay of Hesse's conjunctive title (Klein = little, Wagner = *wagen* = to dare) appropriately signals the two sides of the protagonist's split personality. Yet Klein's dramatic mid-life change does not ultimately lead, like Hesse's own, to a viable identity and a productive life that integrates the two halves. His is a manic-depressive roller-coaster ride between the extremes of self-affirmation and despair that ends in the conventional Hessean escape, suicide. Unable to deal with his guilt and to sustain his positive moods, he fails to achieve that happiness which in a journal of 1918 Hesse defined as the ability to love, and whose precondition is self-love and acceptance.[13] Klein's peak experiences are those of a fleeting self-harmony when he can hear a "voice" which is that of "God" or of "his truest, innermost self" (76). It is this authentic self that leads him to the dancer Teresina, and to recognize in her, despite all the differences between them, the mirror image of genuine selfhood expressed through her art: "there is a resemblance between us; both of us here and now, at rare moments, do what is in us. Nothing is rarer" (94). If Klein's goal is authentic being, its negation and his particular demon is dread or *Angst*, a word Hesse invokes repeatedly for Klein's failure and despair and that may well include a conscious reference back to Kierkegaard, with whose writings Hesse had some familiarity, as manifest in a description (written in the same year as *Klein and Wagner*) that also fits his confessional persona: "how vain he is, how nervous, how suspicious, how full of *Angst* is this Kierkegaard, who said of himself that he is 'as caught up in his own reflection as a reflexive pronoun.'"[14] The *Angst* that preys on Klein is, like Kierkegaard's "dread," not a specific or identifiable fear of something, but a generalized and objectless anxiety. And like that of the founding father of existentialism, Hesse's characterization of *Angst* has a religious context that, though very different from Kierkegaard's version of Christianity, emerges as a major element at the conclusion of his novella. If the Kierkegaardian resonance of Klein's *Angst* suggests that Hesse's reading of the Danish theologian may have carried over into his characterization of Klein, his presentation of the extremes of suicidal "disgust, worry, and surfeit with life" (74) and its abrupt conversion into a resounding hymn of life at the conclusion carries the autobiographical seal of Hesse's experience.

That conclusion, which with its mystical aura is on the spiritual horizon of *Siddhartha*, is certainly not without its problems. The ecstatic finale of Klein's drowning has all the trappings of a religious revelation, for the despairing Klein becomes in death a visionary. Suicide as an apotheosis is a new turn in Hesse's fiction, and one with which he manages up to a point to make his attempted merger of not-so-commensurable elements work through an experimental and highly lyrical prose that resists analysis and disarms judgment. The epiphanic mode that marks the conclusion is already introduced earlier in the narrative (in the extended sequence in section three after Klein has met Teresina), when Hesse projects a Romantic-pantheist awareness of the immanence of the divine in ordinary reality that is quite similar to the ecstatic "sentiment of being" that Wordsworth celebrates in *The Prelude* (Book 2, 1. 420, 1805 text). And Klein's realization "that life becomes meaningful precisely when we lose our grasp of all meanings" is a later, proto-existentialist version of Wordsworth's "wise passiveness" ("Expostulation and Reply"). Through parataxis of style and the rapid accumulation of impressions, Hesse struggles to get around the dilemma that "there were no words for this state," whose best indicator would not be language, but music:

> The wave passed through him like pain and like voluptuous delight. He trembled with sheer emotion. Life roared in him like surf. Everything was incomprehensible. He opened his eyes wide and saw: trees on a street, slivers of silver in the lake, a running dog, bicyclists—and everything was strange, like a fairy tale, and almost too beautiful. Everything looked as if it had come brand-new out of God's toy box. Everything existed for him alone, for Friedrich Klein, and he himself existed solely to feel this stream of wonder and pain and joy pouring through himself. There was beauty everywhere, in every rubbish heap by the wayside; there was deep suffering everywhere; God was everything. (99–100)

With this charged prose Hesse celebrates a sense of the fullness of being synonymous with the "grace" that has been taught "by all the sages of the entire world, Buddha and Schopenhauer, Jesus, the Greeks. There was only one wisdom, only one faith, only one philosophy: the knowledge that God is within us" (87). Yet the strongest support of Hesse's secularized and existential version of Klein's "revelation" is still the New Testament: "'Unless you become as little children ...' occurred to him, and he felt: I have become a child again, I have entered into the Kingdom of Heaven" (103). Hesse's celebration includes art, which "was nothing but regarding the world in a state of grace: illumination" (103). He is so bent on affirming a higher unity that he disregards the basic differences between the religious and philosophic traditions invoked in the canonical catalogue above, just as the novella as a whole seeks to overleap the tension of incommensurable ingredients with its passionate reaching after revelation—and it is perhaps this unreconstructed yearning for revelation that is *Klein and Wagner*'s most poignant and revealing autobiographical statement.

The dying Klein's epiphany certainly supports Hesse's later admission (in a letter of December 1930 to his sister), "despite all my rebelling, I have nevertheless remained the missionary's son."[15] Klein's suicide as a "dropping into the maternal womb, into the arm of God" (138) combines in a characteristic Hessean fashion aspects of the mother and father worlds. The element of surprise is the drowning Klein's realization, as he lets himself sink into the lake, that instead of letting himself fall into death, "he could just as well have let himself fall into life" (138). His belated illumination—"wonderful thought: a life without dread!" (119)—is a complete acceptance of being *as* being: "Let yourself fall! Do not fight back! Die gladly! Live gladly!" (119). The poetic notion of letting oneself "fall" may be tinged with the Schopenhauerian renunciation of the Will (it is relevant that Klein had taken with him on his flight "a small volume of Schopenhauer," 76) and with Oriental mysticism (which influenced Schopenhauer's philosophy): "All life was a breath exhaled by God. All dying was a breath inhaled by God. One who had learned not to resist, to let himself fall, died easily, was born easily. One who resisted, who suffered dread, died hard, was born reluctantly" (118). Yet despite Hesse's interest in Eastern philosophy, his notion of "falling" is not really synonymous with the Buddhist goal of Nirvana, which in the "Journal 1920–1921" he defined as "the redeeming step behind the *principium individuationis*, or, religiously expressed, the return of the individual to the world soul, to God." He finds this goal questionable because "if God casts me out into the world to exist as an individual, is it then my duty to return to the whole as quickly and as easily as possible—or should I not, on the contrary, fulfil God's will precisely by letting myself be borne along (in 'Klein and Wagner' I called it 'letting oneself fall'), so that I expiate with him his desire to forever split himself and live out his life through individual beings?"[16] In the light of this passage, Klein's insight seems closer to modern Western, existentialist modes of thought—for instance, to Heidegger's concept (in *Being and Time*) of *Geworfenheit* (Thrownness).

Klein's final vision of life as a "universal stream of forms" (143) is an earlier version of the ubiquitous river symbol of *Siddhartha*. The metaphysical claim, developed in major key in the novel, that time is an illusion, is also briefly introduced in the novella, as is the idea of music, here the signifier of a cosmic order beyond the reach of language. Hesse's trope of a "dome of music, a cathedral of sound" in whose "midst sat God" (143) is meant to suggest the center toward which Klein is sinking, having been transformed even at the moment of his singing death into "a prophet and proclaimer" (144). For the writer whose actual life fell far short of such achieved concord, this cathedral of sound below the waves is the oddly mixed metaphor of psychic and ontological wholeness. Like Siddhartha's smiling apotheosis, Klein's "falling" death is the idealized self-projection of the Hesse who in the "Journal of 1920–1921" confesses that his "strongest and most tempting exemplary model" is that of the saint.[17]

Yet the sinner in Hesse is also acknowledged in *Klein and Wagner*'s confessional psychomachia, and perhaps nowhere more devastatingly than in the glimpse of Klein's troubled relationship with his wife. His long-festering resentment takes, in the "Wagner" nightmare, the grotesque form of phallic violence:

> He was seized by an overwhelming repugnance for this woman [who is both his wife and an innkeeper's wife with whom he has just had intercourse] and drove a knife into her abdomen. But another woman, like a mirror image of the first, attacked him from behind, drove sharp, powerful claws into his throat and tried to strangle him. (115)

With this stark glimpse of Klein's unconscious, Hesse generalizes the deadlocked relationship between two partners into a psychoanalytic vision of the battle of the sexes. The sexual violence that will crop up again in Harry Haller's stabbing of Hermine also has its counterpart in the last part of *Klein and Wagner*, when Klein resists his irrational impulse to stab the sleeping Teresina and opts instead for killing himself. If these fictional scenarios point up a real pathology, the moralist in Hesse, supported by the perspectives of his psychoanalysis, answers, "the less we shy away from those fantasies which make us into animals and criminals in our waking and our dreaming, the less is the danger that we will in reality and in deed succumb to these evils."[18]

To end this analysis on a somewhat different note, let me point out that *Klein and Wagner* also includes a more prosaic résumé of Hesse's married life: "He ... realized, with sorrow, that he himself had remained a boy and a beginner in love, had become resigned in the course of a long, lukewarm marriage, was timid and yet without innocence, lustful yet full of guilt" (109). Hesse will make up for these inhibitions and repressions in his subsequent writings, which will reflect in heightened form his bold new style of living: Siddhartha, Harry Haller, and Goldmund all become happy adepts in the school of eros and succeed in varying degrees in conquering despair and discovering some meaning in their lives without having, like Klein, to kill themselves in order to do so.

## KLINGSOR'S SELF-PORTRAIT IN AN EXPRESSIONIST MIRROR

Like *Klein and Wagner*, this novella which was written toward the end of Hesse's first summer in Montagnola is a confessional virtuoso performance. It is his highly-stylized self-rendering in a poetic prose redolent of Expressionism, a movement that according to Freedman, Hesse had earlier ignored but was more receptive to when "in the postwar ferment it had become positively fashionable." Hesse rejected, as Field notes, "the extreme demands of Expressionists to throw out the old,"[19] yet the style of *Klingsor* shows the postwar Hesse's willingness to be innovative short of joining the *avant garde*, particularly since some of his assumptions in 1919 sorted well with those of the German Expressionists, including the animus against bourgeois society, the focus on the artist's creative powers, and on a use of words "as charged reservoirs of energy" in order "to bring forth the hidden metaphorical dimension of the poet's subjective vision."[20] From the vantage of the late twentieth century, Hesse's self-portrait in an Expressionist mirror may strike us as impossibly melodramatic:

> The little palette full of pure unmixed colors, intensely luminous, was his comfort, his tower, his arsenal, his prayer book, his cannon. From it he fired upon wicked death. Purple was denial of death, vermilion was mockery of decay. His arsenal was good; his brave troop stood lined up brilliantly, the rapid rounds from his cannon flashed.[21]

To appreciate *Klingsor*'s autobiographical bravura one has to see how the metaphoric leaps of Hesse's startling prose are in fact modulated and controlled by a masterly touch. That he chose the form of the novella for this piece is fitting because it is above all a mood piece, a short but intense lyrical flight, "a pretty rocket."[22]

The Preface asserts that the work of Klingsor, who died at the age of forty-two (Hesse's age at the time of writing) will live on, as will "the legend of his life" (148); conversely, Klingsor's last is Hesse's first Ticino summer turned into a demonic prose poem of the artist that incorporates the polarities of sinner and saint under the aegis of Dionysian intoxication: Klingsor burns the candle at both ends in a desperate surge of living and working. Because these antinomies are momentarily merged in a single persona, there is for once no need for Hesse's characteristic confessional self-splitting. (This is not to deny that there is an obvious self-reference in a very secondary character, Hermann the Poet, who is in any case hardly more than a name.) Hesse also plays some intriguing biographical games, in the manner of the *roman à clef* (something that will peak in *The Journey to the East* a decade later) with the names of places and people dear to him that summer, including Louis the Cruel (the painter Louis Moilliet), the Armenian astrologer (his friend Josef Englert, who cast his horoscope), and the Queen of the Mountain (the young Ruth Wenger, who several years later became his second wife).

The fire imagery so prominent in the opening pages is well-chosen as the governing metaphor of Klingsor's climactic season, an orgiastic triad of the pleasures of wine, sex, and painting. Klingsor's rhapsodic and Nietzschean hunger for life has replaced the Schopenhauerian resignation and pessimism so pronounced in Hesse's earlier art novels: this painter's headlong experiment in intense living is not only fueled by his mid-life desire to make up for lost time, but by the omnipresent fear of death, the psychic equivalent, in this explosive tale, of Klein's *Angst*. The ecstatic sense of cosmic simultaneity that Klein achieves in death Klingsor wants to capture through a late summer binge in which Romantic intensity is translated into a searing metaphysical hunger for the fullness of being: "Why did time exist? Why always this idiotic succession of one thing after another, and not a roaring, surfeiting simultaneity?" (182). Klingsor's hunger expresses itself in an art that is open to "everything that is changing, filled with longing" (182). Fatefully conscious even in his flights of intoxication, this artist knows that his craving (of which eros is in a sense only the immediate instrumentality) brings him that much closer to the inevitability of a death invoked in the grotesqueries of one of the lyrics that intersperse the narrative:

Drunk, I sit at night in the windy wood,
Autumn has gnawed at the singing branches;
The grumbling innkeeper runs to the wine cellar
To fill my empty bottle.

Tomorrow, tomorrow pale death will slice
My red flesh with his humming scythe.
For a long time now that furious fiend
Has lain in wait for me.[23]

With the extremes of *Klingsor's* style, Hesse succeeds in projecting a modern, revitalized Romanticism, something he will do even more effectively in the middle of the next decade in *Steppenwolf.* Indeed, much in this tale—like its name, which is a version of the poet Klingsohr in *Heinrich von Ofterdingen*—harks back to Romanticism, including the mixing of genres and the fragmentary structure, at the same time as it shows the impact of modernism. Thus the Romantic stress on the importance of art and artists is counterbalanced by a nihilistic sense of the futility of art in the modern world. In *Klingsor*, Hesse still presents this idea in the context of World War I and the decline of Europe, but does so less sententiously than in the earlier *Demian* and the Dostoevsky essays (which were in fact written later that fall). In "The Music of Decline" section, Klingsor claims modern art is suicidal and reflects the cultural and political "collapse" of Europe (190). The backdrop to Klingsor's drunken diatribe, the "mechanical music" of the whirling carousel (192) is the cacophonous swan song of a dying culture: half a decade later this music of decline will become the jazz rhythms of an Americanized Europe to which Harry Haller has such an ambivalent response.

*Klingsor's Last Summer* does not shy away from sentimentality, especially in its treatment of the painter's attitude to women. His lurid fantasy of having a host of females of all ages and types fighting over him is fit for the kitschy cover of a contemporary rock album, and his confession, "often I look at every woman like a cunning old libertine, and often like a little boy" (185) suggests that even after psychoanalysis Hesse's attitude to women had not escaped the Romantic stereotyping of his earlier writings.

The frenzied self-portrait that Klingsor achieves "at the end of that summer's ... incredibly fervid, tempestuous period of work," and which is its "crowning glory" (211), is Hesse's pictorial parallel and self-reflexive metaphor for his writing of this novella. And Klingsor's compulsive self-observation in the mirror as he paints his master-piece is of course the symbolic equivalent of the myriad self-mirroring of Hesse's Ticino fictions. In the self-conscious mirror of Klingsor's studied poses and posturings we witness the extremes of the fetishized self as *objet d'art*. The painter's impending death makes for an appropriate end, for such a radical self-reflexivity is in the end also self-devouring:

> In those madly intense days Klingsor lived like an ecstatic. Nights, he loaded himself with wine, and then would stand, candle in his hand, before the old mirror, study his face in the glass ... One night he had a girl with him on the couch in the studio, and while he pressed her naked body against his he stared with reddened eyes over her shoulder into the mirror, saw beside her unbound hair his distorted face, full of lust and full of the abhorrence of lust. (213–214)

With its distorted and exaggerated Expressionist style, the *Klingsor* self-portrait also includes different possibilities for its interpretation "from a wide variety of viewpoints" (212). Surely the most relevant among those suggested by Hesse, the hermeneut of his own work, is that of "Klingsor ... analyzed and interpreted by the artist himself with unsparing psychological insight— an enormous confession, a ruthless, crying, moving, terrifying peccavi" (212). For Hesse, this heightened self-portrait is also a symbolic vision of early twentieth-century European culture. His metaphoric correlation is couched in a hyperbolic language located somewhere between the prophetic voice of *Demian* and the satiric one of *Steppenwolf*, with a significant back-handed compliment to Nietzsche's autobiography:

> This is man, ecce homo, here is the weary, greedy, wild, child-like, and sophisticated man of our late age, dying European man who wants to die, overstrung by every longing, sick from every vice, enraptured by knowledge of his doom, ready for any kind of progress, ripe for any kind of retrogression, submitting to fate and pain like the drug addict to his poison, lonely, hollowed-out, age-old, at once Faust and Karamazov, beast and sage, wholly exposed, wholly without ambition, wholly naked, filled with childish dread of death and filled with weary readiness to die. (213)

In his next major work, Hesse faced East, and uttered his autobiographical *ecce homo* in soothing meditative tones that present a striking lyrical counterpoint to *Klingsor*'s whirling rhetoric of individual and cultural disintegration.

## SIDDHARTHA

Hesse began his "Indian legend"[24] in the winter of 1920; the writing proceeded rapidly, and by spring, he was halfway through Part 2, when he bogged down in the "By the River" chapter. For a time it seemed that the book would be consigned to his collection of unfinished works, but after a painful hiatus of nearly two years, he tackled it anew, and by May 1922 *Siddhartha* was finished. What had been the obstacle? One explanation is that Hesse, like many artists, experienced a letdown after a spell of intensive work, for, as he laments in the journal he kept to fill the void of *not* working on the novel, after the sustained creative high of 1919, 1920 turned out to be "certainly the most unproductive [year] of [his] life."[25] Another reason for the prolonged cold spell is that in the second part of *Siddhartha*, Hesse was reaching, as it were, beyond his confessional shadow: "My Indian poem proceeded splendidly so long as I composed what I had experienced: the mood of the young Brahmin who seeks wisdom and who torments and mortifies himself. But when I had come to the end of Siddhartha the sufferer and acetic, and wanted to write about Siddhartha the victor, the yea-sayer and master, I couldn't proceed any further."[26]

His remedy to this dilemma was at once ingenious and simple: to try and enter imaginatively into and make his own the states of mind he wished to portray in his protagonist. He succeeded in this project to the extent that he managed to bring to a conclusion his most popular "wisdom" book. Yet the catch in his presentation of Siddhartha the "yea-sayer" is that—as with nearly all attempts to formulate religious and spiritual truths—what is intended to be most edifying turns out to be inexpressible save through clichés. As a witty passage in his 1920–1921 journal reveals, Hesse was quite aware of what might be called the Polonius dilemma of proffering words of wisdom:

> There is nothing more difficult than being a father confessor or spiritual guide. When some poor person has told me his story, I can't at bottom say anything else except, "yes, that is sad, as sad as life frequently is, I know it, I too have experienced it. Seek to bear it, and if nothing at all helps, drink a bottle of wine, and if that doesn't help either, know that there is the possibility of

putting a bullet in one's head." Instead of this I seek to produce my consolatory arguments and life-wisdoms, and even if I actually know a few truths, at the instant one utters them aloud and dispenses them as medicine for an actual and immediate sorrow, they are a bit theoretical and hollow, and suddenly one seems to oneself like a priest who seeks to console his people and at the same time has the wretched feeling that he is doing something mechanical.[27]

Hesse's attempt to experience in some measure the spiritual development he wished to portray in the last third of *Siddhartha* led him consciously to re-immerse himself in a world that had been one of the *donneés* of his childhood—Indian religion and culture, as it had been available to him through his missionary parents and his deeply learned, Sanskrit-speaking grandfather Gundert. In the essay "My Belief" (1930), Hesse reminds us that "my father, mother, and grandfather had not only a rich and fairly thorough knowledge of Hindu forms of belief but also a sympathy, though only half admitted, for those forms. I breathed and participated in spiritual Hinduism from childhood just as much as I did in Christianity."[28] Hesse's renewed study of "the Upanishads, the Bhagavad-Gita, and the discourses of the Buddha" in what Mileck calls "a profound spiritual experience"[29] was, however, not the only way out of the impasse of 1920–1921, for as he acknowledged, the Chinese spiritual tradition, chiefly in the form of Taoism, had a significant impact as well on the last part of *Siddhartha*. Finally, even if the novel's exotic setting and hagiographic style do not readily suggest it, psychoanalysis is also a powerful if invisible influence. Freedman has stressed the importance of Hesse's sessions with Jung in early 1921 in helping him to get out from under his literary paralysis, because these may have facilitated "the idea of interior space in which temporal strife is displaced by a transcendent vision."[30] And near the conclusion of his 1920–1921 journal, Hesse summarizes "the path of healing and development" that enabled him to complete *Siddhartha*: "next to the Asiatic teachings (Buddha, Vedanta, and Lao-Tzu)" it included as well "psychoanalysis … not as a therapeutic method … but as the essential element" of a new world view.[31]

If Hesse's turn to the East in *Siddhartha* is a natural extension of his childhood and his family background, it was also reinforced by the Orientalism in vogue at the time he began work on the novel, and which was due in part to the popular *Travel Diary of a Philosopher* (1919) by Count Keyserling, whom Hesse in a review of 1920 praised as "the first European scholar and philosopher who has really understood India."[32] In his own journey to India a decade earlier Hesse had failed, as he admitted to Romain Rolland in 1923, to get beyond "the charm of the exotic" and to enter into "the world of the Indian spirit"—in fact, the only item of his miscellany, *From India: Sketches of an Indian Journey* (1913), that he still considers valuable is "a curious little tale ['Robert Aghion'] which at that time (1911) gave me much pleasure."[33] In striking contrast to his earlier tourist-venture, Hesse's fictional journey to India in *Siddhartha* is an inward and spiritual one that largely eschews picturesque surface and exotic effects in order to explore the sinner-saint polarity within him through the geographic symbolism that Ziolkowski has definitively analyzed as "the landscape of the soul" and "the projection of inner development into the realm of space."[34]

Questions as to the extent and significance of the Oriental influence on this novel, and the related issue of the Indian (Hindu and Buddhist) versus the Chinese (Taoist) components, are difficult to answer, particularly since most Western critics (myself included) simply do not have the necessary expertise to address it authoritatively, and since scholars and critics with an Oriental expertise are understandably prone to overstating the case by taking a part for the whole.[35] In this regard Hesse's ample pronouncements over the years about his intentions in *Siddhartha* are not always helpful, for they can furnish, like the Bible, support for radically differing viewpoints and interpretations. Nevertheless, in my view the gist of these (when considered in the context of the novel) justifies the conclusion that even though the "Eastern" influence is important, the book as a whole expresses a fundamentally Western outlook. Indeed, I would suggest that one of the wonderful ironies of *Siddhartha*'s enthusiastic reception by the American counterculture and student generation of the 1960s is that in the guise of Eastern religion these young readers were taking in, unbeknownst to them, an essentially Western creed.

Perhaps a better way to address the complex matter of the Eastern versus the Western aspects of *Siddhartha* is to describe it as Hesse's mid-life examination of the foundation of his religious beliefs in an undogmatic formulation of his deepest intuitions that draws on three great spiritual traditions: the Christian, the Indian, and the Chinese. Here *Siddhartha* points to a core experience that resists neat or easy definition. Hesse's statement in 1958 that he sought in this book "to discover what all faiths and all forms of human devoutness have in common"[36] assumes a cross-cultural and transconfessional basis of religion, a premise consistent with the three-tiered scheme of humanization outlined in "My Belief" (discussed in the last part of Chapter III). The path of Siddhartha, which leads from the self-will of the second stage to the serene faith of the third, reflects Hesse's own struggles as much as his aspirations toward a higher harmony. Hesse's belief that there is a greater coherence to his career is evident in his insistence that—despite the palpable differences of style and setting—*Demian* and *Siddhartha* are "by no means contradictions, but segments of the same way": *Demian* "stresses the process of individuation, the development of the personality without which no higher life is possible," whereas *Siddhartha* is concerned with "the other side of our task and destiny ... the overcoming of our personality and our being pervaded by God."[37]

The path of Siddhartha's self-realization—which, as Ziolkowski has shown, in some respects resembles that of *Demian*'s Sinclair[38]—indicates both Hesse's assimilation of as well as his critical self-distancing from the Indian element. As Hesse wrote to Stefan Zweig in a revealing statement, "it was only when ... this Indian element began to be no longer important to me that it became possible for me to represent it, just as I am always able to represent only that which in actual life is taking leave of me and departing." Even if Hesse affirms that the Indian "garb" is more than a mere "costume,"[39] Siddhartha obviously bears his author's psychological features. His Sanskrit name, which is also the legendary one of the Buddha, means something like "he who has found the goal," and is ironically appropriate, for Siddhartha can only reach his goal by rejecting the Buddha's teaching of the Eightfold Path and by attending instead to the Buddha's living example of following the voice within, which in Hesse-Siddhartha's view is what brought Gotama his enlightenment under the Bo tree. Therefore it is not surprising that Hesse the perennial Protestant also characterized his book as "the expression of [his] *liberation* from Indian thought" because this "very European book, despite its milieu" takes the concept of individuality "much more seriously than any Asiatic teaching."[40]

Hesse's autobiographical meditation on the spiritual core of all religions can also be read as his further and belated attempt at a reconciliation with his father, an idea first developed by Ball, who notes that Hesse's new closeness to his father during the latter's last years turned into admiration and love after his death in 1916.[41] While Freedman qualifies Ball's terse conclusion that "in *Demian* the father is missing, in *Siddhartha* the mother" with the more balanced view that both aspects "seemed to exist side by side in Hesse's imagination as he settled into his Indian book,"[42] the new ascendancy of the father world is evident in *Siddhartha*'s series of guru and guide figures. While the novel by no means excludes the mother world, which is suggested by Kamala and the realm of the senses (Samsara), the unresolved father-son conflict of Hesse's youth is now transposed and spiritualized through a set of strategic rejections of father figures. With the possible exception of

Siddhartha's confrontation with the head Samana, these are respectful partings-of-the-way without any of the overt resentment and even contempt that burden most of the father-son relationships in Hesse's writings up to *Siddhartha*. Now the legend of self-will is presented with a delicate but masterly touch: unlike Sinclair, who seeks repeatedly to flee back into the Eden of childhood and whose weak self continues to rely on strong guides, Siddhartha makes a definitive break at the beginning of the novel with the tradition of his family, and appreciates early in his quest that he must reject all gurus to find himself. That, incidentally, is why Govinda, Siddhartha's friend and early disciple who depends on mentors as a roadmap to salvation, is still searching at the end of the book. He may well represent, as Field has suggested, "passive Oriental acceptance,"[43] but he is also the type of the perpetual follower who can never find the proper rhythm of his own life.

In the stately modulations of its lyrical and liturgical prose *Siddhartha* develops with synoptic clarity the stages of its hero's spiritual development from the exemplary "Brahmin's son"[44] of the opening to the smiling saint of the conclusion. Hesse's paradigmatic patterning is everywhere evident: more so than any of his previous alter egos, Siddhartha—true to his name—achieves his goal; in his life's pilgrimage, the polarities of sinner/saint, mind/nature are symmetrically balanced and mediated by the unifying symbol of the river. Hesse's new maturity is also evident in the balance of objectivity and empathy with which both the roles of father and son are presented, and in the wry but pervasive humor that seems to have eluded most of his critics—this, after all, is a wisdom book in which even the River Mystical is known to laugh at an apprentice saint.

Surely the influential Augustinian model of conversion and the genre of the saint's life (with which Hesse was familiar because of his long-standing interest in the Middle Ages and Saint Francis, about whom he had written a poetic biography) must have helped him frame the hagiographic *vita* of Siddhartha.[45] Thus what sometimes seems in *Demian* like a series of chaotic transformations is unfolded in *Siddhartha* as a coherent progression. The earlier novel's "light" and "dark" worlds are now two landscapes separated by the river, and the hero's life is both a geographic and spiritual journey that culminates in an experienced unity of self and world. However, if Hesse's saint reaches the third level of humanization, his life is also characterized by the Romantic-existential sense, to borrow Kierkegaard's title, of "stages on life's way." The experience of "awakening," so important later in *The Glass Bead Game*, depends on a periodic self-renewal symbolized by the age-old trope of the snake shedding its skin (37). The informing dynamic of Siddhartha's life, "awakening," though marked by a feeling of utter aloneness and "icy despair" (41), differs from Klein's existential *Angst*, because it is a function of higher self-realization. It is a proleptic force, as Siddhartha realizes when at the end of Part 1 he decides *not* to return home to his father. Moreover, in this novel the diachronic succession of identity stages is countered by a synchronic perception of the atemporal totality of the self, which is in turn posited on the larger unity of the cosmos.

Siddhartha's "awakening" is already implicit in his dissatisfaction with the Brahminic faith of his forebears as a viable way "toward the Self, toward Atman" (6). His subsequent adolescent confrontation with his priestly father over his decision to join the wandering ascetics, the Samanas, is an ironic rescripting of the young Hesse's active and not-so-successful rebellion into a successful passive resistance (6–7). Unlike the adolescent Hesse, and like Demian, Siddhartha uses his uncanny self-control to master others. Thus the identity crisis of Hesse's youth is transformed into an amusing episode from which the son emerges victorious, but which also shows the figure of the father as compassionate and dignified. Siddhartha's subsequent rejection of the ascetic-Samana ideal as a "flight from the Self" that can be achieved with less trouble, as he explains to Govinda, by the ox-driver "asleep over his bowl of rice wine" (17), is his second step away from external authority figures and toward himself. Like his earlier departure from home, his parting with the Samanas turns on a sly assertion of his self-will, in a scene whose humor has a satiric edge when Siddhartha hypnotizes the head Samana and forces him into fawning acquiescence.

Siddhartha's subsequent encounter with the Buddha—who shares with him not only a name, but a similar *vita*—is the final exercise of his *Eigensinn* against the figure whom he recognizes instantly as the greatest of all teachers and saints ("Never had Siddhartha esteemed a man so much, never had he loved a man so much," 28). Yet he refuses to subscribe to Gotama's doctrine, raising instead, in this subtly comic encounter, objections to the Buddhist gospel of the Eightfold Path to Nirvana, because he knows now that the road to enlightenment simply cannot be taught: the one thing the Buddha's teachings do not contain, as Siddhartha points out like some forward sophomore, is the incommunicable secret of "what the Illustrious One himself experienced" in the hour of *his* illumination (34). The youthful critic then concludes his Protestant rebuff of the Buddha with the assertion that he must judge for himself, which earns him the well-deserved reprimand, "you speak cleverly, my friend. Be on your guard against too much cleverness" (35).

Siddhartha's "awakening" in the last section of Part 1 cuts specifically against the grain of the Buddha's teachings, for it is his entry into the maternal sphere of nature and the senses that marks the emergence of a radically this-worldly self. A psychoanalytic passage from the "Journal 1920–1921" throws some light on Siddhartha's sudden *volte face*: "All heroic demands and virtues are repressions … In fact, virtues, like talents, are a sort of dangerous if at times useful hypertrophy, like goose livers grown to abnormal size."[46] Like the later Goldmund's flight from the monastery, Siddhartha's transformation is one from the austerities of the father world to a life of pleasure whose focus is the courtesan Kamala. And like Klein's passionate transports after his meeting with Teresina, Siddhartha's "awakening" is the revelation, not of a transcendent meaning, but of one immanent in the everyday world. The lyrical meditation below may have an "Indian" cast, but its larger drift should be familiar to anyone acquainted with the epiphanic mode in English literature from Wordsworth to Joyce:

> He looked around him as if seeing the world for the first time. The world was beautiful, strange, and mysterious. Here was blue, here was yellow, here was green, sky and river, woods and mountains, all beautiful, all mysterious and enchanting, and in the midst of it, he, Siddhartha, the awakened one, on the way to himself. All this, all this yellow and blue, river and wood, passed for the first time across Siddhartha's eyes. It was no longer the magic of Mara, it was no more the veil of Maya, it was no longer meaningless and the chance diversities of the appearances of the world, despised by deep-thinking Brahmins, who scorned diversity, who sought unity. River was river, and if the One and Divine in Siddhartha secretly lived in blue and river, it was just the divine art and intention that there should be yellow and blue, there sky and wood—and here Siddhartha. Meaning and reality were not hidden somewhere behind things, they were in them, in all of them. (39–40)

Siddhartha's childlike and unreflective immersion in the world of the senses on the other side of the river brings him a sexual awakening through an encounter with a teacher that is just as stylized and replete with gentle humor as his earlier confrontations with male preceptors. The poem that earns him his first kiss from Kamala throws his earlier spirit-exercises into a wonderfully ironic light:

> Into her grove went the fair Kamala,
> At the entrance of the grove stood the brown Samana.

As he saw the lotus flower,
Deeply he bowed.
Smiling, acknowledged Kamala,
Better, thought the young Samana,
To make sacrifices to the fair Kamala
Than to offer sacrifices to the gods. (56)

It is characteristic of Hesse's light touch in this novel that the young man who has just abjured all teachers should now seek out a new mentor—but one who teaches not any dogma, but engages her new pupil in a protracted *practicum* in the *Kama Sutra*. And unlike many of Hesse's earlier protagonists who prove misfits in Cupid's school, from Giebenrath who almost falls down the cellar stairs at Emma's advances, to Sinclair's pallid cult of Beatrice, Siddhartha proves an apt student. In the fictions of his middle period Hesse may still stereotype sexual relationships through Romantic spectacles, but at least his confessional personas are now a far cry from the neurasthenic virgins of his early fiction—a fact that no doubt reflects his changed outlook and lifestyle after his move from Bern. Indeed, Hesse's request to a friend to return his copy of the *Kama Sutra*, because he "needed it very badly, as soon as possible"[47] may stand as a humorous footnote to the Kamala sequence in *Siddhartha*.

Siddhartha's immersion in worldly pleasures can be no more than a way station, for Hesse's aim is to show that, as he wrote in 1921, "the highest toward which humans can aspire" is the most advanced degree of "harmony within the individual soul." Hesse saw this issue in both religious and psychological terms, as evident in his gloss, "who achieves this harmony has at the same time what psychoanalysis would call the free disposability of the libido, and that of which the New Testament states, 'everything is yours'."[48] In *Siddhartha* this "harmony" is more effectively conceived than it was with the Abraxas symbol of *Demian*, as the dialectical integration of antithetical aspects of the self. Siddhartha has learned that the road of asceticism is a dead end; now he has to learn that the same holds true for the contrary path of sense-indulgence. In the four segments from "Kamala" to "By the River," Hesse the moralist demonstrates the old lesson, preached from many a Christian pulpit, that the pursuit of sense pleasure is in the end destructive of the very wonder and delight it first occasioned in us. Siddhartha has awakened to the innocent senses, only to lose himself in the headlong pursuit of hedonism under the combined tutelage of Kamala (*kama* = love) and the merchant Kamaswami ("Master of this World"=materialism). What began in naive joy ends in "By the River" in suicidal disgust and surfeit of the greedy round of pleasure. Siddhartha has succumbed to "the soul sickness of the rich" (78) and has lost "the divine voice in his own heart" (76)—something symbolized by his dream of the dead songbird, whose actual release by Kamala is a metaphor of his renewed "awakening."

Having experienced the extremes of self-denial and self-gratification—this noble spirit, after all, does nothing half-heartedly—and discovered that each is a cul-de-sac, Siddhartha is ready for the greater synthesis adumbrated in the third part of the novel. It should not surprise us that the Hesse who in the "Journal 1920–1921" contrasted Augustine's religious with Rousseau's secular *Confessions* should, in his depiction of Siddhartha's turn from the corrupt pleasures of the world (Samsara) to a saintly life (symbolized by Vasudeva, the Ferryman), follow the well-known Augustinian model of a right-angle turn from sin to salvation. In fact I may not be straining too far if I discern a further parallel between Siddhartha's life and Augustine's: just as the young Augustine pursued false systems and practiced erroneous arts before finding the true faith—as a follower of the Manicheans, as a professor of rhetoric, and as a student of neo-Platonic philosophy, all of which nevertheless contributed something essential to the saint's final identity—so Siddhartha looked into three different teachings (as Brahmin, Samana, and Buddhist) that proved inappropriate to his needs but that were instrumental in shaping his final outlook. In any event, after rejecting the suicidal impulse that Klein succumbed to, Siddhartha experiences yet another "awakening" to a higher self. Now the metaphor is literalized as he wakes up from a deep and healing sleep to a new awareness synonymous with the basic message of Christianity: "he loved everything, he was full of joyous love towards everything he saw. And it seemed to him that was just why he was previously ill—because he could love nothing and nobody" (94). Cured of his self-hatred and despair, Siddhartha has become again "like a small child" (95) and is ready, like the dying Klein, to enter into the kingdom of heaven—or, to invoke the Chinese equivalent that is just as relevant to the last third of *Siddhartha*, into the mystery of the Tao.

Even a cursory examination of Taoist sayings will reveal basic similarities with the religious ideas of the last part of *Siddhartha*. We know that Hesse's interest in the Chinese tradition and particularly the figure of Lao-Tzu dates back to at least a decade earlier, when he characterized the *Tao Te Ching* as a "fashionable book" in Europe for the "past fifteen years."[49] His renewed interest in Taoism may have been stimulated by his father's pamphlet (published in 1914, the year before his death) on "Lao-Tzu as a Pre-Christian Witness to the Truth." In 1919 Hesse published in the first issue of *Vivos Voco* (a journal he co-edited for a short time after the war) "Tao:

A Selection of the Sayings of Lao-Tzu" from a new translation of the *Tao Te Ching*.[50] Two years later he epitomized Lao-Tzu's Tao as "the quintessence of wisdom," and in 1922 he described *Siddhartha* as a work in "Indian garb that begins with Brahman and Buddha and ends with the Tao."[51] In the light of these avowals Hsia's conclusion that Vasudeva and the river are both versions of the Tao, and that, moreover, the former is also "a portrait of Lao-Tzu" seems plausible.[52] The impact of Taoist ideas on the latter portion of *Siddhartha* is most discernible through the imprint of Lao-Tzu's model of the wise man: the belief in the complementarity of opposites based on an underlying unity, the stress on a life of extreme simplicity, the heuristic use of humor and wit, the lack of a systematic doctrine, the ideal of non-action (Wu Wei) and silence (which, like Wordsworth's "wise passiveness," is not mere passivity), the paradox that in striving too hard for enlightenment we are blinded, and the idea that wisdom cannot be formulated.

The central meditative emblem of *Siddhartha* is the most apt and natural image of the river. Siddhartha's devotion to it (when he joins Vasudeva as his fellow ferryman) is based on his discovery of the age-old paradox, "the water continually flowed and flowed and yet it was always there; it was always the same and yet every moment it was new. Who could understand, conceive this?" (102). Hesse's invocation of this long-standing trope (from Heraclitus and Confucius[53] to Wordsworth's *Prelude* and Thomas Wolfe's *Of Time and the River*) of flux and permanence, the temporal and the timeless, shows that he is capable of varying the expressive range of his favorite metaphors: water, which in his fiction typically functions as the token of the mother world, now signifies, as Ziolkowski has shown, "the natural synthesis" of "the familiar polarity of spirit and nature."[54] It is also to Hesse's credit that once he has demonstrated Siddhartha reaching the point, under Vasudeva's silent tutelage, of being able to hear the holy OM in the many voices of the river, he resists an easy "happy end," for Siddhartha must now suffer the trials he once imposed on his father when he left home to follow the Samanas.

Here there is a real autobiographical symmetry to the book's design, for if at the beginning Hesse identified with "the Brahmin's son" striking out on his own, in "The Son" (117) he identified with the grief of Siddhartha the father—and by extension, with that of his own father—at the revolt of a headstrong child. With his depiction of "the festering wound" of Siddhartha's anxiety about his recently discovered and now prodigal son (left to him by the dying Kamala), Hesse shows suffering as a humanizing force (a "Western" and Romantic idea) as well as an instance of the cosmic rhythm of recurrence (a mystical and "Eastern" motif). We may read the poignant and ironic passage below as Hesse's confession of his belated reconciliation with a father with whom the middle-aged author is now able to sympathize:

> One day, when the wound [of his son's flight] was smarting terribly, Siddhartha rowed across the river, consumed by longing, and got out of the boat with the purpose of going to town to seek his son ... The river was laughing clearly and merrily at the old ferryman. Siddhartha stood still; he bent over the water in order to hear better. He saw his face reflected in the quietly moving water, and there was something in this reflection that reminded him of something he had forgotten and when he reflected on it, he remembered. His face resembled that of another person, whom he had once known and loved and even feared. It resembled the face of his father, the Brahmin. He remembered how once, as a youth, he had compelled his father to let him go and join the ascetics, how he had taken leave of him, how he had gone and never returned. Had not his father also suffered the same pain that he was now suffering for his son? Had not his father died long ago, alone, without having seen his son again? Did he not expect the same fate? Was it not a comedy, a strange and stupid thing, this repetition ... of events in a fateful circle? (131–132)

When Siddhartha first crossed this river, Vasudeva had prophesied that "everything comes back" (49). Now, as Siddhartha experiences this with a perplexed resentment of which the old ferryman is the sympathetic onlooker, Siddhartha is suddenly rewarded with an intuition of the simultaneity of all being that Hesse seeks to render in a lyric-epiphanic prose that parallels Klein's final illumination, including the metaphoric conversion of water into music as a symbol of a higher unity beyond the reach of language:

> He could no longer distinguish the different voices [of the river] ... They all belonged to each other ... They were all interwoven and interlocked, entwined in a thousand ways. And all the voices, all the goals, all the yearnings, all the sorrows, all the pleasures, all the good and evil, all of them together the world. All of them together was the stream of events, the music of life. (135–136)

The mystical note developed in Klein's ecstatic drowning is now further amplified in Siddhartha's spirit-hearing of "the great song of a thousand voices" merging into "one word: OM—perfection" (136). In this religious experience of higher self-realization, Siddhartha's individual identity merges into cosmic unity: the metaphysical ground of self and world are one and the same; to reach the one is to touch the other. The icon of such a self-surrender, or *un*becoming—the problematic goal of Hesse's final phase—is already introduced here in Vasudeva's "going into the unity of all things" with a radiant smile and "a form full of light" (137) that we shall encounter again in the dying Music Master of *The Glass Bead Game* nearly two decades later.

Obviously the final hagiographic glimpses of Vasudeva and Siddhartha are at a far remove from the fractured reality of Hesse's actual life and experience, something implicit in the shift of the concluding "Govinda" section from the point of view of the enlightened saints to that of the forever-frustrated seeker.[55] After the metaphysical uplift of "OM," the reappearance of Siddhartha's old "shadow" and friend brings the novel back down to the second level of humanization and the world of unreconciled oppositions that is Hesse's true habitat. In addition to restoring the dialectical tension between faith and despair, salvation and seeking, the episode of the final encounter between Siddhartha and Govinda recaps the basic themes of the book: seeking precludes finding, loving the world is more important than understanding it, words fail to grasp the nature of reality. Yet Hesse is able to lighten these didactic concerns with the presence of humor, as the hapless Govinda, who earlier failed to recognize Siddhartha in the man of the world (when he guarded his sleep by the river) now fails again to recognize his friend in the saint. Govinda's need for a dogmatic faith typifies the hopeless quest of this mental traveler, for as Siddhartha teases him, "you do not see many things that are under your nose" (140).

Yet despite its ironic and light touches, the sermon of the concluding chapter cannot rise above the contradictions inherent in its logic, something that makes Hesse's most popular wisdom book a problematic achievement: it aspires to communicate wisdom even as it maintains that "wisdom is not communicable" (142); it seeks truth knowing full well that "a truth can be expressed and enveloped in words if it is one-sided" (143); it maintains that "time is not real" when the form of the novel, both as narrative and as print, is a mode of temporality. Moreover, the sentence about the unreality of time, already entertained by Klein, is reversible by the very law of the identity of opposites proclaimed in *Siddhartha* and elsewhere in Hesse ("in every truth the opposite is true," 143): *time, indeed, is most real*, a contrary sentence already vividly dramatized as the fear of death that fuels *Klingsor's Last Summer*, in many ways the stylistic and thematic counter-fiction to *Siddhartha*.

True, the concluding transformational sequence of the river, the parable of the stone, and Siddhartha's farewell kiss to Govinda is an impressive stylistic experiment in suggesting the greater unity of being. Asserting that time is not real, however, is ultimately only a verbal solution to the existential dilemma of our being irremediably in time, something Siddhartha had earlier recognized "by the river": "He had died and a new Siddhartha had awakened from his sleep. He also would grow old and die. Siddhartha was transitory, all forms were transitory" (100). To extrapolate from the perception of eternal transitoriness and flux (what Goethe in the title of a famous poem calls "Permanence in Change") that temporality is an illusion is not a logical move but requires a metaphysical leap of faith. Hesse was willing to take the plunge with a poetic prose that invokes cosmic plenitude and omnipresence through the rapid accumulation of myriad "flowing forms … of simultaneousness" in Siddhartha's "mask-like" smile of enlightenment (151). Seen in this light, the paean of presence of *Siddhartha*'s closing pages is Hesse's attempted escape, with an Eastern and metaphysical fiction, from the *ecce homo* of the *Klingsor* confession and the existential dilemma of our being in time and history that we Westerners have been painfully afflicted with since at least the eighteenth century and the rise of Romanticism.

## NOTES

1. Hesse, *Wandering: Notes and Sketches*, trans. James Wright (New York: Farrar, Straus & Giroux, 1972), 5–6.
2. GB I, 405, letter of July 2, 1919.
3. AS, 130.
4. "Journal 1920–1921," AS, 130.
5. "Life Story Briefly Told," AW, 56.
6. GB I, 412, 437, letters of August 8, 1919, and January 5, 1920.
7. Hesse, "Self-Communion," in *Materialen zu Hermann Hesses "Siddhartha,"* vol. 2, ed. Volker Michels (Frankfurt: Suhrkamp Verlag, 1974), 360–363. Subsequently this volume will be cited as MATSID2.
8. In the essay cited in the previous note Hesse claims that he is "at a further remove from every truth than ever before," MATSID2, 360.
9. "Journal 1920–1921," AS, 122.
10. For example, Boulby calls it "probably one of the most ruthlessly direct and merciless pieces of self-exposure in the whole range of modern German literature" (130), and Mileck similarly describes it as "perhaps … the most ruthless of Hesse's many self-exposures" (242).

11. Field has objected that "the psychoanalytic and mystic-philosophical" perspectives are not harmonized; *Hermann Hesse: Kommentar* (cited in Chapter V, note 17).

12. Hesse, *Klein and Wagner*, in *Klingsor's Last Summer*, trans. Richard and Clara Winston (New York: Farrar, Straus & Giroux, 1971), 49. Subsequent citations of *Klein and Wagner* are of this edition and translation and will appear in the text.

13. Hesse, "From Martin's Journal," in *Materialen zu Hermann Hesses "Siddhartha,"* vol. 1, ed. Volker Michels (Frankfurt: Suhrkamp Verlag, 1975), 300–304. Subsequently this volume will be cited as MATSID1.

14. GW, vol. 12, 284.

15. MATSID1, 202.

16. AS, 132–133.

17. AS, 124.

18. GB I, 424, letter of ca. fall 1919.

19. Freedman, 213; Field, 69.

20. Richard Sheppard, "German Expressionism," in *Modernism 1890–1930*, ed. Malcolm Bradbury and James McFarlane (New York: Penguin Books, 1976), 278.

21. Hesse, *Klingsor's Last Summer* (see note 12), 187–188. Subsequent citations of this novella are of this edition and translation and will appear in the text.

22. MATSID1, 192, letter of ca. December 1919.

23. "Klingsor Sends His Friend Thu Fu a Poem," GW vol. 5, 346.

24. AB, 45, letter of April 6, 1953.

25. "Journal 1920–1921," AS, 130.

26. "Journal 1920–1921," 119.

27. "Journal 1920–1921," 129–130.

28. MB, 177.

29. MB, 176; Mileck, 160.

30. Freedman, 225. As Freedman notes (224), we know next to nothing "about the content of these sessions," save that Hesse found them very trying.

31. AS, 146.

32. MATSID1, 112. See also Ziolkowski, 146–147.

33. GB II, 56, letter of April 6, 1923.

34. Ziolkowski, 161.

35. For such specialized yet illuminating readings of *Siddhartha* in terms of its Indian and Chinese elements respectively, see Adrian Hsia, *Hermann Hesse und China: Darstellungen, Materialen, und Interpretationen*

(Frankfurt: Suhrkamp Verlag, 1974), 237–248; and Vridhagiri Ganeshan, "Siddhartha und Indien," MATSID2, 225–254.

36. GW, vol. 11, 50.

37. GB II, 48, letter of February 3, 1923.

38. Ziolkowski, 153.

39. GB II, 52, 55, letters of February 10 and March 12, 1923.

40. GB II, 96, letter of June 18, 1925.

41. Ball, 147–151.

42. Ball, 151; Freedman, 217.

43. Field, 81.

44. Hesse, *Siddhartha*, trans. Hilda Rosner (New York: Bantam, 1971), 3. Subsequent citations of the novel are of this edition and translation and will appear in the text.

45. Cf., Boulby has emphasized that "*Siddhartha* discloses finally and unmistakably the significance of hagiography, of the saintly *vita*, as a formal conditioning factor in Hesse's work," 152.

46. AS, 137.

47. MATSID1, 98, letter of February 23, 1920.

48. GB I, 468, letter of March 23, 1921.

49. MB, 385–386.

50. Freedman, 217, MATSID1, 86–91.

51. GB I, 480 (letter of November 11, 1921); MATSID1, 152, letter of February 1922.

52. Hsia, *Hesse und China*, 240, 246.

53. Hsia cites the Confucian saying, "thus like this river everything flows on day and night without cease" (*Hesse und China*, 244).

54. Ziolkowski, 166–167. Hans Jürg Lüthi's claim that the river represents the mother world that is otherwise absent in the novel (*Hermann Hesse: Natur und Geist* [cited in Chapter IV, note 20], 68) misses the mark twice, because the mother world is symbolized not by the river but by Kamala and the world of the senses.

55. Boulby has drawn attention to the "very interesting … change of [authorial] standpoint" (157) in the last chapter.

# Chronology

| | |
|---|---|
| 1877 | Hermann Hesse born July 2 in Calw, Württemberg, near Stuttgart, to Johannes Hesse and Marie Gundert Isenberg Hesse, former Pietist missionaries in India. |
| 1881 | Family moves to Basel, Switzerland, returning to Calw five years later. |
| 1890 | Prepares to attend Maulbronn Seminary. Suffers collapse after seven months at Maulbronn and enters sanatorium. Begins at a Cannstatt Gymnasium in 1892. |
| 1893 | Depression persists through the school year. Drops out the following fall, returning to Calw on October 18, 1893. |
| 1894 | Reads extensively in history, philosophy, poetry, and fiction while working as an apprentice in a machine shop. |
| 1895 | Serves an apprenticeship at a bookstore in Tübingen as his studies continue. |
| 1899 | Publishes *An Hour beyond Midnight*, which deepens his estrangement from his family, as his mother finds parts of the book indecent. Starts work at a Basel bookstore. |
| 1901 | Publishes *Hermann Lauscher* and makes trips to Italy to follow up his studies in art history. |
| 1902 | Mother dies in April, but Hesse does not attend her funeral. |
| 1903 | Becomes engaged to Maria Bernoulli in the spring. Resigns from bookstore job after signing contract with Fischer Publishing House. |

| 1904 | Publishes *Peter Camenzind*, his first major work, the success of which enables him to marry. Writes essays on Boccaccio and St. Francis of Assisi. Moves with Maria to remote farmhouse in Gaienhofen. |
| 1905 | Maria gives birth to Bruno, their first son. |
| 1906 | Publishes *Beneath the Wheel*. Becomes co-editor of *März*, a liberal journal. |
| 1909 | Second son, Heiner, is born. |
| 1910 | Third novel, *Gertrud*, is his first work to receive negative critical response. |
| 1911 | Martin, the couple's third son, is born. Journeys east to India with friend Hans Sturzenegger. Marital tensions develop. |
| 1912 | Moves family to house outside Bern. |
| 1914 | Publishes *Rosshalde*. Hesse's advocacy of peace and his Swiss residence prompt charges of cowardice. During the war, he edits and publishes books for German prisoners of war in cooperation with the German embassy. |
| 1916 | Father dies. Enters a sanatorium following nervous breakdown and is treated by Dr. Joseph Lang, a Jungian psychotherapist. |
| 1919 | Publication of *Demian* under the pseudonym Emil Sinclair marks the beginning of artistic maturity. Leaves his family to live in Montagnola in southern Switzerland, where he takes up painting to relieve stress. |
| 1922 | Publishes *Siddhartha*. |
| 1924 | Marries Ruth Wenger after divorcing Maria in 1923, but the couple separates before long. |
| 1927 | Divorces Ruth. Publishes *Steppenwolf*. Close friend Hugo Ball publishes first biography of Hesse. |
| 1930 | Publishes *Narcissus and Goldmund*. |
| 1931 | Marries Ninon Dolbin, with whom Hesse had remained in contact after receiving an admiring letter from her, written when she was fourteen. The marriage succeeds, and they spend their remaining years in Montagnola in a house they designed themselves. |

| 1932 | Publishes *Journey to the East*. Begins work on *The Glass Bead Game*. |
| 1933 | During the Hitler era, the Hesses shelter refugee-artists fleeing the Third Reich. |
| 1942 | Publishes *Collected Poems*. |
| 1943 | Publishes *The Glass Bead Game*, his magnum opus. |
| 1946 | Publishes *War and Peace*, a collection of essays on politics since the First World War. Receives both the Goethe Prize and the Nobel Prize for Literature. |
| 1951 | Publishes a selection of his massive correspondence, which accumulated as Hesse not only kept in touch with a number of the era's major intellectuals, but continued to answer all letters from his readers personally well into the 1940's. |
| 1955 | Recieves the Peace Prize of the German Book Trade. |
| 1962 | Dies August 9 in Montagnola and is buried in nearby San Abbondio. |

# Contributors

HAROLD BLOOM is Sterling Professor of the Humanities at Yale University and Henry W. and Albert A. Berg Professor of English at the New York University Graduate School. He is the author of over 20 books, including *Shelley's Mythmaking* (1959), *The Visionary Company* (1961), *Blake's Apocalypse* (1963), *Yeats* (1970), *A Map of Misreading* (1975), *Kabbalah and Criticism* (1975), *Agon: Toward a Theory of Revisionism* (1982), *The American Religion* (1992), *The Western Canon* (1994), and *Omens of Millennium: The Gnosis of Angels, Dreams, and Resurrection* (1996). *The Anxiety of Influence* (1973) sets forth Professor Bloom's provocative theory of the literary relationships between the great writers and their predecessors. His most recent books include *Shakespeare: The Invention of the Human* (1998), a 1998 National Book Award finalist, *How to Read and Why* (2000), and *Genius: A Mosaic of One Hundred Exemplary Creative Minds* (2002). In 1999, Professor Bloom received the prestigious American Academy of Arts and Letters Gold Medal for Criticism, and in 2002 he received the Catalonia International Prize.

ERNST ROBERT CURTIUS (1886-1956) was one of Germany's most eminent men of letters. The author of a highly influential study entitled *European Literature and the Latin Middle Ages*, Curtius taught for much of his career at the University of Bonn.

THOMAS MANN (1875-1955), Nobel Prize Laureate, is the author of such modern classics as *Death in Venice*, *Doctor Faustus*, and *The Magic Mountain*.

Mann and Hesse were close friends for many years and corresponded extensively.

RALPH FREEDMAN is Professor Emeritus of Comparative Literature at Princeton University. He has been the editor of a collection of essays on Virginia Woolf as well as a biography of Hermann Hesse. His biography of Rilke appeared from Farrar, Straus and Giroux in 1996.

THEODORE ZIOLKOWSKI is Class of 1900 Professor of Modern Languages at Princeton University. His books include *Fictional Transfigurations of Jesus*, *The Mirror of Justice: Literary Reflections on Legal Crises*, and *The Sin of Knowledge: Ancient Themes and Modern Variations*.

MARK BOULBY is Emeritus Professor of German at the University of British Columbia. His publications include *Karl Phillip Moritz: At the Fringe of Genius* and a study of Uwe Johnson.

HENRY HATFIELD (1912-1995) taught German language and literature at Columbia and Harvard universities. In addition to editing a collection of essays on Thomas Mann, he authored a critical introduction to Goethe and *Clashing Myths in German Literature from Heine to Rilke*.

JOSEPH MILECK is Emeritus Professor of German at the University of California at Berkeley. His publications include *Hermann Hesse and his Critics* and *Hermann Hesse: Life, Work, and Criticism*, as well as a full-length biography of Hesse.

MARTIN SWALES teaches at University College, London. He is co-editor of *The Art of Detective Fiction* and co-author of *Reading Goethe*. His other publications include *Studies of German Prose Fiction in the Age of European Realism* and a study of Thomas Mann.

EUGENE STELZIG is Distinguished Teaching Professor in the Department of English at SUNY Geneseo. In addition to his study of Hesse, he has written a book on Wordsworth and, more recently, a study entitled *The Romantic Subject in Autobiography: Rousseau and Goethe*.

SIEGFRIED UNSELD directs Suhrkamp Verlag, Germany's most prestigious literary and scholarly publishing company. Works of his that have been translated into English include *The Author and his Publisher* and *Goethe and his Publishers*.

# Bibliography

Abood, Edward. "Jung's Concept of Individuation in Hesse's *Steppenwolf.*" *Southern Humanities Review* 3 (Summer 1968): 1-12.

Andrews, R.C. "The Poetry of Hermann Hesse." *German Life and Letters* 6 (1952-53): 117-27.

Antosik, Stanley. "Utopian Machines: Leibniz's 'Computer' and Hesse's Glass Bead Game." *Germanic Review* 67, no. 1 (Winter 1992): 35-45.

Benn, Maurice. "An Interpretation of the Work of Hermann Hesse." *German Life and Letters* 3 (1949-50): 202-11.

Boulby, Mark. *Hermann Hesse: His Mind and His Art.* Ithaca, NY: Cornell University Press, 1967.

Breugelmann, René. "Hermann Hesse and Depth Psychology." *Canadian Review of Comparative Literature* (Winter 1981): 10-47.

Casebeer, Edwin F. *Hermann Hesse.* New York: Warner Paperback Library, 1972.

Cohn, Hilda. "The Symbolic End of Hesse's *Glasperlenspiel.*" *Modern Language Quarterly* 11 (September 1950): 347-57.

Colby, Thomas E. "The Impenitent Prodigal: Hermann Hesse's Hero." *German Quarterly* 40 (1967): 14-23.

Curtius, E. R. "Hermann Hesse." *Essays on European Literature.* Trans. Michael Kowal. Princeton, NJ: Princeton University Press, 1973.

Farquharson, Robert H. "The Identity and Sgnificance of Leo in Hesse's *Morgenlandfahrt.*" *Monatshefte* 55 (1963): 122-28.

Field, George Wallis. *Hermann Hesse*. New York: Twayne, 1970.

———. "Hermann Hesse as Critic of English and American Literature." *Monatshefte* 53 (1961): 147-58.

———. "Hermann Hesse: Polarities and Symbols of Synthesis." *Queens Quarterly* 81 (1974): 87-101.

———. "On the Genesis of *Glasperlenspiel*." *German Quarterly* 41 (November 1968): 673-88.

Flaxman, Seymour L. "*Der Steppenwolf*: Hesse's Portrait of the Intellectual." *Modern Language Quarterly* 15 (December 1954): 349-58.

Freedman, Ralph. *Hermann Hesse: Pilgrim of Crisis*. New York: Pantheon, 1978.

———. "Romantic Imagination: Hermann Hesse as a Lyrical Novelist." *The Lyrical Novel: Studies in Hermann Hesse, André Gide*, and Virginia Woolf. Princeton, NJ: Princeton University Press, 1963.

Gontrum, Peter. "Oracle and Shrine: Hesse's *Lebensbaum*." *Monatshefte* 56 (April-May 1964): 183-90.

Hatfield, Henry. "Accepting the Universe: Hermann Hesse's *Steppenwolf*." *Crisis and Continuity in Modern Fiction*. Ithaca, N.Y.: Cornell University Press, 1969.

Johnson, Sydney. "The Autobiographies in Hermann Hesse's *Das Glasperlenspiel*." *German Quarterly* 29 (May 1956): 160-71.

Koester, Rudolf. "The Portrayal of Age in Hesse's Narrative Prose." *Germanic Review* 41 (1961): 111-19.

Mann, Thomas. "Introduction to Hermann Hesse's *Demian*." *Demian*. Trans. Michael Roloff and Michael Lebeck. New York: Harper and Row, 1965.

Mayer, Hans. "Hermann Hesse's *Steppenwolf*." *Steppenwolf and Everyman*. Trans. Jack D. Zipes. New York: Thomas Y. Crowell, 1971.

Middleton, J. C. "An Enigma Transfigured in Hermann Hesse's *Glasperlenspiel*." *German Life and Letters* 10 (1957): 298-302.

Mileck, Joseph. *Hermann Hesse: Life and Art*. Berkeley, CA: University of California Press, 1978.

———. "Names and the Creative Process: A Study of Names in Hesse's *Lauscher, Demian, Steppenwolf*, and *Glasperlenspiel*." *Monatshefte* 53 (1961): 167-80.

———. "The Poetry of Hermann Hesse." *Monatshefte* 46 (1954): 192-98.

———. "The Prose of Hermann Hesse: Life, Substance and Form." *German Quarterly* 27 (1954): 163-74.

Nauman, Walter. "The Individual and Society in the Work of Hermann Hesse." *Monatshefte* 41 (Spring 1949): 33-42.

Negus, Kenneth. "On the Death of Joseph Knecht in Hermann Hesse's *Glasperlenspiel.*" *Monatshefte* 53 (Summer 1961): 181-9.

Neuer, Johanna. "Jungian Archetypes in Hermann Hesse's *Demian.*" *Germanic Review* 57 (Winter 1982): 9-15.

Norton, Roger C. "Variant Endings of Hesse's *Glasperlenspiel.*" *Monatshefte* 60 (1968): 141-46.

Otten, Anna. *Hesse Companion.* Albuquerque, NM: University of New Mexico Press, 1977.

Reichert, Herbert W. *The Impact of Nietzche on Hermann Hesse.* Mt. Pleasant, MI: The Enigma Press, 1972.

Rockwood, Heidi M. "The Function of Pablo in Hesse's *Steppenwolf.*" *South Atlantic Review* 59 (November 1994): 47-61.

Rose, Ernst. *Faith from the Abyss: Hermann Hesse's Way from Romanticism to Modernity.* New York: New York University Press, 1965.

Seidlin, Oskar. "Hermann Hesse: The Exorcism of the Demon." *Symposium* 4 (1950): 325-48.

Serrano, Miguel. *C. G. Jung and Hermann Hesse: A Record of Two Friendships.* Trans. Frank McShane. New York: Schocken, 1966.

Shaw, Leroy R. "Time and the Structure of Hermann Hesse's *Siddartha.*" *Symposium* 11 (1957): 204-24.

Stelzig, Eugene L. "The Aesthetics of Confession: Hermann Hesse's *Crisis* Poems in the Context of the *Steppenwolf* Period." *Criticism* 21, no. 1 (Winter 1979): 49-70.

———. *Hermann Hesse's Fictions of the Self: Autobiography and the Confessional Imagination.* Princeton, NJ: Princeton University Press, 1988.

Swales, Martin. *The German Bildungsroman from Wieland to Hesse.* Princeton, NJ: Princeton University Press, 1978.

Tusken, Lewis W. "A Mixing of Metaphors: Masculine-Feminine Interplay in the Novels of Hermann Hesse." *Modern Language Review* 87 (July 1992): 626-35.

———. "Thematic Unity in Hermann Hesse's *Narziss and Goldmund*: The Tree Symbol as Interpretive Key." *Modern Fiction Studies* 29 (Summer 1983): 245-51.

————. *Understanding Hermann Hesse: The Man, His Myth, His Metaphor.* Columbia, SC: University of South Carolina Press, 1998.

Unseld, Siegfried. "Hermann Hesse's Influence: Ethics or Aesthetics?" *Hermann Hesse: Politische und wirkungsgeschichtliche Aspekte.* eds. Sigrid Bauschinger and Albert M. Reh. Bern: Francke, 1986.

Ziolkowski, Theodore, ed. *Herman Hesse: A Collection of Critical Essays.* Englewood Cliffs, NJ: Prentice-Hall, 1973.

————. *The Novels of Hermann Hesse: A Study in Theme and Structure.* Princeton, NJ: Princeton University Press, 1965.

# *Acknowledgments*

Curtius, E. R. "Hermann Hesse," from *Essays on European Literature*. © 1973 by Princeton University Press. Reprinted by permission of Princeton University Press.

"Introduction," by Thomas Mann. From *Demian: The Story of Emil Sinclair's Youth*. © 1948 by Holt, Rinehart and Winston, Incorporated. Reprinted by permission.

Freedman, Ralph. "The Novel as Disguised Lyric," from *The Lyrical Novel: Studies in Hermann Hesse, André Gide, and Virginia Woolf*. © 1963 by Princeton University Press. Reprinted by permission of Princeton University Press.

Ziolkowski, Theodore. "*The Glass Bead Game*: Beyond Castalia," From *The Novels of Hermann Hesse: A Study in Theme and Structure*. © 1965 by Theodore Ziolkowski. Reprinted by permission of Theodore Ziolkowski.

"*Narziss and Goldmund*," by Mark Boulby. From *Hermann Hesse: His Mind and Art*. © 1967 by Cornell University. Used by permission of the publisher, Cornell University Press.

"Accepting the Universe: Hermann Hesse's *Steppenwolf*," by Henry Hatfield.

233

From *Crisis and Continuity in Modern German Fiction.* © 1969 by Cornell University. Used by permission of the publisher, Cornell University Press.

"*Narziss und Goldmund*: Life's Double Melody," by Joseph Mileck. From *Hermann Hesse: Life and Art.* © 1978 by The Regents of the University of California. Reprinted by permission.

Swales, Martin. "Hesse: *The Glass Bead Game*," from *The German Bildungsroman from Wieland to Hesse.* © 1978 by Princeton University Press. Reprinted by permission of Princeton University Press.

"The Aesthetics of Confession: Hermann Hesse's *Crisis* Poems in the Context of the *Steppenwolf* Period," by Eugene L. Stelzig. From *Criticism* 21, no. 1 (Winter 1979): 49-70. © 1979 by Wayne State University Press. Reprinted by permission.

"Hermann Hesse's Influence: Ethics or Esthetics," by Siegfried Unseld. From *Hermann Hesse: Politische und wirkungsgeschichtliche Aspekte.* © 1986 Siegfried Unseld. Reprinted by permission.

Stelzig, Eugene. "Ticino Legends of Saints and Sinners," from *Hermann Hesse's Fictions of the Self: Autobiography and the Confessional Imagination.* © 1988 by Princeton University Press. Reprinted by permission of Princeton University Press.

# Index